Left: Disney's iconic castle dominates the Magic Kingdom.

Atlas

Downtown, Loch Haven
  and Winter Park **134**
International Drive
  and Universal
  Orlando Resort **136**
Walt Disney World
  Resort and US 192 ..**138**

*City Locator: Inside
  Front Cover*
*Theme Parks: Inside
  Back Cover*
CityWalk: p.50
Downtown Disney: p.92

Street Index: 140
General Index: 141–4

Nightlife **92**
Pampering **96**
Restaurants **98**
Shopping **112**
Sport **116**
Themed Attractions **118**
Thrill Rides **124**
Transportation **128**

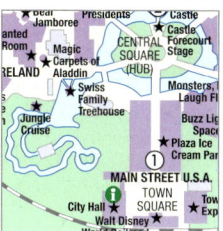

Below: a rare chance to meet a star.

Orlando

Not many destinations promise to take you to the 'Happiest Place on Earth'. Cynics might argue Orlando should not promise this either, but there is no denying that this modern city in the heart of sub-tropical Florida has become a tourist mecca, not for its natural wildlife and agreeable climate, which it has in abundance, but because of one pair of ears, recognized the world over.

Orlando Facts and Figures

Size of Walt Disney World Resort: **47sq miles (122 sq km)**
Number of hotel rooms in Orlando: **115,200**
Number of restaurants in Orlando: **5,390**
Orlando's total shopping space: **52.1 million sq ft (4.8 million sq m)**
Number of residents in Greater Orlando: **1.9 million**
Number of visitors to Orlando each year: **46.6 million**
Economic impact of visitors: **$27.6 billion**
Cost of land purchased by Walt Disney for his resort: **$5 million**
Number of public or semi-private golf courses: **176**
Ratio oak trees to residents in Winter Park: **3:4**

The Land Built for a Mouse

Even before Disney's unique brand of entertainment arrived, the climate and savage beauty of Florida's landscape were attracting over 50,000 visitors each year – and that was in the 1870s. Roughly 100 years later Walt Disney's dreamlands arrived and everything about central Florida changed. Swamplands were reclaimed for theme parks, identikit holiday homes were built with alligator fences to protect their private pools, the cattle and citrus industries that had for so long dominated the state's economy were quickly forced into the backseat with tourism driving development, and the heart of Orlando began its never-erending battle with the whims of Disney.

For most youngsters and even some oldsters, Disney is synonymous with a dream vacation. This is not just because of a price that forces people into months, if not years, of planning and saving, but because of the childhood dreams that Disney promises to fulfill. When a little girl meets Snow White or a boy shakes the hand of Peter Pan it is a dream that has come true and who could begrudge a young child for calling this moment 'magical.'

Although not cheap by any means, a Disney vacation may be better value than you imagine. By the time you've checked out of a well-appointed Disney Resort, having been consistently greeted with a smile and had constant entertainment for your children, you may find you've bagged a bargain. The Disney experience is so unique that any price seems a steal. Added into this value is that everything at Disney, from cleaning maids to Cinderella's smile, works like clockwork thanks to a terrifyingly efficient management structure that seems capable of eliminating all potential problems. This may not really be the 'Happiest Place on Earth', but it is not from lack of trying.

Imaginary Lands and Tourist Traps

Disney's draw knows no socio-economic bounds and for those unwilling to pay inflated resort prices, there are countless places to eat, sleep, and play along International Drive

Below: often overlooked by tourists, Downtown Orlando has a thriving art and nightlife scene.

Contents

Areas

Orlando 4
Magic Kingdom 6
Epcot 10
Animal Kingdom..............14
Hollywood Studios 16
Kissimmee and
    Celebration 18
Universal Studios 20
Islands of Adventure........22
International Drive
    and Lake
    Buena Vista 24
SeaWorld 26
Downtown
    Orlando and Loch
    Haven Park 28
Winter Park and
    Maitland......................30
Space Coast 32

Below: astronauts preparing for launch.

A–Z

Accommodations............36
Bars and Cafés 50
Behind the Scenes..........54
Budgeting and
    Survival 56
Children 60
Essentials........................62
Food and Drink 68
Golf 70
History 74
Live Shows, Parades,
    and Fireworks 76
Museums and
    Galleries......................82
Music, Dance, and
    Theater 88
Natural World 90

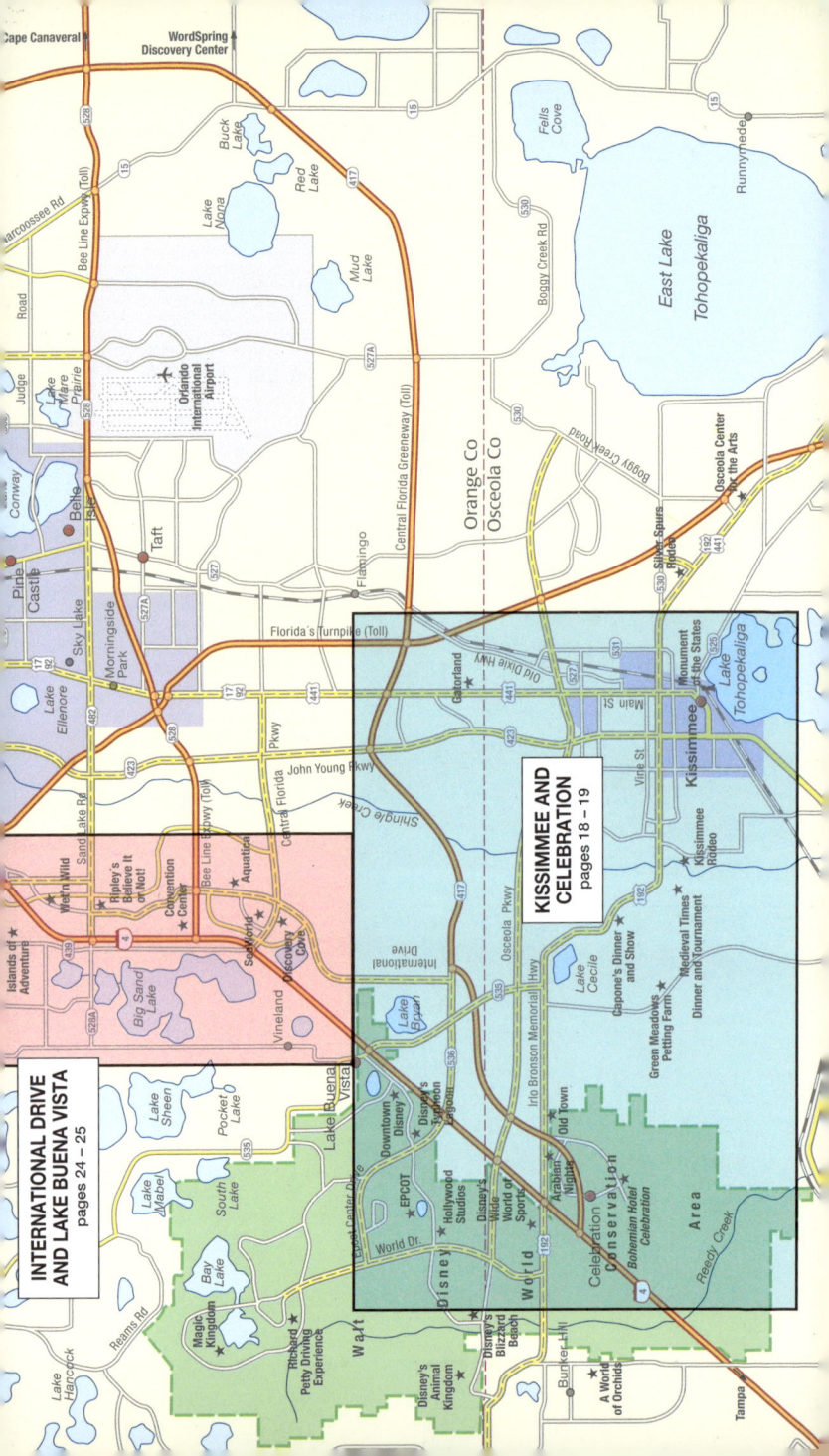

and US192 that offer discounted deals and cheap thrills in an effort to entice the weary hordes away from the all-inclusive resorts.

Some attractions such as Universal Resorts and SeaWorld can compete with The Mouse; others are poor imitations. Hotels may offer more family-friendly options at better prices than Disney, while other cheap stays are shabby beyond repair, and for every fine restaurant there are at least two poor fast-food outlets looking to make a quick buck. The gaudiness of these off-resort areas should be experienced, if only to increase your appreciation of the well-designed theme parks, but be wary. For some businesses, once proximity to Disney is secured, emphasis on quality of service or goods receives little attention.

The Cultural Heart: Downtown and Winter Park

This makes it such a pity that the distance to Orlando's 'real life' is so great. Downtown Orlando is an important business center with a budding nightlife and arts scene. Winter Park, home of Rollins College, is rich in culture and has fantastic shopping, gourmet dining, and European-style cafés.

Don't let these gems go overlooked. Disney may go to any length to appeal to the child inside, but these real, functioning communities offer the indulgences of a grown-up vacation.

Highlights

▲ **Epcot's** famous sphere marks the entrance to a park revealing technological wonders and cultures from around the globe.
▶ Real wildlife and models of dinosaurs dominate the attractions at the **Animal Kingdom**.

▶ **SeaWorld** provides an opportunity to interact with sea animals, such as dolphins, penguins and killer whales.

▲ The **thrill rides** of Orlando's theme parks, especially Islands of Adventure, attract adrenaline junkies from around the world.

▲ Kids can't get enough of the **Magic Kingdom's** characters and attractions.
▶ Visiting the **Kennedy Space Center** is a true once in a lifetime opportunity.

The Magic Kingdom

For most visitors the charming, child-friendly Magic Kingdom is synonymous with Disney World. This was the resort's original park and is still its best. For younger children the chance to meet Cinderella or Peter Pan really is a dream come true, and many of the slow, dark rides here are perfectly weighted to spark their imagination without igniting fear. Some teenagers may find this park a bit too 'kiddy,' but there is no shortage of adults fulfilling long-held childhood dreams by shaking Mickey's hand or wearing a pair of ears all day long. It's hard not to admire the attention to detail, and the fireworks show that ends each day is superb.

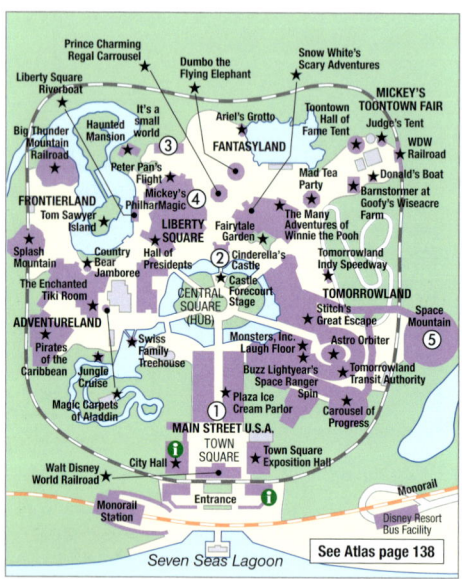

If you are not staying at a Disney Resort, allow plenty of time to get to and from your car to the park entrance. Trams from the parking lot drop guests off at the Ticket and Transportation Center, where you can buy your ticket and then board a boat or the monorail to reach the main entrance. From here you join the other crowds that have been directly deposited from their Disney Resort transportation.

Town Square Exposition Hall. When not being used for conventions or presentations, the auditorium shows continuous reels of classic Disney films. This quiet and cool retreat on the fringes of the park is almost always empty.

Otherwise, Main Street is meant to be explored. In addition to the highly decorated souvenir shops there are such gems as the barber's shop with a barbershop quartet and the **Chapeau Hat Shop**, which sells a variety of colorful caps to get you in the spirit.

Of course, any visit to Main Street, U.S.A. would not be complete without dropping in to the **Plaza Ice Cream Parlor** for a sundae.

SEE ALSO SHOPPING, P.112

Main Street, U.S.A.

The Magic Kingdom hits you the minute you walk through the gates. Music sets a dreamy tone, and suddenly the real world is replaced by an idealized version of a Victorian-era American small town – this is **Main Street, U.S.A.** ① Before you explore its collection of shops and attractions, use the practical facilities at **Town Square** to get yourself orientated.

The **City Hall** to the left of the park entrance has maps and information and can book meals. It also contains the park's lost and found office.

Above the park's entrance gates is one of the stations for the **Walt Disney World Railroad**, which also has stations in Frontierland and Mickey's Toontown Fair.

To the right of the main entrance is the tucked-away

Left: some girls get a handsome prince charming…

from the film, making Johnny Depp one of the few human film stars to feature in a Magic Kingdom ride.

The other attractions in Adventureland serve to entertain kids with time to spare. These include the **Magic Carpets of Aladdin**, a basic hub-and-spoke ride; the **Swiss Family Treehouse**, a free play area based on the Robinsons' fictional home, and **The Enchanted Tiki Room**, a short show featuring animatronic birds. It does provide a chance to cool off, if not much else.

Frontierland

The home of good ol' fashioned country living, Frontierland features characters such as Song of the South's Brer Rabbit and Tom Sawyer. It also has two of the park's thrill rides – **Splash Mountain** and **Big Thunder Mountain Railroad**. Though both rides are tame in comparison to other parks' roller coasters, they make a good stepping stone for children who have recently outgrown kiddie-coasters.

Tucked away in Frontierland's corner is **Tom Sawyer Island**, a free play area for children that includes rope

The Hub and Cinderella's Castle

The Magic Kingdom was designed in a hub-and-spoke style. At the end of Main Street, U.S.A. the hub connects four spokes to Adventureland, Liberty Square and Frontierland, Fantasyland and Mickey's Toontown Fair, and Tomorrowland. At the center of the connecting hub is **Cinderella's Castle** ②: its Forecourt Stage is home to **Dream Along with Mickey**, the park's musical live show.

Though the castle serves as the park's signature backdrop, inside there is only **Cinderella's Royal Table**, a sit-down restaurant that lets you dine with the entire gaggle of Disney princesses. Little girls and, let's face it, some fathers have dreamt of this opportunity for years.

SEE ALSO LIVE SHOWS, P.76;
RESTAURANTS, P.98

Adventureland

There is more than a hint of Disney nostalgia at Adventureland. Many of its attractions, though updated, date from the Magic Kingdom's beginning and provide a unique insight into the early days of theme parks.

Jungle Cruise is the most charming of the early attractions. This light-hearted cruise through the jungle rivers of the world is frequently disrupted by attacks from disgruntled natives, crocs, hippos, and elephants.

Next door is the legendary **Pirates of the Caribbean**, which has the notoriety of being the only theme park ride later to become a movie. This dark ride has been frequently updated since its opening to conform to changing codes of decency, yet it still paints a colorful portrait of pirate life. Its most recent adaptation has seen the addition of an animatronic Captain Jack Sparrow

Below: …while others get stuck with Goofy.

7

  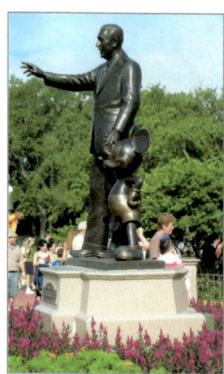

Above: familiar Disney characters from classic films and modern creations.

bridges to cross and caves and trails to explore.

Along the road to Liberty Square there are several shops and smaller attractions such as a shooting arcade. Also here is the **Country Bear Jamboree**, a stage show featuring animatronic bears leading children in songs.
SEE ALSO THRILL RIDES, P.124

Liberty Square

Sandwiched between Frontierland and Fantasyland, Liberty Square recreates a New England town center. In addition to the leisurely **Liberty Square Riverboat** ride along the Rivers of America, there is the **Hall of Presidents**. This patriotic attraction features every US president in animatronic form, with the current president leading the show.

Without a doubt the most enjoyable attraction on Liberty Square is the slightly scary **Haunted Mansion**. This more sophisticated dark ride explores a dusty old house in which holograms, lasers, and other special effects make ghosts appear all around you, even in your carriage.

Fantasyland

For most visitors under the age of ten Fantasyland could be a destination in itself. Cinderella's Castle creates the perfect backdrop, and every attraction celebrates a childhood favorite, from Mickey Mouse to Peter Pan.

One of the park's original attractions is **it's a small world** ③. This voyage through animatronic nations of the world is accompanied by a song that is sung in various languages throughout the boat ride, but sticks in everyone's head after they disembark. It's curious to see just how Disney saw the world in the late 1960s – a tableau of superficial stereotypes that today would shame any travel publication.

Across from here are two of Fantasyland's finest children's attractions. **Peter Pan's Flight** is a fantastic dark ride over the streets of London to Neverland. Your pirate ship flies past key scenes from the classic Disney film before touching down. **Mickey's Philharmagic** ④ plays on vintage films, too, incorporating countless songs and characters into this 4-D movie aimed at younger children (most other 4-D films in Orlando are much too scary for the little ones).

Other attractions in Fantasyland include **Prince Charming Regal Carrousel** and **Dumbo the Flying Elephant**, a hub-and-spoke ride that lifts riders in the air. Not to be missed is a ride on the dizzying tea-cups of the **Mad Tea Party** – a classic funfair ride. All three are good options when short waiting times are at a premium.

Fantasyland has two more slow rides aimed at children. **Snow White's Scary Adventures**, though recently toned down, may still be too intense for the youngest guests; meanwhile, **The Many Adventures of Winnie the Pooh** is a ride that is worth no one's time, as it feels in every way a poor imi-

> Character greetings play a huge part of the experience at the Magic Kingdom and other theme parks. These occur in two different formats. The first is the regularly scheduled events, which you can find listed on your Times Guide. But unexpected appearances often occur, too, when anyone from the famous Cinderella to a recent unknown will appear in the park for a limited time to pose for pictures and sign autographs.

tation of the slow rides Disney normally does so well.

Quieter times are to be had at **Ariel's Grotto**, home of the Little Mermaid, at **Pooh's Playful Spot**, a playground for younger children, and at the **Fairytale Garden** between **Cinderella's Castle** and the entrance to Tomorrowland, where Belle from *Beauty and the Beast* tells stories.

Mickey's Toontown Fair

Mickey's Toontown Fair has the mildest attractions in the Magic Kingdom and focuses squarely on young children, giving them a chance to meet characters, especially Mickey Mouse in the **Judge's Tent**. Little ones can also look through either Minnie or Mickey's house (despite their years together the royal couple still do not cohabitate).

Other characters greet children throughout the day at the **Toontown Hall of Fame Tent**. The only ride at the fair is the **Barnstormer at Goofy's Wiseacre Farm**, an introductory roller coaster with a height requirement of 35in. There is also a water playground called **Donald's Boat** and a station for the **Walt Disney World Railroad** that can take you straight back to the entrance or around the park to Frontierland.

Tomorrowland

Built to resemble a Jules Verne-esque world of the future, Tomorrowland now feels slightly faded, but is not without its charms. The biggest draw is **Space Mountain** ⑤, the Magic Kingdom's most intense thrill ride.

If you arrive at Tomorrowland from Fantasyland you will pass the noisy **Tomorrow-**

Right: little princesses wait for the parade.

land Indy Speedway, a souped-up go-cart track that takes many of the controls out of the drivers' hands.

Tomorrowland has many smaller attractions to explore. The **Astro Orbiter** is a traditional hub-and-spoke ride that goes much higher than most. Also over-head is the **Tomorrowland Transit Authority**, a mini-monorail that circles the area with little drama.

Two dark alien adventures await. In **Buzz Lightyear's Space Ranger Spin**, you get the chance to shoot aliens with a ray gun from a spinning spaceship, while at **Stitch's Great Escape** (minimum height: 40in), a slightly scary teleport simulator tricks you into thinking that an alien has gotten loose in the room, and includes long periods of complete darkness.

A popular attraction is **Monsters, Inc. Laugh Floor**, an interactive show that lets guests submit jokes to be retold by the Monsters themselves.
SEE ALSO THRILL RIDES, P.124

Seeing It All

Though the Magic Kingdom stays open from 9am until late every day of the week, it is nearly impossible for a young family (this park's target market) to see it all in one day and still have the energy to enjoy the fantastic fireworks that end the day.

If you are staying nearby or at a Disney resort, the best approach for this park is to get here in time to see the whimsical opening ceremony and then head back to your hotel for lunchtime and a break. Come back around 4pm to finish the park. Though this will mean missing the afternoon **Celebrate a Dream Come True Parade**, it will allow you plenty of time to find a choice place for the much more elaborate **Main Street Electrical** parade and **Wishes**, the nighttime fireworks show. After a day this full, few will find it hard to get to sleep once they finally return to the hotel.
SEE ALSO LIVE SHOWS, P.76

9

Epcot

While the Magic Kingdom focuses on the child in us all, the two halves of Epcot appeal to a more mature palate. What began as Walt Disney's 'Experimental Prototype Community of Tomorrow' has become one of Disney's most enigmatic parks; its sprawling layout invites slow exploration and demands a lot of walking. The environmental messages of Futureworld, however, are sponsored by corporations with less than green reputations, while the fine ethnic cuisines served at World Showcase are surrounded by souvenir shops making a quick buck on global cultures. For many the enigma gives way to intrigue, making Epcot their best day out.

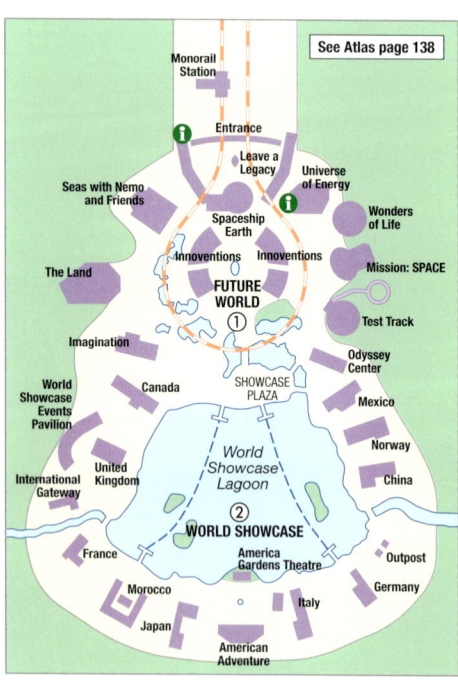

See Atlas page 138

Monorail Station

Entrance

Leave a Legacy

Universe of Energy

Seas with Nemo and Friends

Spaceship Earth

Wonders of Life

Innoventions — Innoventions

The Land

FUTURE WORLD ①

Mission: SPACE

Imagination

Test Track

Odyssey Center

World Showcase Events Pavilion

Canada

SHOWCASE PLAZA

Mexico

International Gateway

United Kingdom

World Showcase Lagoon

Norway

China

② **WORLD SHOWCASE**

France

America Gardens Theatre

Outpost

Morocco

Germany

Italy

Japan

American Adventure

If you are staying at any of the Epcot resorts or coming from Hollywood Studios, you may find it easier to enter the park via boat at the International Gateway located between France and the United Kingdom: it's a smoother ride than the genuine English Channel.

resort's second theme park. Future World, anchored by Spaceship Earth, pays homage to Walt's original idea and is where the tour begins.

Future World ①

Beyond the entrance and below the orb of **Spaceship Earth** is the **Leave a Legacy** sculpture – plinths covered in steel etchings of past visitors. The Spaceship itself, forever the park's icon, is the home of **Project Tomorrow**, a slow ride that traces communication from Cro-Magnon man to the future. As is the case in many of Disney World's older attractions, the future is beginning to look a lot like the past.

UNIVERSE OF ENERGY
Turn to the left and you could find yourself confronted by **Universe of Energy**, spon-

The Disney Dream that Didn't Come True

When Walt Disney pitched the original Epcot in the 1970s, the 'Experimental Prototype Community of Tomorrow' vision was of a controlled, planned community that showcased American innovation in technology and showed how its application could improve everyday life. Unlike modern America, this vision relied on public transportation and relegated cars underground. Unfortunately for green living, this vision died alongside Walt in 1966. In its place sprang Epcot, the

Left: Spaceship Earth.

slow, dark ride featuring characters from the *Finding Nemo* film. Once at Sea Base Alpha you have the chance to see all sorts of aquatic creatures, from clownfish to dolphins, and even humans participating in **DiveQuest**. Its **Coral Reef Restaurant** is one of the finest dining experiences this side of Showcase Lagoon.

SEE ALSO BEHIND THE SCENES, P.54–5; RESTAURANTS, P.99

THE LAND

The strongest environmental message in the whole park is sponsored by Nestlé and found inside **The Land** pavilion – if only an environmentalist's discomfort ended there. The Circle of Life features characters from *The Lion King* who are persuaded by Simba to stop the needless destruction of their native habitat for a useless holiday resort – a paradoxical sentiment for Disney to endorse by anyone's standards.

Living with the Land is an intriguing, slow boat ride through different exhibits about maximizing agricultural production without destroying natural habitat. Nothing wrong there, but when the 'revolutionary' methods discussed include

sored by ExxonMobil. The only attraction here is **Ellen's Energy Adventure**. This positive spin on energy acquisition and production is easily the park's worst attraction; don't let it ruin the start to an intriguing park.

MISSION: SPACE AND TEST TRACK

Even more reason to move on is that next comes **Mission: SPACE**, the park's best thrill ride. There is a milder version now available for those who'd like to experience the visuals of lift-off without feeling the G-force. Either way you'll exit to the **Advanced Training Lab**, an intriguing interactive and play area.

Next door is the park's long-time favorite, **Test Track**. Sponsored by General Motors, this ride simulates the tests new cars endure before being cleared for safety.

SEE ALSO THRILL RIDES, P.124

In the center of the park there are Innoventions East and West, filled with interactive exhibitions showing off the latest in video games and robotics.

THE SEAS WITH NEMO AND FRIENDS

To the right of Spaceship Earth as you enter are three more pavilions. The **Seas with Nemo and Friends** is an enormous aquarium called Sea Base Alpha and reached via a Clam-mobile through a

Below: Mission: SPACE – G-forces await.

Left: looking at the lagoon from Japan.

natural pest control and composting (techniques any hobby gardener could describe) one begins to fear the stewardship of commercial agriculture. You will see many of the crops grown here on the menu at the **Garden Grill**.

One unqualified success in The Land is **Soarin'** (minimum height: 40in) a hanggliding simulator that takes you over sights of outstanding beauty in California.

IMAGINATION

The main attraction in this pavilion is **Captain EO starring Michael Jackson**, a 4-D musical film featuring the King of Pop and a host of intergalactic characters. Produced by Star Wars' George Lucas, this sight and sound spectacular promises stunning visual effects, fantastic dance sequences and music you'll never forget.

Other attractions include **Journey into Imagination with Figment**, which starts out as a typical dark ride, but has periods of complete darkness and loud noises. **ImageWorks** is an interactive playground that uses various tricks of photography.

World Showcase ②

Some children may find World Showcase – a quick tour through 11 nations of the world – a bore, but most adults, at least those that like to shop, eat or drink, will love it. Each pavilion gives you the chance to experience a nation's consumables without actually visiting the country.

As this half of Epcot usually stays open later than Future World, a couple could easily make a romantic, if early, night of it here. In some ways it's even better than Downtown Disney as the food is more varied and the atmosphere, especially at night, less hectic.

MEXICO

Top of the romantic destination list would be the dimly lit **San Angel Inn Restaurante**, set under a recreated

> Numerous live acts perform around Epcot daily, including the World Showcase Players (a drama group). More land-specific entertainment includes Mo'Rockin, Morocco's lively musicians, China's impressive Dragon Legend Acrobats, and the *lederhosen*-clad Oktoberfest Musikanten in Germany.

Mayan temple. The only ride in Mexico is the **Gran Fiesta Tour Starring the Three Caballeros**, a poor dark ride featuring Donald Duck touring various Mexican landscapes.
SEE ALSO RESTAURANTS, P.100

NORWAY

The land of the Vikings is retold in **Maelstrom**, a slow boat ride with unexpected turns and drops that finishes with a short film about the Norwegian way of life. The main features of the pavilion are a recreated stave church and a Norwegian castle that houses the **Akershus Royal Banquet Hall.**
SEE ALSO RESTAURANTS, P.98

CHINA

China features one of the best shops in World Showcase, a fine restaurant in the **Nine Dragons**, and an enjoyable Circle-Vision (the screen wraps completely around the audience) film called ***Reflections of China***. Set in a recreated temple, it takes you from the Great Wall of China to Hong Kong and shows some of the most remarkable natural environments, not just in China but the world.
SEE ALSO RESTAURANTS, P.99

GERMANY

There are no proper attractions at Germany, but with a year-round *Oktoberfest* atmosphere and several fine German beers on offer, no one ever really seems to notice. The **Biergarten Restaurant** is the main attraction here, but shops in half-timber houses also sell some fine Christmas ornaments and quality wooden toys for younger children.
SEE ALSO RESTAURANTS, P.98

ITALY

Designer labels, fine wines, and even ashtrays are for sale in the Italy pavilion, which is a collage of Venetian architecture that includes the Doge's Palace and the Campanile from St Mark's Square. Italian cuisine is served up in **Tutto Italia Ristorante**.

SEE ALSO RESTAURANTS, P.100

AMERICAN ADVENTURE

Portraying one's own country in a land of sweeping generalizations was always going to make interesting viewing for outsiders. No one will be surprised by the patriotic nature of the attractions, but the **Spirit of America Fife and Drum Corps**, the **Voices of Liberty**, and even the **American Adventure** film do their best to explain this patriotism to foreign guests. The film, which features an animatronic Ben Franklin and Mark Twain among others, does its best to provide a balanced view of American history by including the destruction of Native American culture and the horrors of slavery. By the end, though, emotive patriotism replaces historical accuracy. Even more disappointing is that with America's rich culinary scope, from Cajun cornbread to New England clam chowder, Disney chose for the **Liberty Inn** to serve burgers and fries.

JAPAN

Just like the real country, many people could come to Japan just to shop. There is a huge selection of smartly designed sushi plates and knives, silk garments, eccentric toys, and other delicate trinkets. Though the quick-service restaurants here serve fine sushi, the **Teppan Edo** Restaurant is the best place for a sit-down meal.

SEE ALSO RESTAURANTS, P.100

MOROCCO

The Morocco pavilion has some of the finest faux architecture in World Showcase. You can even have a go at getting lost in the warren of shops selling Eastern art and dress, including fine rugs and bronzework. The country's cuisine is summed up at **Restaurant Marrakesh**.

SEE ALSO RESTAURANTS, P.99

FRANCE

It should be no surprise that you get two fine restaurants, **Les Chefs de France** and **Bistro de Paris**, and an accomplished patisserie in France. There is also a fine wine shop and, in the ultimate sign of good taste, a store selling Insight Guides.

Impressions de France is a panoramic film shown throughout the day that takes you on a sweeping journey over the French countryside.

SEE ALSO RESTAURANTS, P.98–9

UNITED KINGDOM

Get your gourmandizing done before you leave France – fish and chips are the main fare in the UK. This little Britain has everything from Blighty, including a Beatles cover band at the Rose and Crown Pub (binge drinkers not supplied).

CANADA

America's neighbor gets a rugged interpretation with mountainous terrain and the Circle-Vision Film, **O Canada!** The signature restaurant **Le Cellier Steakhouse** serves meals hearty enough for any lumberjack.

SEE ALSO RESTAURANTS, P.99

SEEING IT ALL

If you are a quick walker you can see all of Epcot in one day, albeit a very long one. Though the distances to be covered are vast, the park has less time spent waiting for rides than others, as much of World Showcase can be seen at your own pace. Do make reservations if you have your heart set on a particular restaurant, as tables fill quickly.

Left: a great imitation of Venetian landmarks.

13

Animal Kingdom

For nearly 30 years Disney World believed animatronic animals were a more easily maintained attraction than their real counterparts, but then success at SeaWorld and Busch Gardens showed the value of genuine wildlife. In 1998 Disney opened the Animal Kingdom – a well-designed zoo loaded with big attractions. While animals and conservation are the main themes in areas such as Rafiki's Planet Watch, Discovery Island, and Oasis, they are quickly brushed aside in other areas, letting themed dinosaur digs, the Expedition Everest thrill ride, and live shows like the Festival of the Lion King entertain the kids.

Seeing it Slowly

The crowds filing through **Oasis**, and youngsters driving parents on, mean few guests take time to appreciate the exhibitions here, which include everything from jewel-blue macaws to snuffling warthogs.

This is why the Animal Kingdom should be savored slowly. When watched patiently, animals do the darnedest things. Spending even two full days here is barely enough time to appreciate the park in full.

The **Rainforest Café** is one of only two table-service restaurants in the park.

SEE ALSO RESTAURANTS, P.100

See Atlas page 138

Discovery Island ①

Discovery Island is the hub of the park, with the 14-story artificial banyan tree, called the **Tree of Life**, providing orientation for guests. The **Discovery Island Trails** are meandering walks punctuated by unique creatures in artificial habitats.

The main reason people come to Discovery Island, other than to cross to a new land, is to see the 4-D show, **It's Tough to be a Bug**, based on the film *A Bug's Life* and starring the same creatures. Older kids will find the special effects amusing, but under-8s may find the unexpected smells, sprays, and sensations a bit too lifelike.

As the island is at the center of things, there are several cafeteria-style restaurants here where you can grab a bite, and several standard souvenir shops where you can spend a buck.

Camp Minnie Mickey

This land features the park's best live show, **Festival of the Lion King** ②, and the conservation-minded **Pocahontas and Her Forest Friends**. The former should not be missed, while the latter serves little purpose other than an excuse to get off your feet.

Left: close encounters.

is guaranteed to get you wet, whether you like it or not.

Like the Pangani Forest Trail, the **Maharajah Jungle Trek** is a walk through traditional, though highly themed, zoo enclosures. It's your chance to see tapirs, Komodo dragons, and tigers living amid ancient palace ruins. **Flights of Wonder** is a chance to get out of the sun to see some birdlife do amazing tricks.
SEE ALSO LIVE SHOWS, P.78; THRILL RIDES, P.125

DinoLand U.S.A.

DinoLand U.S.A. creates a fairground atmosphere with traditional games you can pay to play. **TriceraTop Spin** is a traditional hub-and-spoke ride, while **Primeval Whirl** is an old-timey-looking roller coaster with a twist: the car spins as you go.

While kids love to play in **The Boneyard**, a playground that recreates a dinosaur dig, most adults come here either to ride **DINOSAUR** ⑤, a thrilling dark ride that takes you back in time to capture DNA from the last remaining dinosaur on the planet, or to spend their spare time while waiting to see **Finding Nemo – the Musical** ⑥.
SEE ALSO LIVE SHOWS, P.77–8

The **Greeting Trails** are the area's other attraction. The characters change throughout the day and the lines can get long, but it is a handy way to kill time while waiting to see the Festival of the Lion King.
SEE ALSO LIVE SHOWS, P.77

Africa

Kilimanjaro Safaris ③ is the main attraction in the recreated African town of Harambe. This ride showcases Disney's clever design skills that make the barriers between you and the giraffes, elephants, and rhinos invisible – an attempt to create a genuine safari experience; the ride is bumpy once the poachers get involved.

The **Pangani Forest Exploration Trail** is a more

Kodak estimates that roughly 4 percent of all the amateur photographs taken in the US are snapped at either Walt Disney World or Disneyland.

---

traditional zoo experience, with reinforced glass protecting you from the many gorillas and other animals. Not to be missed is the underwater hippo-viewing pool. This enormous creature is absolutely amazing to see as it swims past viewers.

Rafiki's Planet Watch

From Africa you can board a train to Rafiki's Planet Watch. This mini-land has interactive exhibits that focus on animal conservation and teach you how to encourage wildlife to live in your garden back home. There is also a petting zoo called **Affection Section**.

Asia

Thrill rides dominate Anandapur, Disney's collage of the Indian subcontinent. The big attraction is **Expedition Everest** ④, Disney World's high-speed roller coaster. **Kali River Rapids** is a much tamer affair, but this whitewater ride

Below: Kilimanjaro Safaris.

Hollywood Studios

It is no coincidence that Hollywood Studios opened the same year as Universal Studios. Disney believes strongly in giving competition to the competition. What makes Hollywood Studios more attractive to most guests, other than it being handily located on the Disney World Resort, is its more child-friendly nature and Disney's faultless 'imagineering.' Though it is hardly the resort's most successful park, it provides behind-the-scenes access to not just loud and flashy film stunts, but to quiet, retiring animators, too. And there are thrill rides here that not even a grumpy teenager could call lame. An extra bonus is that you can easily see it all in one day.

Hollywood Boulevard

Just past Hollywood Studio's Art Deco entrance gates you enter a square, the beginning of Hollywood Boulevard, with facilities to help you get oriented and one of the best shops in the entire Disney World Resort, **Sid**

Cahuenga's One of Kind, which sells one-off movie memorabilia. At the other end of Hollywood Boulevard stands the park's centerpiece, **Mickey's Sorcerer's Hat** ①.

Behind the Sorcerer's Hat is the **Great Movie Ride**, a Magic Kingdom-style dark

ride through sets from classic film scenes, from the romantic ending to *Casablanca* to scarier scenes from *Alien*.
SEE ALSO SHOPPING, P.112

Sunset Boulevard

At the Sorcerer's Hat, adrenaline addicts are most likely to make a dash to the right to reach the **Rock 'n' Roller Coaster Starring Aerosmith** ② and the **Twilight Zone Tower of Terror** ③, both at the far end of Sunset Boulevard. These are the park's only thrill rides.

Other than the standard souvenir shops, the only other attraction here is **Beauty and the Beast – Live on Stage** ④, a shortened musical production of the Disney film. The nighttime spectacular **Fantasmic!** ⑤ takes place at a special stadium just behind Beauty and the Beast.
SEE ALSO LIVE SHOWS, P.78;
THRILL RIDES, P.125

Mickey Avenue and Animation Courtyard

Behind the Sorcerer's Hat lies Mickey Avenue and Animation Courtyard, two areas with popular behind-the-scenes attractions. **The Backlot Tour** is a half-hour tour that includes walking and riding a tram through sets used in

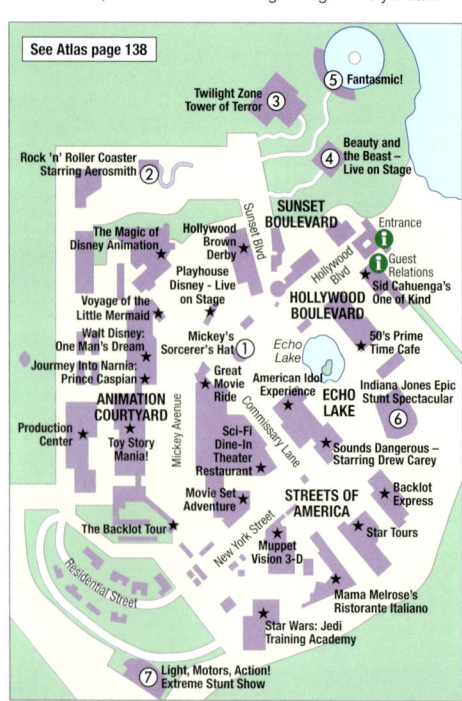

See Atlas page 138

⑤ Fantasmic!

Twilight Zone Tower of Terror ③

Beauty and the Beast – Live on Stage ④

Rock 'n' Roller Coaster Starring Aerosmith ②

The Magic of Disney Animation ★
Hollywood Brown Derby ★
SUNSET BOULEVARD
Entrance

Playhouse Disney - Live on Stage ★
Guest Relations

Voyage of the Little Mermaid ★
Sid Cahuenga's One of Kind
HOLLYWOOD BOULEVARD

Walt Disney: One Man's Dream ★
Mickey's Sorcerer's Hat ①
Echo Lake
50's Prime Time Cafe ★

Journey Into Narnia: Prince Caspian ★
Great Movie Ride ★
American Idol Experience ★
ECHO LAKE
Indiana Jones Epic Stunt Spectacular ★
⑥

ANIMATION COURTYARD

Production Center
Toy Story Mania! ★
Sci-Fi Dine-In Theater Restaurant ★
Sounds Dangerous – Starring Drew Carey ★

Movie Set Adventure ★
STREETS OF AMERICA
Backlot Express

The Backlot Tour ★
Star Tours ★

Muppet Vision 3-D ★

Mama Melrose's Ristorante Italiano ★

Star Wars: Jedi Training Academy ★

⑦ Light, Motors, Action! Extreme Stunt Show

Left: the streets of San Francisco.

a bumpy ride alongside a trainee pilot who comes into too much contact with the evil empire. Then feel the Force yourself at **Star Wars: Jedi Training Academy**, a live show where kids learn to use a light saber from a Jedi Master and do battle with Darth Vader. **Sounds Dangerous – Starring Drew Carey** does its best to create an auditory 3-D film, while the **American Idol Experience** lets you make your own music on stage. SEE ALSO LIVE SHOWS, P.78

Streets of America and Commissary Lane

There's more movie magic at Streets of America. The main attraction again is a stunt show, but the **Lights, Motors, Action! Extreme Stunt Show** ⑦ only appeals to those keen on loud cars.

For the little ones the **Muppet Vision 3-D** show is a pleasant break from the heat and features Kermit and friends in a short film. The *Honey, I Shrunk the Kids* films make an appearance at their own **Movie Set Adventure**, which lets kids slide down enormous blades of grass and run away from giant insects. SEE ALSO LIVE SHOWS, P.78

If you'd like to learn more about the man who started it all, **Walt Disney: One Man's Dream** on Mickey Avenue tells a sugar-coated story of Walt's life and how he began what is now one of the world's largest entertainment companies.

---

films and television shows. All is not always as calm as it seems, especially when you reach Catastrophe Canyon. Nearby on Mickey Avenue, **Journey Into Narnia: Prince Caspian** lets you see how this fantasyland was created for these magical movies. **Toy Story Mania!** is an interactive 4-D attraction with carnival-style games based on the movie characters.

The **Magic of Disney Animation** is a much tamer affair and gives you the opportunity to see Disney animators at work. Animation Courtyard also features two live shows aimed at the little ones: the

pleasant **Voyage of the Little Mermaid** and **Playhouse Disney – Live on Stage.** SEE ALSO LIVE SHOWS, P.78

Echo Lake

Stunts, stars and nostalgic dining are the attractions around Echo Lake. The **Indiana Jones Epic Stunt Spectacular** ⑥ features a Harrison Ford double recreating some of the hero archeologist's most famous stunts. **Star Tours** (minimum height: 40in) simulates

Below: one of the 'casting' directors who entertain the crowds.

Kissimmee and Celebration

South of Walt Disney World Resort, the Irlo Bronson Memorial Highway (US 192) links the southern fringes of the park to Kissimmee and has developed into a more sprawled-out version of International Drive *(see p.24)*. Affordable accommodations dominate this long stretch of highway, with more chain restaurants and gaudy gift shops than you can count. US 192 is also the main artery for visitors staying in vacation homes. In addition to the touristy tat, there are two unique communities along this corridor: Kissimmee has a long history as the center of Florida's cattle market, while Celebration looks like a traditional small town, but was conceived by Walt Disney.

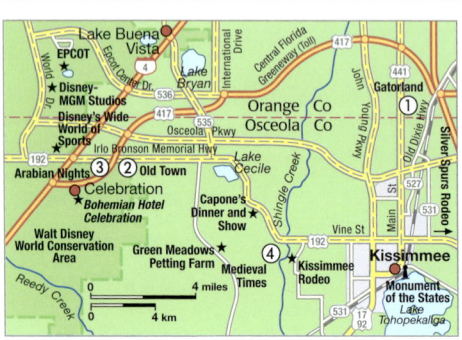

Above: home-grown art.

Kissimmee and Where it all Began

It seems impossible to imagine that before Disney burst onto the scene, the sleepy town of Kissimmee was a sizeable tourist destination in its own right. People's reasons for coming were very different. Instead of families escaping for a bit of R&R, Kissimmee would get overrun by cowboys and farmers from the surrounding areas coming into town for the cattle market, rodeo, or just a bit of socializing.

Kissimmee still has a **rodeo**, and it is common to come across cattle farms alongside vacation home developments in this area, but the past is dwindling, and Kissimmee doesn't have as much to offer as it used to.

Still, the tiny streets that surround its historic center are charming for their variety of houses and people, and though the shopping will never compare with the latest malls, it does provide a flavor of small-town American life, pure and simple.

One original attraction that is still going strong is **Gator-**

Buildings by well-known architects have made Celebration an even bigger tourist attraction. Philip Johnson, known for the New York State Theater at Lincoln Center and the Glass House of New Canaan, Connecticut, designed the town hall. Michael Graves, whose projects include Disney World's Swan and Dolphin hotels, gets credit for the post office.

---

land ①, one of the Orlando area's first tourist attractions. Much like its featured creature, it is proving a survivor.
SEE ALSO SPORT, P.116–7; THEMED ATTRACTIONS, P.118

Between Kissimmee and Celebration

The stretch of US 192 that winds northwest from Kissimmee to Celebration is a long strip of motels, gift shops, and unique attractions that would not look out of place at a rundown funfair, if they were not so enormous.

Obviously these are built to attract idle tourists between visits to the area's larger attractions, but none of these seem to be a roaring success. One of the most disappointing is the **Old Town** ② complex. Built to resemble an old-time

Left: Celebration is full of recreated traditional American homes.

place to stay is the very well-appointed **Bohemian Hotel Celebration**, set on the town's lake. The rest of downtown arcs around the waterfront and includes several shops and places to eat. There is a noticeable lack of chains – not what you'd expect from a corporate city. It may be no surprise that the tiny little bookshop has a section devoted to Disney, but the fact that it contains anti-Disney literature is indeed refreshing; perhaps Disney is a more relaxed puppeteer than it is usually given credit for.

One can't help feeling depressed when leaving Celebration and returning to US 192. After having spent the day in such considered environs, a land where zoning regulations are considered a limit on free speech is enough to make the most hardened patriot a bit of a socialist.

If Celebration's global planning decisions were allowed throughout Orlando, the main arteries for a tourist's stay would no longer be scars on the land, but as beautiful as either the imagined theme parks the tourists enjoy or the remarkable nature the state has always possessed.

SEE ALSO ACCOMMODATIONS, P.41

main street, it does not have a worthy shop in it, though the bars and clubs like **Sun on the Beach** and funfair rides do provide plenty of distraction at night, and there is special weekend entertainment.

Dinner theaters play a large part in Orlando's nightlife. Some make a fantastic night out, others are less rewarding. US 192 has many to choose from, including the highly rated **Arabian Nights** ③, **Medieval Times** ④, and **Capone's Dinner and Show**.

SEE ALSO LIVE SHOWS, P.80–1; NIGHTLIFE, P.93

Celebration – the Town that Walt Built

Just south of the junction of Interstate 4 and US 192 is the idealized town of Celebration, a planned settlement originally designed and owned by

the Walt Disney Corporation. All of this makes it sound very intimidating, and it does have its limitations for residents and businesses; for visitors the overall effect is of an old-fashioned American small town. The attention to detail and well-conceived planning make a welcome relief from the brash anarchy of both US 192 and International Drive, where the only driving tenet behind construction seems to be bigger, better, louder.

There are plenty of holiday homes to be found in the town of Celebration, but the only

Right: lakeside setting for Bohemian Hotel Celebration.

19

Universal Studios

Universal Orlando's first theme park is now part of a complete resort capable of competing with Disney World. So, why choose Universal over Disney? Universal may not have the dreams and romance of classic Disney characters to back it up, but it isn't afraid to treat you as an adult, it revels in terrifying you, and it has bars… with happy hours. Like Hollywood Studios, Universal recreates stunts and special effects, but is happier to stick you in the middle of the action. On the downside Universal seems unable to compete with Disney in attention to detail. One trump is that Express access is available on all attractions. It is free for resort guests, for others there is a price.

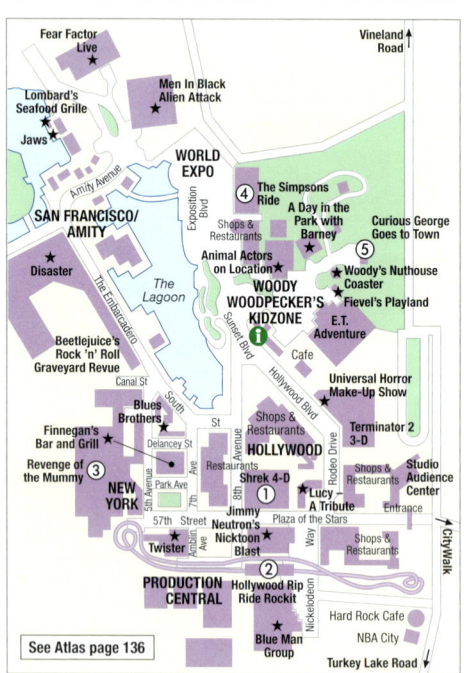

See Atlas page 136

Production Central

Plaza of the Stars and friendly actors on set greet you as you enter the park. Beware, if you dawdle the actors may try and pull you into their scene. Straight ahead is Production Central, or you could take 'Rodeo Drive' to Hollywood on the right.

Production Central has three attractions. The charm and humor of DreamWorks' Shrek films comes through in **Shrek 4-D** ①. Shrek and Princess Fiona are trying to enjoy their honeymoon, but Lord Farquaad returns from the dead to ruin their plans. It is undoubtedly one of the

more enjoyable special-effects films in Orlando. The seats also move, but no height restrictions apply.

Across the road **Jimmy Neutron's Nicktoon Blast** (minimum height: 40in) puts you in a mini-rocket motion simulator to chase after characters from Nickelodeon, including SpongeBob Square Pants and the Rugrats. Towering above is Universal's newest thrill ride, **Hollywood Rip Ride Rockit** ②. Before you board, you choose which song you want to play as you soar 17 stories high along Orlando's tallest roller coaster. You can even re-live the thrills as it's all captured on video.

SEE ALSO THRILL RIDES, P. 126

New York

Continuing along Plaza of the Stars, Production Central becomes New York, but this big apple feels spacious and empty. Universal's biggest ride, **Revenge of the Mummy** ③ awaits, and unless you are an Express pass holder you will probably find the line anything but empty.

Less challenging for most would be a gentle exploration of **Twister**. This special-effects demonstration recreates scenes from the film of

Left: the Blue Man Group.

Woody Woodpecker's Kidzone

Devoted to keeping the little ones occupied, Kidzone features two shows, the **Animal Actors on Location** and the singalong **A Day in the Park with Barney**. There are two playgrounds: **Fievel's Playland**, which presents the world from a mouse's point of view, and **Curious George Goes to Town** ⑤, an interactive playground that is guaranteed to get you soaked. **Woody's Nuthouse Coaster** is a gentle beginner's rollercoaster ride.

The **E.T. Adventure** recreates the classic film, including the bike ride past the moon, in a dark ride as good as any created by Disney.

Hollywood

Surely Tinseltown should make the biggest impact in a motion-picture theme park, but the attractions here are disappointing. The cheeky street entertainers bring the most laughs. For those curious about make-up special effects, the **Universal Horror Make-Up Show** will teach you how some of the most gruesome injuries can be created.

Lucy – A Tribute pays homage to Lucille Ball, the star of the classic American sitcom *I Love Lucy*.

---

the same name to dramatic effect; some children may find this far too scary.
SEE ALSO THRILL RIDES, P.126

San Francisco/Amity

Two worlds collide in this recreation of America's east and west coasts that features two very cheesy rides. In **Disaster** you board an underground train minutes before a huge earthquake strikes: it floods the tracks and threatens to dump a tanker truck on your head. While young children may find this attraction a bit scary, only young people could fall for the daftness of **Jaws**. The great white shark that disturbs this gentle cruise through Amity looks so inauthentic that the technology of Disney's Jungle Cruise *(see p.7)* makes it look dated. The ocean theme continues at **Lombard's Seafood Grille**.
SEE ALSO RESTAURANTS, P.104

World Expo

Tucked into the corner of the park, this is a re-creation of a world's fair minus all the exhibitions. **Men in Black Alien Attack** (minimum height: 42in), is a fun and challenging ride through the universe zapping aliens along the way. On **The Simpsons Ride** ④ you accompany the hapless cartoon family on a hair-raising, animated ride through Krustyland, a dodgy theme park run by Krusty the Clown.

Below: the vintage streets of New York.

Islands of Adventure

The screams are audible as soon as you enter the park. Look up and you'll see why – the Incredible Hulk roller coaster twists and drops riders at speeds few would think sensible. This is Orlando's finest theme park for those seeking big thrills. In total there are four roller coasters, three drenching river rides, a sensational motion simulator ride, and various fairground-style rides that throw you, spin you, drench you, and otherwise shake you all around. But it's not necessarily a kid-free zone. The comic-book-laden themes will appeal to young boys as well as overgrown ones, and the dreamlike Seuss Landing celebrates a childhood classic.

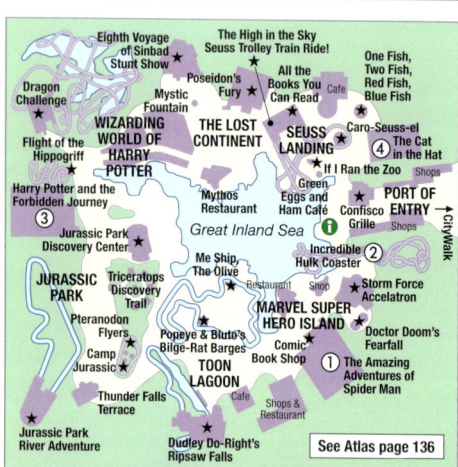

See Atlas page 136

Marvel Super Hero Island

For boys weaned on Marvel comic books, this island is a dream come true, especially at the **Comic Book Shop**, but no cultish fascination is needed to appreciate the thrill rides here. You don't need to know anything about Peter Parker to realize that **The Amazing Adventures of Spider Man** ① is the finest motion simulator ride in Orlando. The **Incredible Hulk Coaster** ② is the park's signature ride and not for the faint-hearted. Two standard fairground rides will please those wanting slightly tamer thrills. **Storm Force**

Accelatron is a variation on the spinning teacup theme, while **Doctor Doom's Fearfall** (minimum height: 52in) lifts riders 150ft (46m) in the air before dropping them to the ground. SEE ALSO SHOPPING, P.113; THRILL RIDES, P.126–7

Toon Lagoon

Toon Lagoon celebrates tamer cartoon characters such as Betty Boop, a spinach-craving sailor and a Canadian mountie, but the rides still pack a punch and are guaranteed to get you wet. **Dudley Do-Right's Ripsaw Falls** (minimum height: 44in) is a tame log ride

for most of the journey, but its finale boasts one of the steepest water drops ever created. It is impossible to stay dry on **Popeye & Bluto's Bilge-Rat Barges** (minimum height: 42in) – if the whitewater rapids don't drench you the overhead fountains are sure to get you soaked. To make matters even worse, mischievous children can shoot water cannons at you from Popeye's **Me Ship, The Olive**.

Jurassic Park

Dinosaurs set the theme in this jungle-like land. The **Jurassic Park Discovery Center** provides educational insight into the great beasts. You can create a dinosaur with your DNA, take control of models of these enormous

Below: a happy fan.

Left: Marvel Super Hero Island.

roller coasters intertwined in the sky, or opt for a gentler ride on the family-friendly **Flight of the Hippogrift**. Then visit the shops and taverns of Hogsmeade for wizard fare.

SEE ALSO THRILL RIDES, P.126–7

Seuss Landing

This is the most magical land outside of the Magic Kingdom. Dr Seuss's stories lend themselves to fantastic realizations, including a **Green Eggs and Ham Café**. Most remarkable is how ordinary plants and trees have been grown and pruned to resemble the zany illustrated plants in the children's book series.

Needless to say, kids are well catered for here. **If I Ran the Zoo** is an imaginative play area, and the **Caro-Seuss-el** replaces the traditional horses with Dog-alopes, Cowfish, and Aqua Mop Tops. **The High in the Sky Seuss Trolley Train Ride!** and **One Fish, Two Fish, Red Fish, Blue Fish** both lift riders above the park, with the latter promising to soak you if you can't drive your fish properly.

The Cat in the Hat ④ ride is an accomplished dark ride through the famous children's story. The couch you ride has a notorious habit of going in a spin. If you're a fan of the Cat don't leave without a trip to **All the Books You Can Read**.

SEE ALSO SHOPPING, P.113

animals, and if you're lucky you'll get to watch a dinosaur hatchling emerge from its shell. **Camp Jurassic** is a remarkable playground that includes a terrifying maze of caverns that little children will find frightening and big ones could lose themselves in for an entire day. Above, the **Pteranodon Flyers** whisk kids around the camp in a ski-lift-style ride.

The **Jurassic Park River Adventure** (minimum height: 42in) recreates the theme of the original film: a tourist jaunt through a park filled with dinosaurs that goes horribly wrong. Escaped raptors make trouble, but it's the T-Rex that nearly eats your boat, which is most frightening; the steep, dark drop that lets you escape him is no picnic either.

The Lost Continent

Poseidon's Fury is a drawn-out special-effects show set in a haunted temple. Though the live-action host is amusing, the show is not worth the wait. The **Eighth Voyage of Sindbad Stunt Show** does little to improve the standards with its stilted acting. Both attractions are saved by spectacular sets. The **Mythos** restaurant is the finest place to have a meal in the park.

SEE ALSO LIVE SHOWS, P.79;
RESTAURANTS, P.105

The Wizarding World of Harry Potter

The chance to experience the world of the now-legendary boy wizard has made this the most sensational new theme park attraction in years. **Harry Potter and the Forbidden Journey** ③ takes you through the classrooms and corridors of Hogwarts Castle, then high into the air on a thrilling magical journey with Harry and his friends. Take the **Dragon Challenge** and ride one of two high-speed

As you enter the park you may find you need a bit of liquid courage before boarding the thrill rides. The **Confisco Grille** is a good place to steel your nerves. For most it's the area's shops that are more likely to be visited. *See also Restaurants, p.105.*

International Drive and Lake Buena Vista

After the plans for Disney World were announced, Orlando Hilton owner Finley Hamilton built a hotel at the Sand Lake Road/I-4 interchange, the southern end of a road that he dubbed International Drive. The lodging seemed a long shot and became known as 'Finley's Folly,' but he was vindicated when Disney made the hotel its headquarters during the resort's construction, setting off a rush to develop hotels, restaurants, and competing attractions along the 12-mile commercial strip now known as I-Drive.

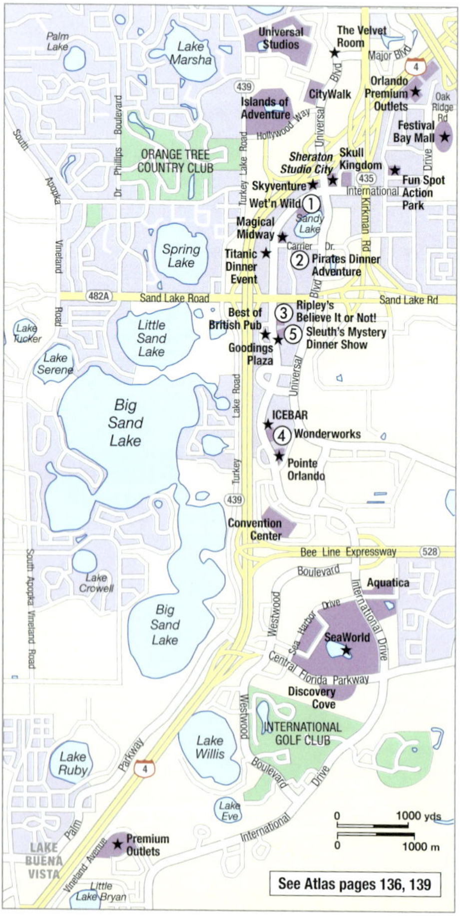

Above: Wonderworks.

I-4 to Sand Lake Road

One of Orlando's most recognizable hotels, the **Sheraton Studio City**, towers over the northern section of International Drive, which is otherwise dominated by bargain shopping and cheap thrills. Just north of Oak Ridge Road are the **Orlando Premium Outlets**, the city's newest and largest outlet mall, while not much further south is the **Festival Bay Mall**, which includes the **Ron Jon Surf Shop** and the **Ron Jon Surfpark**.

Opposite Festival Bay Mall is the **Fun Spot Action Park**, with over a dozen amusement park rides, including an enormous go-cart track. **Wet'n Wild** ①, more or less across the road, is an extensive water park with slides and a wave pool, **Skyventure** is an indoor skydiving venue, while the **Magical Midway** offers more

Map labels

Palm Lake
Lake Marsha
Universal Studios
The Velvet Room
Major Blvd
439
CityWalk
Islands of Adventure
Orlando Premium Outlets
Oak Ridge Rd
Festival Bay Mall
Hollywood Way
ORANGE TREE COUNTRY CLUB
Dr. Phillips Boulevard
South Apopka
Turkey Lake Road
Sheraton Studio City
Skull Kingdom
435
Skyventure
Wet'n Wild
Fun Spot Action Park
International Dr
Kirkman Rd
Universal Blvd
Vineland
Sandy Lake
Spring Lake
Magical Midway
Titanic
Titanic Dinner Event
Carrier Dr.
② Pirates Dinner Adventure
482A
Sand Lake Road
Sand Lake Rd
Lake Tucker
Little Sand Lake
Best of British Pub
③ Ripley's Believe It or Not!
⑤ Sleuth's Mystery Dinner Show
Lake Serene
Goodings Plaza
Universal Blvd
Big Sand Lake
ICEBAR
Turkey
④ Wonderworks
Pointe Orlando
439
Convention Center
South Apopka Vineland Road
Bee Line Expressway
528
Boulevard
Lake Crowell
Westwood
Aquatica
Big Sand Lake
International Drive
Sea Harbor Drive
SeaWorld
Central Florida Parkway
Discovery Cove
INTERNATIONAL GOLF CLUB
Lake Ruby
Lake Willis
Westwood Boulevard
4
Lake Eve
LAKE BUENA VISTA
Palm Parkway
★ Premium Outlets
International Drive
Little Lake Bryan
Vineland Avenue

0   1000 yds
0   1000 m

See Atlas pages 136, 139

Most visitors to I-Drive and Lake Buena Vista are here for the same reason as the hoteliers and restaurateurs serving them: Disney. Even before Walt Disney officially announced the new park, developers had jumped aboard the Mouse wagon.

SHOWS, P.81; THEMED ATTRACTIONS, P.118, 120

Pointe Orlando

Opposite the Orange County Convention Center, **Pointe Orlando** is the undisputed center of International Drive's retail life. This shopping center has several bars, some of the best restaurants along the strip, and a branch of Regal Cinemas with 20 screens, including an IMAX.
SEE ALSO SHOPPING, P.114

go-carts and fairground rides. East of International Drive on Carrier Drive is the popular **Pirate's Dinner Adventure** ②. The huge painting of the Titanic at the same intersection marks the venue for Orlando's newest dinner theater, the **Titanic Dinner Event**.
SEE ALSO LIVE SHOWS, P.81; SHOPPING, P.114–5; THEMED ATTRACTIONS, P.119–21, 123

South of Sand Lake Road

From Sand Lake Road to the Point, I-Drive takes on a character all its own. The I-Drive Trolley transports visitors up and down the street and, in a rare American sight, people can be seen walking along the sidewalk between restaurants and hotels that are tucked behind parking lots.

No one can call this area classy, but it is the only tourist center that combines food, drink, and hotels in such proximity that driving, much less drink-driving, is not necessary.

Ripley's Believe It or Not! ③, in a subsided building, provides oddities galore, but is not to be outdone by **Wonderworks** ④ – a completely upside-down house full of interactive exhibits and video games. **Sleuth's Mystery Dinner Show** ⑤, in the same complex as **Goodings**, is one of the city's better dinner theaters, while expats flock to the **Best of British** pub.
SEE ALSO BARS AND CAFÉS, P.51; FOOD AND DRINK, P.69; LIVE

South International Drive and Lake Buena Vista

From here International Drive continues past **SeaWorld**, but loses any inherent attraction until it terminates near the other location for **Premium Outlets**.

West of I-4 there is an assortment of hotels that take advantage of the proximity to Disney World that **Lake Buena Vista** provides.
SEE ALSO SEAWORLD, P.26–7; SHOPPING, P.115

Below: I–Drive has little visual appeal, but plenty of activities.

SeaWorld

With three top rides, five shows, and over a dozen restaurants, SeaWorld is much more than just the world's foremost aquarium. But the animals are the stars, and with careful planning, you can see most of them in one full day. As the emphasis is on shows and exhibits rather than rides, there tend to be fewer lines and a more easygoing pace than at other parks. Spacious grounds and the absence of themed lands encourage visitors to meander between attractions instead of marching doggedly from beginning to end. Unfortunately there is no way of avoiding the long waits for Kraken, Manta and Journey to Atlantis, unless you ride during one of the main show times.

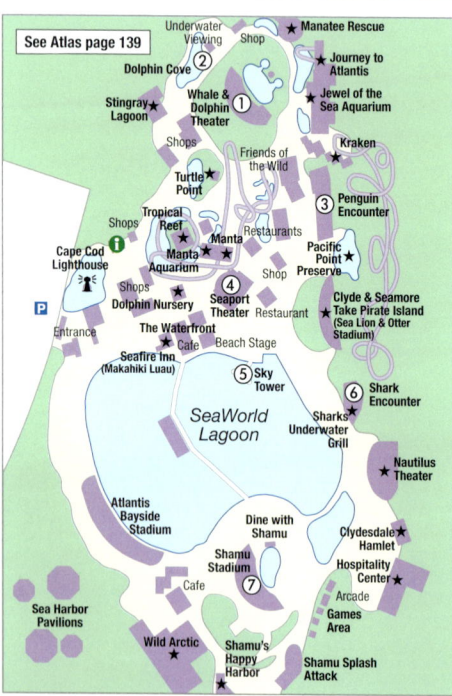

See Atlas page 139

SeaWorld operates two other theme parks. The all-inclusive **Discovery Cove** gives you an up-close view of sealife and includes a chance to swim with dolphins. At first glance **Aquatica** seems like any other old water park, until you realize that water slides pass underwater and through a pod of dolphins. *See Themed Attractions, p.121.*

Whale and Dolphin Theater

To the left of the entrance is a path that meanders past some modest, animal-specific attractions to the **Whale and Dolphin Theater** ①, home of the **Blue Horizons** show featuring tricky dolphins and wetsuited acrobats.

Turtle Point is a recreated lagoon that houses several endangered species of turtles. **Stingray Lagoon** is a large shallow pool filled with the creatures. Stick your hand in to feel their smooth skin. Undoubtedly the main animal attraction here is **Dolphin Cove** ②. For a couple of dollars you can buy a plate of fish at feeding time and stroke the dolphins as you feed them. There is also an underwater viewing area from which to see these playful mammals.

Plan Your Day

You'll find everything you need to organize your visit to Sea-World at the park's entrance, and as shows play such a big part here, it is worth getting a copy of the show times, sitting down with a cup of coffee at Cypress bakery and properly planning how to spend your day here – if you don't you could easily miss out on the bigger productions.

Guest Services also organizes reservations for meals and **Discovery Cove**. SEE ALSO THEMED ATTRACTIONS, P.122

Left: friendly faces at feeding time.

with sharks of all descriptions. The best view is had while dining at the **Sharks Underwater Grill**. Next door is the **Nautilus Theater**, home to **A'Lure, The Call of the Ocean**, a mesmerizing Cirque du Soleil-style show. A short walk through the **Clydesdale Hamlet** brings you to the **Hospitality Center**, where every guest that is old enough is entitled to a free glass of beer.

SEE ALSO LIVE SHOWS, P.79; RESTAURANTS, P.109

Shamu Stadium

Opposite the SeaWorld lagoon is **Shamu Stadium** ⑦, home of the famous killer whale and his show **Believe**. **Shamu's Happy Harbor** is a disappointing play area for kids though: the rides don't feel as substantial as they should, and the enormous climbing frame makes keeping an eye on your child nearly impossible.

The **Wild Arctic** hosts beluga whales and polar bears. You access the zoo section of the area via a simulated helicopter ride that goes horribly wrong.

SEE ALSO LIVE SHOWS, P.79

Things hit closer to home at **Manatee Rescue**, where the story of Florida's cuddliest-looking and most endangered sea mammal is told. An alligator pond lies just outside, displaying the state's most long-term residents.

SEE ALSO LIVE SHOWS, P.80

Thrill, Spills, and Penguins

Thrill rides and ice slides dominate the area around **Penguin Encounter** ③. The penguins themselves are fascinating to watch, and their chilled home is a perfect retreat for humans, too, during the hot summer months. The two nearby thrill rides, **Kraken** and **Journey to Atlantis**, provide danger-seeking guests with other distractions.

SEE ALSO THRILL RIDES, P.127

From Sea Lions to the Waterfront

Under the screaming shadow of Kraken sit the barking sea lions at **Pacific Point Preserve** who are more than persistent in their request for food. A trained sea lion features in **Clyde and Seamore Take Pirate Island** at the Sea Lion and Otter Stadium.

An archway leads to the **Seaport Theater** ④, home to the **Pets Ahoy** show. Beyond is **Manta**, a thrill ride that lets you glide face down on an inverted roller coaster.

Under the **Sky Tower** ⑤, a fixture since the park opened in 1973, the **Waterfront** area stretches along a lake at the center of the park and is the main location for sit-down restaurants such as the **Seafire Inn**.

SEE LIVE SHOWS, P.80, RESTAURANTS, P.109; THRILL RIDES, P.127

Sharks, Acrobats and Free Beer

At the top of the Waterfont are three attractions not to be missed. **Shark Encounter** ⑥ is a walk-through aquarium

Below: an underwater surprise.

Downtown Orlando and Loch Haven Park

Orlando's Downtown, though the center of 'real life' in central Florida, is on the fringes of Orlando's imaginary, tourist-oriented world and hence often overlooked. It shouldn't be. Around this thriving business area are quality restaurants not reliant on heavy themes to attract customers, and a thriving nightlife district meant for adults, not children. There are historic houses, grand hotels, and relaxing lakeside walks to be explored. And in Loch Haven Park, just to the north, there is another novelty: culture.

See Atlas pages 134–135

Heading west from Downtown you will find that Division Street carries its name for a reason. To its east lies commerce-driven Downtown Orlando, to the west the city's traditional African-American neighborhood, which dates back to the early 1900s. The **Wells' Built Museum** documents the area's vibrant past. *See also Museums and Galleries, p.84*

atmospheric setting for the high-concept restaurants and trendy nightlife spots that are making a comeback here.

From Church Street to Washington Street, there is a medley of bars that would seem more appropriate on a college campus than in a business center.

But there is culture here, too. At 29 Orange Avenue is the **Cityartsfactory**, now housed in the old Philips Theater. This is the center for the Downtown Arts District and features a large exhibition space and several commercial art galleries.

North of Central Boulevard is **Wall Street Plaza**, a bar and restaurant complex with happy-hour specials to tempt in the office workers. Most nights feature live music in one of the bars. Walk through

Downtown

Orange Avenue from South Street to East Colonial Drive is the spine of Downtown Orlando. At its southern base is the **Grand Bohemian Hotel Orlando** ①, a top-class hotel that includes the **Boheme**, one of the city's finest restaurants, and the **Grand Bohemian Gallery**, which fea-

tures a fine collection of European and American art.

Just west of here, between I-4 and Orange Avenue, is the revitalized **Church Street Station** ② area. Set around the old train depot, the historic buildings date from the 1880s and early 1900s. Retaining many of their period features, they make an

Left: Downtown's Lake Eola.

complex, hosting the Philharmonic orchestra, theater productions, and the **Orlando Magic** basketball team.
SEE ALSO, MUSIC, DANCE, AND THEATRE, P.88; SPORT, P.116

Loch Haven Park

Loch Haven was created as a cultural anchor, a counterbalance to the theme parks' domination, and includes heavy hitters such as the **Orlando Science Center** ⑤ and **Orlando Museum of Art** ⑥. But culture shouldn't have to be treated like this.

Though originally meant as a cultural oasis, it feels more like a ghetto. While intriguing institutions such as **The Rep Theatre**, the **Orlando Shakespeare Theater** ⑦ and the **Mennello Museum of American Art** are located here, there is nothing tempting you to stay beyond your visit – the nearest restaurants, bars, and cafés are Downtown – a 10-minute drive away. Each attraction has its own isolated parking lot, hardly an invitation to walk between institutions.

Just to the east of Loch Haven Park are the extensive **Harry P. Leu Gardens**, which include wide-ranging examples of Florida's natural flora.
SEE ALSO MUSEUMS AND GALLERIES, P.83–4, 87; MUSIC, DANCE, AND THEATER, P.89; NATURAL WORLD, P.91

Wall Street Plaza to Heritage Square and the **Orange County Regional History Center**. This old courthouse now tells the story of central Florida's development.

Magnolia Avenue ③ is worth exploring as well; in some ways it's an artier Orange Avenue. It has several galleries, the **Mad Cow Theatre** and more sophisticated drinking spots like **The Celt Irish Pub**.
SEE ALSO ACCOMMODATIONS, P.47–8; BARS AND CAFÉS, P.52; MUSEUMS AND GALLERIES, P.82, 83; MUSIC, DANCE, AND THEATER, P.89; RESTAURANTS, P.109

Lake Eola and Thornton Park

To the east of Downtown between Central and Robinson streets, the 43-acre (17 hectare) Lake Eola Park has a gentle walking trail and a café. Paddleboats can be rented if you'd like to venture out to the central fountain, and a small amphitheater hosts concerts.

Overlooking the lake is the **Eō Inn**, a historic boutique hotel with the full-service **Urban Spa**. South of the lake is the Thornton Park area, where you'll find trendy places to eat and drink such as **HUE Restaurant.** SEE ALSO ACCOMMODATIONS, P.47; PAMPERING, P.97; RESTAURANTS, P.110

Centroplex

Home to the **Bob Carr Performing Arts** ④ venue and **Amway Arena**, this is Orlando's main entertainment

Below: a vintage train at the refurbished Church Street Station.

Winter Park and Maitland

North of Orlando lies an oasis of small-town American life with a healthy helping of sophisticated European atmosphere – Winter Park. This town thrives on the energy of Rollins College, an elite liberal arts institution that runs several museums open to students and tourists alike. Park Avenue is the center of day- and nightlife in Winter Park, with numerous independently owned shops, some fantastic cafés for lunch, and fine dining options for dinner. Beyond Winter Park to the northeast are Maitland, whose historical society commemorates all aspects of its history, and Eatonville, the first African-American township in the United States.

Park Avenue

If you find yourself in Orlando for reasons not entirely of your own choosing – kids' vacation, a convention, visiting in-laws in holiday homes – then Park Avenue could prove the perfect antidote to the theme-park atmosphere.

This tiny main street of Winter Park is lined with places for adults to enjoy such pleasures as a quiet glass of red at the **Wine Room**, a fine meal at **Café de France** and other treats more sophisticated than Mickey Mouse ice creams – all without a themed restaurant in sight.

At the northern end of Park Avenue's string of shops and restaurants is the **Charles Hosmer Morse Museum of American Art** ①, which celebrates the leaded-glass works of Louis Comfort Tiffany.

SEE ALSO FOOD AND DRINK, P.69; MUSEUMS AND GALLERIES, P.85; RESTAURANTS, P.111.

Rollins College ②

The graceful Spanish-style architecture that constitutes the campus of **Rollins College** helps create a tranquil retreat on the shores of Lake Virginia, east of Park Avenue and south of Holt Avenue.

In addition to providing a terrific setting for an afternoon

Below: the romantic setting of Rollins College.

Left: small shops dominate Park Avenue.

It does not take an avid 'twitcher' to spot the numerous birds of prey circling Florida's skies and even rummaging through the garbage bins on I-Drive. If these feathered friends have intrigued you, then this is the perfect place to find out more as injured birds are nursed back to health on the premises.

Eatonville today is a nice, quiet small town that you could easily drive straight through, but it has great significance in US history. After the Emancipation Proclamation freed the slaves in 1863, Eatonville became one of the first all-black towns in America. In 1887 it officially became the first incorporated African-American town in the United States. Unless you visit during the annual festival, this history is hard to spot. Only the **Zora Neale Hurston National Museum of Arts** ⑥ stands out. Named after the Harlem Renaissance writer who grew up here, it now celebrates African-American art.

SEE ALSO MUSEUMS AND GALLERIES, P.86, 87; NATURAL WORLD, P.90

Below: the Aztec-inspired Maitland Art Center.

stroll, the college maintains some fine museums, on and off campus, in the Orlando area. The small but refined **Cornell Fine Arts Museum** ③ features strong temporary exhibitions and a modest collection of European art. Also on campus is the eclectic **Annie Russell Theatre**.

SEE ALSO MUSEUMS AND GALLERIES, P.85; MUSIC, DANCE, AND THEATER, P.89

Greater Winter Park

Rollins College's cultural institutions extend beyond the campus grounds. To the northeast along Osceola Avenue are the **Albin Polasek Museum and Sculpture Gardens** ④, which exhibit the Czech sculptor's work. Attractions become more Floridian at the **Winter Park Village** shopping center, which includes several restaurants and bars.

SEE ALSO MUSEUMS AND GALLERIES, P.85; SHOPPING, P.115

Maitland and Eatonville

Sleepy Maitland has tried its best to tag along to Winter Park's 'real world' ability to attract tourists, but lacking a genuine main street, it doesn't receive the same attention. Instead it has the Maitland Historical Society, which runs two intriguing museums. The **Waterhouse Residence Museum and Carpentry Shop Museum** on the shores of Lake Lily preserve what life was like in central Florida at the beginning of the 20th century, while the **Maitland Historical Museum and Telephone Museum** keep an eclectic collection based on local lore. Next door to the Telephone Museum, the **Maitland Art Center** runs courses and has a small gallery set amid its remarkable Aztec-inspired grounds.

Between Maitland and Eatonville lies the **Audubon Center for Birds of Prey** ⑤.

The Space Coast

There is more than enough to do in Orlando, but the Space Coast offers a once-in-a-lifetime opportunity. Nowhere else in the world are you able to visit up close a location that launches satellites and humans into space. The visitor center is full of compelling exhibitions, from how man first reached the Moon to the latest developments in the International Space Station. The security necessary for these operations has preserved Florida's natural habitats all along this stretch of coast – don't be surprised to spot an alligator outside your tour bus – and nearby towns such as Cocoa Beach provide fine surfing and more earthly distractions.

Above: a rare chance to meet an astronaut.

Kennedy Space Center ①

Though you may initially think the Space Center's Visitor Complex is small, it takes an entire day to see it, as the bus tour itself takes 2–3 hours.

Educational exhibits are to the left as you exit the Information Center. **Eye on the Universe: The Hubble Space Telescope** reveals stunning images from the depths of outer space. **Early Space Exploration** tells of the traumas and triumphs that led to the first landing on the Moon, while in the **Rocket Garden** genuine examples from these early days tower above visitors. The **Children's Play Dome** will entertain any young ones not interested in space – it's usually rather empty.

Opposite the Information Center is **Astronaut Encounter** where you meet real astronauts, and **Exploration Space: Explorers Wanted**, an interactive, live theater exhibit. Beyond that is the **IMAX** theater which shows two features: *Space Station 3D* and *Hubble 3D*.

To the right of the Information Center is a quirky exhibit called **Robot Scouts**, which celebrates these often forgotten, mechanical space heroes. Beyond that is a life-size shuttle that you can explore independently, and the **Shuttle Launch Experience**, which lets you know just what

it feels like to be on a shuttle mission. This lacks the centrifugal force of Mission: SPACE at Epcot *(see p.124)*, so don't be put off by it.

Also in the Space Shuttle Plaza is the **Mission Status Center** that briefs visitors about upcoming missions, and the **Astronaut Memorial**, which honors those who have given their life in the cause of space exploration.

The bus tour from the visitor complex takes in two main sights. The first is the **LC-39 Observation Gantry**, which has a short film about the early space program, but the key objective is to gain good views of the dozen or so launch pads from the gantry above.

For those looking to continue their journey into space, the **U.S. Astronaut Hall of Fame** is just across the Indian River from the Visitor Center along SR 405. *See Themed Attractions, p.119.*

Many of these launch pads are still active. You'll pass the Space Shuttle's enormous **Vehicle Assembly Building** on your way to and from here.

The **Apollo/Saturn V Center** contains a 363ft-long Apollo rocket, a re-creation of an Apollo launch and the first Moon landing.

A separate tour, **Discover KSC: Today & Tomorrow**,

Left: the Rocket Garden.

focuses on NASA's Space Shuttle program, with visits to the shuttle landing facility and the closest possible viewpoint of the launch pad.
SEE ALSO THRILL RIDES, P.127

Merritt Island and Canaveral Seashore

In contrast to all this high-tech adventure are two nearby nature preserves: the **Merritt Island National Wildlife Refuge** ②, home to manatees and leatherback turtles alike, and the barrier dunes and sea-swept beaches of **Canaveral National Seashore** ③.
SEE ALSO NATURAL WORLD, P.90–1

Cocoa Beach ④

Those who prefer beaches in a more developed setting will find Cocoa Beach to their liking – an old-time seaside town with an abundance of chain motels, restaurants, and souvenir shops, as well as first-rate beaches. The biggest attraction is the **Ron Jon Surf Shop**, a neon-lit palace devoted to surf gear. Famous surfers occasionally drop in for autograph sessions; scuba diving and surfing lessons are also available.
SEE ALSO SHOPPING, P.115

Below: Cocoa Beach Pier as the sun goes down.

A–Z

In the following section Orlando's attractions and services are organized by theme, under alphabetical headings. Items that link to another theme are cross-referenced. All sights that fall within the bounds of the atlas section at the end of the book are given a page number and grid reference.

Accommodations 36
Bars and Cafés 50
Behind the Scenes 54
Budgeting and Survival 56
Children 60
Essentials 62
Food and Drink 68
Golf 70
History 74
Live Shows, Parades, and Fireworks 76
Museums and Galleries 82
Music, Dance, and Theater 88
Natural World 90
Nightlife 92
Pampering 96
Restaurants 98
Shopping 112
Sport 116
Themed Attractions 118
Thrill Rides 124
Transportation 128

Accommodations

Accommodations in Orlando range from luxury resorts that cater to your every whim to modest mom-and-pop motels, antique-filled bed & breakfasts, and campgrounds. Although standards for service and facilities are generally quite high, there is the occasional bad apple. Indeed, some of the cheapest accommodations offered by tour operators are positively miserable, so be sure you know what you're getting into before signing on the dotted line. If you're staying at Disney spend the extra money to stay at a resort they classify as Moderate or Deluxe – the attention to detail at these resorts guarantee a magical vacation.

Reservations and Prices

Reservations are generally required, and if you are traveling during the high season you should book several months ahead if you have your heart set on a particular hotel or if you want to stay inside Walt Disney World.

Room rates vary enormously between the high season and the low season *(see box p.42)*. There is plenty of scope to ask for a discount if you are staying for a week or more, or if you are visiting during the off-season.

Left: the monorail travels through the Contemporary's main lobby.

Florida also imposes a resort tax, in addition to the usual sales tax, which is added to the price of all hotel rooms. It varies from county to county and ranges from between 2 and 5 percent.

Magic Kingdom Resorts

Contemporary Resort
4600 North World Drive, Lake Buena Vista; tel: 407-824-1000; $$$; Monorail to Epcot and Magic Kingdom, Link: 302; map p.138 B4

The monorail passes through the middle of this 15-story A-frame built over a quarter-century ago. Most rooms have two queen-size beds and a daybed. Tower rooms have private balconies overlooking the Magic Kingdom or Bay Lake; those in the Garden Wings have nice views but are somewhat distant from the central property. There are several bars and restaurants, including the elegant **California Grill** – a popular

Information on all of Disney's resort hotels can be found at http://disneyworld.disney.go.com. Reservations can be made there or by phoning: 407-939-7675.

spot for watching Magic Kingdom fireworks. Amenities include a supervised evening children's program, salon, water activities, a health club and tennis center, two swimming pools, and a video arcade.
SEE ALSO RESTAURANTS, P.102

Grand Floridian Resort & Spa
4401 Grand Floridian Way, Lake Buena Vista; tel: 407-824-3000; $$$; Monorail to Epcot and Magic Kingdom, boat to Magic Kingdom; map p.138 A4

The Victorian era in all its splendor is recreated at Disney's flagship property, an elegant confection of glistening white, wooden buildings with red shingled roofs, gracious verandas, and turrets. Open-cage elevators in the plant-filled, five-story, chandeliered lobby serve second-floor shops and

All of Disney's resorts are connected to all of Disney's parks by bus. Some resorts are connected to individual parks by monorail or boat – a great way to arrive. We have listed these unique links in our listings.

restaurants. Most rooms in the four- and five-story lodge buildings have two queen-size beds and a daybed; many overlook the Seven Seas Lagoon. Amenities include some of Disney's finest dining experiences at **Victoria and Albert's** and **Citricos**, and a fine water-side restaurant, **Narcoossee's**; several bars, a supervised evening children's program, the Grand Floridian Spa and Health Club, two swimming pools, and water activities.

SEE ALSO PAMPERING, P.96;
RESTAURANTS, P.102–3

Polynesian Resort
1600 Seven Seas Drive, Lake Buena Vista; tel: 407-824-2000; $$$; Monorail to Magic Kingdom and Epcot, boat to Magic Kingdom, Link: 302; map p.138 A4
One of Disney's most authentic theme hotels re-creates a Pacific Islands

retreat. The centerpiece is the Great Ceremonial House, a tropical extravaganza of plants and waterfalls. Rooms, in 11 two- and three-story 'longhouses,' vary in size, but most have two queen-size beds, a daybed and balconies. Those overlooking the Seven Seas Lagoon afford front-row seats for Magic Kingdom fireworks. There are several restaurants and

bars, two pools, a playground, supervised evening children's programs, and water activities.

Wilderness Lodge and Villas
901 Timberline Drive, Lake Buena Vista; tel: 407-824-3200; $$$; boat to Magic Kingdom, Link: 302; map p.138 B4
A skillful blending of wood and stone replicates the look of an early 20th-century National Park lodge. Although the eight-story lakefront dwelling appears rustic, accommodations are anything but. Most rooms have two queen-size beds, tables and chairs, and balconies. Villas, in a five-story adjoining

Below: the Grand Floridian Resort and Spa.

Prices for a standard double room:
$ under $100
$$ $100–$200
$$$ over $200

building, range from studios with kitchenettes to two-bedroom units with dining areas, kitchens and whirlpool tubs. There are several restaurants and bars, a supervised evening children's program, a health club, video arcade, two swimming pools, sand beach, and boat rental. Boats sail to the Magic Kingdom; buses serve the other parks.

Epcot Resorts

BoardWalk Inn and Villas
2101 Epcot Resorts Boulevard, Lake Buena Vista; tel: 407-939-5100; $$$; boat to Epcot; map p.138 B2

Elaborately detailed buildings with turreted, brightly colored facades and twinkling lights recreate an East Coast boardwalk circa 1920. Spacious rooms with ocean-blue and sea-green furnishings have two queen-size brass beds, daybeds, and ceiling fans; two-story garden suites have private gardens. The villas – Disney Vacation Club timeshare units – sleep 4 to 12 and have kitchens, laundries and whirlpool tubs. A nightclub, piano bar, restaurants, midway games, and shops line the boardwalk. There's a supervised evening children's program, a health club, and a large swimming pool with a 200ft water slide.

Caribbean Beach Resort
900 Cayman Way, Lake Buena Vista; tel: 407-934-3400; $$; Link 301; map p.138 C2

Each of the five areas at this brightly colored resort that circles 45-acre Barefoot Bay recreates a Caribbean island and has its own pool, beach, and laundry room. Accommodations in each of the two-story buildings are the same: two double beds, a table and chairs, a coffeemaker, and bath. Rates vary only according to view. A food court and several casual restaurants cater to the resort's family-oriented clientele, and there are water sports, bike rentals, playgrounds, a shopping complex, and a video arcade.

Dolphin Resort
1500 Epcot Resorts Boulevard, Lake Buena Vista; tel: 407-934-4000; $$$; boat to Epcot; map p.138 B2

Two 56ft-high dolphins and hundreds of seven-story banana leaves festoon the facade of this 27-story, triangular, turquoise hotel with four nine-story wings. The lobby has a circus theme, and the spacious rooms, with turquoise and peach furnishings, have two queen-size beds, desks, and chairs. Some have balconies. There is a supervised evening children's program. In addition to

the seashell-shaped pool there are several restaurants and lounges on the property, which is within walking distance of Epcot and the BoardWalk.

Old Key West Resort
1510 North Cove Road, Lake Buena Vista; tel: 407-827-7700; $$$; boat to Downtown Disney; map p.138 C2

Although it's miles from the ocean, this hotel's color scheme and architecture bear an uncanny resemblance to buildings in the seaside resort town far to the south. Studios have two queen-size beds, tables and chairs, small refrigerators, microwaves, and coffeemakers. One-bedroom villas have king-size beds in the main bedroom and queen-size sleeper sofas in the living room. Two- and three-bedroom villas have full kitchens and porches or balconies. All units except studios have private whirlpool tubs. There are grills and picnic tables, several restaurants, a health club, swimming pools, shopping, tennis courts, a video arcade, and playgrounds.

Port Orleans Resort – French Quarter
2201 Orleans Drive, Lake Buena Vista; tel: 407-934-5000; $$; boat to Downtown Disney; map p.138 C3

This moderate hotel is reminiscent of New Orleans, and its landscaping makes it very suitable for couples

Left: the Boardwalk Villas are part of Disney's timeshare scheme.

wanting to get away as there are many quiet, romantic spots in which to linger. On the other hand, kids will love the Doubloon Lagoon pool with its colorfully themed attractions that include alligator and dragon slides.

Port Orleans – Riverside
1251 Riverside Drive, Lake Buena Vista; tel: 407-934-6000; $$; boat to Downtown Disney; map p.138 C3

With a feel for the Old South, the Riverside brings the Louisiana bayou to Florida. Accommodations are in two- and three-story buildings divided into 'parishes.' All rooms are the same size, and most have two double beds. Mansion rooms are in antebellum-style 'estates,' while Bayou rooms are in rustic-appearing buildings surrounding Man Island, a sprawling water complex. Only mansions have elevators. Amenities include six swimming pools, a restaurant and food court, shops, bars, bike and boat rentals, and fishing excursions.

Swan Resort
1200 Epcot Resorts Boulevard; tel: 407-934-3000; $$$; boat to Epcot; map p.138 B2

Fort Wilderness Resort within Walt Disney World has more than 800 campsites for tents and RVs. Another option is to rent a trailer (decked out like a log cabin) that sleeps up to six people and has air conditioning, color TV, radio, cookware and linen, i.e. all the equipment you'll need. The resort is located amid 750 acres (304 hectares) of woods and streams at 4510 North Fort Wilderness Trail, Lake Buena Vista, east of the Magic Kingdom. For information and reservations, tel: 407-824-2900.

Above: the Swan Resort is one of Disney's finest and is especially suitable for people traveling without children.

Just across the road from the Dolphin is this property, topped by two 47ft-tall swans. Rooms in the 12-story main building and two seven-story towers are a bit smaller in size than those in the Dolphin *(see p.38)*, but similar in color and amenities. There's a pool as well as several restaurants and bars, including the fine **Il Mulino New York Trattoria** and **Kimonos** sushi bar, and a supervised evening children's program.

SEE ALSO RESTAURANTS, P.103

Yacht and Beach Club Resorts and Beach Club Villas
1700–1800 Epcot Boulevard, Lake Buena Vista; tel: 407-934-7000 (Yacht Club) and 407-934-8000 (Beach Club); $$$; boat to Epcot, Link: 303; map p.138 B2

Each of the three properties overlooking a 25-acre lake has a distinct theme, but they share many facilities. Yacht Club rooms are finished in a nautical motif; those in the Beach Club are reminiscent of a private seaside retreat. Most, however, have either one king-size or two queen-size beds (some with daybeds), ceiling fans, and a table with chairs. The studios and one- to three-bedroom villas sleep up to eight. The resort's highlight is Stormalong Bay, an elaborate swimming area with whirlpools, water slides, and a private beach. In addition, there are several pools, a miniature golf course, a health club, restaurants and bars, boating, a supervised evening children's program, a salon, tennis courts, a video arcade, and shops.

Animal Kingdom Resorts

All-Star Movies, Music, and Sports
1901 (Movies) 1801 (Music) and 1701 (Sports) West Buena Vista Drive, Lake Buena Vista; tel: 407-939-7000 (All-Star Movies), 407-939-6000 (All-Star Music), 407-939-5000 (All-Star Sports); $–$$; Link: 303, 305; map p.138 A1–B1

This was Disney's only budget complex until the Pop Century *(see p.40)* opened. It has 30 three-story buildings divided by themes. Each has a distinctive facade, but aside from a few decorative touches, the size and decor of most rooms are identical: they're 260sq ft, have two double beds, small bureaus, a table with chairs, and bathrooms with separate vanity areas. Popular with families, the resort has a game room,

39

Above: the wildlife comes to see you at the Animal Kingdom Lodge.

playground, two pools, shopping, and food court. Buses transport guests to the parks.

Animal Kingdom Lodge
2901 Osceola Parkway, Lake Buena Vista; tel: 407-938-8000; $$$; Link: 301; map p.138 A1

Built to resemble a southern African game lodge, the hotel has an elaborately furnished lobby with a four-story observation window looking out onto a 33-acre savanna, which teems with wildlife. All standard and deluxe rooms have hand-crafted furniture and traditional tapestries, plus balconies; most have two queen-size beds. Many of the balconies overlook the savanna. Amenities include three restaurants, several bars, a children's play area that opens at 4.30pm, a health club, playground, shopping area, video arcade, and outdoor pool.

Coronado Springs Resort
1000 West Buena Vista Drive, Lake Buena Vista; tel: 407-939-1000; $$; Link: 303, 305; map p.138 B2

The American Southwest and Mexico are elaborately re-created at this lakefront complex with outdoor fountains, a Mayan pyramid, and the country's largest ballroom (the property is a popular spot for conventions). Each of three buildings is evocative of a different setting – the oceanfront, the city, and the countryside – with rooms decorated accordingly. Standard rooms have two double beds: some queens and kings are also available. There are several pools, a large whirlpool, a health club

and spa, a playground, video arcades, shops, a restaurant and food court, several bars, and water sports.

Wide World of Sports

Pop Century Resort
1050 Century Drive, Lake Buena Vista; tel: 407-938-4000; $$; Link 301; map p.138 C1

Encompassing 10 four-story buildings, this resort is divided into two sections: the Legendary Years, depicting the first 50 years of the 20th century, and the Classic Years, depicting the second 50 years. Statues representing various aspects of pop culture are used to carry the themes. Rooms, smaller than at other Disney properties at 260sq ft, have two double beds, bathrooms with a separate vanity area, and small dressers, tables, and chairs. Each section has a food court, swimming pool, playground, shopping area, and video arcade.

Other Disney Resorts

Buena Vista Palace
1900 Buena Vista Drive, Lake Buena Vista; tel: 866-397-6516; www.buenavistapalace.com; $–$$; map p.139 D2

Located across the lagoon from Downtown Disney, the Palace's rooms are all very well appointed in sleek modern furnishings and pillow-

Right: Downtown Disney as seen from the Hilton.

Prices for a standard double room:
$ under $100
$$ $100–$200
$$$ over $200

Above: the stylishly southern Bohemian Hotel Celebration.

top beds. Most have balconies, and some even offer a view of the lake. The Island Suites provide more space than the smallish rooms. The resort has large spa and pool facilities and six restaurants to choose from.

Hilton
1751 Hotel Plaza Boulevard, Lake Buena Vista; tel: 407-827-4000; www.hilton-wdwv.com; $$$; map p.139 D2

Within walking distance of Downtown Disney, this large hotel is set among 23 acres of tropical landscaping. Guests receive similar benefits as Disney Resort guests, including Extra Magic Hours, an on-site Disney Character breakfast, free transportation to the parks, and access to five Disney golf courses. Several grades of suite are available for those needing more space. All rooms have Hilton Serenity Beds to provide extra comfort and an MP3 compatible clock radio.

Royal Plaza Hotel
1905 Hotel Plaza Boulevard, Lake Buena Vista; tel: 407-828-2828; www.royalplaza.com; $$; map p.139 D2

Located near Downtown Disney, the Royal Plaza has 394 rooms. Its standard rooms are the largest in the Downtown Disney area, are appointed with subtle contemporary decor and furnishings, and have all the modern amenities you'd expect. Suites are also available. The pool is nothing to shout about, but being this close to Disney, you may not find time to use it.

Wyndham Lake Buena Vista Resort
1850 Hotel Plaza Blvd, Lake Buena Vista; tel: 407-828-4444; www.regalsunresort.com; $; map p.139 D2

Across the street from Downtown Disney, the new Wyndham Resort is a good option for those on a budget, especially if you opt for one of the standard rooms. Superior rooms offer views of either Downtown Disney and the theme parks, the lake, or towards downtown Orlando. All rooms have TVs, high-speed internet, fridges, safes and other basic amenities, while the resort itself offers a Disney Character Breakfast, a two-pool swimming area with its own bar and grill, a fine-dining restaurant and other bars too.

Celebration and Kissimmee

Bohemian Hotel Celebration
700 Bloom Street, Celebration; tel: 407-566-6000 or 888-249-4007; www.celebration hotel.com; $$$; map p.18

Located in the town of Celebration, this quietly elegant, out-of-the-way boutique hotel seems like a million miles away from Disney-World, which is close by. Guests feel like they are stepping back into Old Florida. Registration is concierge-style in the low-key lobby, which features comfy sofas, fans, a bar, and hand-painted murals and hand-tinted photos of orange groves, wildlife, and historic scenes. The peaceful terrace has rocking chairs and overlooks the pool, lake, and adjoining workout room. The 115 rooms have a classic southern feel, with pinstriped wallpaper, reproduction antique furnishings, interactive televisions, and high-speed internet access; some have balconies. Guests may play Celebration's renowned 18-hole golf course and work out at the state-of-the-art fitness

Orlando hotel prices vary quite dramatically between the seasons, which are unsurprisingly linked to the US school calendar. The Christmas break period, mid–Dec until New Year, is the most expensive, followed by spring break, mid-Feb until the end of Mar, and summer, end of May until the beginning of August. The cheapest times to visit are from New Year until mid-Feb, Aug and Sept (but be prepared for extraordinary heat), and the first half of Dec.

Above: arriving in style at Portofino Bay.

center at Celebration's nearby hospital.

Celebrity Resorts

2800 North Poinciana Boulevard, Kissimmee; tel: 407-997-5000; www.celebrity resorts.com; $$

This timeshare establishment has several different sizes of accommodation, from standard rooms to three-bedroom villas. All are quite affordable and available for short lets. The resort has tennis, basketball and racquetball courts, a fitness center, three outdoor pools and one indoor pool, and a playground. The rooms and suites are well designed, making the most of their space.

Mystic Dunes Resort & Golf Club

7900 Mystic Dunes Lane, Celebration; tel: 877-747-4747; www.mystic-dunes-resort.com; $$$

Located on 600 acres (243 hectares) of meticulously landscaped grounds, this timeshare resort makes for a grand short-term retreat. The sleekly furnished, one- to three-bed villas all have a fully equipped kitchen, washer and dryer, and a whirlpool bath. Resort amenities include the **Mystic**

Dunes Golf Club, four heated swimming pools (one of which has a two-story water slide and children's wading pool), and mini-golf. Tennis and basketball courts also feature.
SEE ALSO GOLF, P.71–2

Omni Orlando Resort at ChampionsGate

1500 Masters Boulevard, ChampionsGate; tel: 407-390-6664; www.omniorlando resort.com; $$$

Located southwest of Celebration along the I-4 corridor, this luxury resort is surrounded by 36 holes of golf, all designed by Greg Norman. It is also home to the **David Leadbetter Golf Academy**. No prizes for guessing what brings most guests here. For those not wanting to hit the green, there is a big pool with water slide, a lazy river, and several restaurants to keep you busy.
SEE ALSO GOLF, P.70

Prices for a standard double room:
$ under $100
$$ $100–$200
$$$ over $200

Palisades Resort

14200 Avalon Road, Orlando; tel: 321-250-3030 or 866-455-4062; www.palisadesresort orlando.com; $$

The Palisades Resort is a good choice for nature lovers. It's a little out of the way for some of the main theme parks, though only a 15-minute drive to Animal Kingdom, but its location adjoining a 400-acre nature preserve more than makes up for that. Rooms are more basic than you'll find at Disney resorts, but they all have TVs, fridges, complimentary internet, washer, dryer and a proper kitchen. The resort has a fitness centre, sauna and an outdoor pool overlooking the nature preserve.

Palm Lakefront Resort & Hostel

4840 West Irlo Bronson Highway (US 192), Kissimmee; tel: 407-396-1759; www.orlando hostels.com; $; Link: 54, 55

The only place in Orlando that properly caters to the backpacking crowd: you can get a bed for less than twenty bucks at times, and a public bus connects it directly to Disney and other theme parks. Of course this

For reservations at Universal Orlando, telephone 888-273-1311 or go online to www.universalorlando.com.

Above: the Royal Pacific Resort.

isn't luxury accommodation, but it sure ain't bad. With a clean pool and a lakeside view, it is more than serviceable.

Seralago Hotel & Suites Main Gate East
5678 West Irlo Bronson Memorial Highway (US 192), Kissimmee; tel: 407-396-4488 or 800-366-5437; www.seralago hotel.com; $; map p.139 D1

The concept behind this large, family-oriented hotel near the Magic Kingdom is a winner: kidsuites and two-room suites that cost less than $100 dollars a night – ideal if you are on a budget and insist on putting little ones to bed in a different space. The quality of the hotel, though, is no better than you'd expect for these prices. The rooms are as dull and dreary as any Motel 6 chain, the kidsuites are only one room with a fort built around the children's bunk beds, and even the 2-room suites feel a bit cramped (though they are still the best bargain in the area). The pool not only lacks any unique design, but

is also missing the most essential quality for most families: shade. There is a shuttle service to the park once a day.

Universal Studios Resorts
Hard Rock Hotel
5800 Universal Boulevard, Orlando; tel: 407-503-2000; www.hardrockhotelorlando.com; $$$; map p.136 A3

Not quite as lavish or expensive as the Portofino, the accommodations at this Mission-style hotel range from very comfortable standard rooms to large and opulent suites. An eclectic array of rock-and-roll memorabilia is displayed tastefully around the building, which

nearly surrounds a huge pool with a sandy beach, water slide, and underwater sound system. Several restaurants and bars, a fitness room, an indoor play area, and a Hard Rock store round out the picture.

Loews Portofino Bay Hotel
5601 Universal Boulevard, Orlando; tel: 407-503-1000; $$$; map p.136 A3

This is such a beautifully designed and constructed recreation of the real Portofino, you'd be forgiven for calling out *buon giorno* from your window first thing in the morning, especially after that first cup of stiff Italian coffee. Set on a harbor filled with fishing boats, the hotel offers some of the most luxurious accommodations in Orlando, with large, sumptuous rooms, three elaborate pools, a spa, an indoor children's play area, and several restaurants, including the elegant Bice Ristorante. Very expensive, but worth it. Free water taxis transport guests between the theme parks and the three Universal hotels. Best of all, guests at all on-site hotels are given Express access to nearly all rides and attractions.

Below: all the mod cons, and a guitar at the Hard Rock Hotel.

43

Don't forget to check the hidden charges when booking a hotel. All hotels add a Bed Tax, which varies from county to county and can be as high as 6 percent. Also, do not make any in-room calls until you check the rates (these should be provided near the phone). Local and toll-free calls are usually free, but not always, and when they are not, they usually cost much, much more than they should.

Above: the candlelit pool at Gaylord Palms – a romantic place for a rendezvous.

Loews Royal Pacific Resort
6300 Hollywood Way, Orlando; tel: 407-503-3000; $$$; map p.136 A3

Attempting to recreate the South Pacific in central Florida, this resort is centered around a lagoon-like pool fringed with palm trees, waterfalls, a sandy beach, and cabanas. Accommodations are priced slightly lower than the Hard Rock Hotel but sacrifice little in the way of comfort or amenities, which include several good restaurants and bars, a children's activity room, a fitness room, and convention facilities.

International Drive and Lake Buena Vista

Arnold Palmer's Bay Hill Club & Lodge
9000 Bay Hill Boulevard, Orlando; tel: 888-422-9445; www.bayhill.com; $$$

Duffers are in heaven at this golf resort, where they can play two championship courses or brush up their techniques in the **Arnold Palmer Golf Academy**. The atmosphere at the wood-and-stone lodge is low-key and clubby, with nicely appointed rooms. Arnie is often in residence during the winter.
SEE ALSO GOLF, P.70

Caribe Royale
8101 World Center Drive, Orlando; tel: 800-823-8300; www.thecaribeorlando.com; $$; Link 304; map p.139 D2

This enormous resort has over 1,300 suites and 120 villas. Each suite has either two queen beds or one king, a wet bar, microwave, coffeemaker, full kitchen including a refrigerator, washer and dryer. The main pool has a 75ft (23m) water slide. Other amenities include tennis courts, a video arcade, fitness centre, basketball court, and free transportation to Disney World. Their flagship restaurant, **The Venetian Room,** offers fine Italian cuisine.

Below: inside the Gaylord Palms Hotel.

Doubletree Resort Orlando
10100 International Drive, Orlando; tel: 407-352-1100 or 800-327-0363; www.doubletree orlandodrive.com; $$$; I-Ride: Greenline; map p.139 E4

This 17-story mock Spanish tower at the center of this sprawling hotel complex resembles an old Californian mission on growth hormones. Set in 28 acres of tropical landscaping, it has three pools, two kiddie pools, and a day spa. And it's within walking distance of SeaWorld. Other amenities include a fitness center and miniature golf. A refrigerator and coffee-maker are in each room.

Enclave Suites Hotel & Suites
6165 Carrier Drive, Orlando; tel: 407-351-1155 or 800-457-0077; www.enclavesuites.com; $$; I-Ride: mainline; map p.136 A2

Located just off International Drive, this all-suites hotel offers a lot more than the average chain. All rooms include a fully-fitted kitchen, and the Kid Suites are decorated in theme-park style. There are two outdoor pools and one indoor pool, two kiddie pools, and a playground.

Four Points by Sheraton Orlando Studio City
5905 International Drive, Orlando; tel: 407-351-2100;

Above: ice slide at the Gaylord Palms Hotel.

www.starwoodhotels.com; $$;
I-Ride: main and green lines,
Link: 8, 38; map p.136 A2
The design of Studio City is
much more than you'd
expect for a mid-priced
hotel. The rooms are a bit
too trendy, with zebra-
striped shower curtains and
other 'trying too hard'
touches, but the views in the
upper rooms make up for
this shortcoming, and all the
rooms are generously sized.

**Gaylord Palms Hotel
& Convention Center**
6000 West Osceola Parkway,
Kissimmee; tel: 407-586-2000;
www.gaylordpalms.com; $$$;
map p.139 C1
As the name suggests, this is
one of Orlando's best convention hotels, with a large
amount of its sprawling
grounds devoted to meeting
spaces. Families may feel a
bit out of their element here,
but there is so much space
you should be able to avoid
the suits if need be. The 4.5-
acre glass atrium recreates
various destinations in
Florida from St Augustine to
Key West. The rooms carry

on this theme. The **Relâche
Spa** may be on site to help
execs de-stress, but after a
long vacation in Orlando
mom and dad may need to
use its services as well.
SEE ALSO PAMPERING, P.96

Grand Cypress Resort
One Grand Cypress Boulevard,
Orlando; tel: 407-239-1234;
www.grandcypress.hyatt.com;
$$$; map p.139 C4
This luxurious resort has a
lush garden setting near
Downtown Disney. Amenities
include the famous **Grand
Cypress Golf Academy** and
four exclusive Jack Nicklaus-
designed golf courses, a rac-
quet club, windsurfing on the
lake, a 'Kids' Club,' and an
equestrian center, as well as
convention facilities.
SEE ALSO GOLF, P.71

**Holiday Inn Resort
Orlando – The Castle**
8629 International Drive,
Orlando; tel: 407-345-1511;
www.thecastleorlando.com; $$;
I-Ride: mainline; map p.136 A1
Spires, mosaics, banners,
and rich purple-and-gold
drapes and bedspreads give
this mid-range hotel a touch
of medieval whimsy. Amen-
ities include one restaurant,
two cafes, a fitness center,
free shuttles to the theme
parks, and a pleasant courtyard pool.

Lake Eve Resort
12388 International Drive,
Orlando; tel: 407-597-0370 or
866-934-7985; www.lakeeve
resort.com; $$; map p.139 E3
All 176 suites here have
views of Lake Eve, at the
southern end of Interna-
tional Drive not far from
SeaWorld and Discovery
Cove. It's an ideal place for
families as you can rent 1-,
2- or 3-room apartments,
and they all come with TVs,
washer, dryer and a fully-
fitted kitchen. There's an
outdoor pool as well as a

kids' pool and a water play
area, children's activities, a
restaurant, lounge, free
internet and a complimen-
tary shopping service.

The Peabody Orlando
9801 International Drive,
Orlando; tel: 407-352-4000;
www.peabodyorlando.com; $$$;
I-Ride: main and green lines;
map p.136 A1
This 27-story landmark hotel
in the tourist corridor has an
Olympic-size pool and takes
pride in being Orlando's convention hotel of choice.

Chain hotels and motels are
both common and popular, but
we have chosen not to cover
them here in detail. Some
people dislike chains because
they offer no variety and lack a
personal touch; on the other
hand, once you have been to a
hotel run by a particular chain,
you can predict what kind of
service and facilities to expect
wherever else you are in the
world. However, due to the
intense competition in Orlando,
especially at the budget end of
the market, many chain hotels
struggle to make much money
here, and you may find that
their facilities do not quite
measure up to those in other
areas. Below are the central
reservation numbers and websites for some of the chains
located near Disney:

La Quinta
Tel: 800-753-3757
www.lq.com

Marriott Courtyard
Tel: 888-236-2427
www.marriott.com

Comfort Suites
Tel: 877-424-6423
www.choicehotels.com

Holiday Inn
Tel: 800-465-4329
www.ichotelsgroup.com

Best Western
Tel: 800-780-7234
www.bestwestern.com

Above: the Ritz Carlton Grande Lakes is surrounded by exquisitely designed grounds.

Though known for its twice-daily 'March of the Peabody Ducks,' this is not really a place for kids. Guests looking for high tea and fine room service will feel more at home.

Renaissance Orlando at SeaWorld™
6677 Sea Harbor Drive, Orlando; tel: 407-351-5555; www.renaissanceseaworld.com; $$$; I-Ride: mainline; map p.139 E4
This elegant 10-story tower and convention complex is perfect for business travelers as well as families. Rooms are huge and well appointed, and the service is first rate. A grand, sunlit atrium with what appears to be acres of marble flooring encompass meeting facilities, waterfalls, goldfish ponds, and several shops and restaurants. A coffee shop and deli are good for a quick breakfast or lunch. The location is ideal for guests who want to explore several parks. The hotel is across the street from SeaWorld and Discovery Cove, and 15 minutes or less from Universal Orlando and Disney World. Amenities include a pool, an exercise room, a nearby spa and tennis courts. All in all, it's great value in a prime location.

Ritz Carlton Orlando Grande Lakes
4012 Central Florida Parkway, Orlando; tel: 407-206-2400; www.ritzcarlton.com; $$$
Located to the east of International Drive, this luxury

Bed & breakfasts vary greatly in terms of price and quality, but the thing they have in common is that they are almost always in a private and/or historic home. Few have restaurants, and the facilities will not be as good as in a regular hotel, but some travelers prefer the more personal ambience (and the often wonderful home-cooked breakfasts). These lovely old homes are often decorated with antiques and family mementos, and give you a glimpse of real life in this highly touristic region. Several national hotel booking websites provide information about and photographs of bed-and-breakfast establishments in the Orlando region. These include www.bedandbreakfast.com, www.bnbfinder.com and www.bbonline.com. The tourist information office can also help you find accommodations with a more personal touch.

resort is designed to resemble a grand Italian *palazzo*. The rooms feature marble baths, are generously sized, and are impeccably appointed. Amenities include a 40,000sq-ft spa and a Greg Norman-designed golf course.
SEE ALSO GOLF, P.72

Rosen Shingle Creek
9939 Universal Boulevard, Orlando; tel: 866-996-9939 or 866-996-6338; www.shinglecreekresort.com; $$$; Link 58; map p.136 B1
This enormous resort seems to come out of nowhere. Though it is situated near I-Drive it stands alone and requires transportation to reach anything else. The rooms here are very well appointed and generously oversized compared to the average Orlando hotel room. Two fine restaurants, **Cala Bella** and **A Land Remembered** can keep guests more than happy on site. Among the other amenities are four heated pools, including a child's wading pool and a lap pool, the award-winning **Shingle Creek Golf Club,** and the **Shingle Creek Spa**.
SEE ALSO GOLF, P.72–3;

Prices for a standard double room:
$ under $100
$$ $100–$200
$$$ over $200

PAMPERING, P.97; RESTAURANTS, P.107–8

Sheraton Safari Hotel
12205 South Apopka Vineland Road, Orlando; tel: 407-239-0444 or 800-325-3535; www.sheratonsafari.com; $$; map p.139 D3

This African-themed hotel has elaborate decor inside and out, with an over-the-top swimming pool that has a 79-ft python water slide, a lobby filled with indigenous sculpture, and animal print fabrics decorating every room. Free transportation to all Disney parks.

Wyndham Resort
8001 International Drive, Orlando; tel: 407-351-2420; www.wyndhamorlando resort.com; $$$; I-Ride: mainline; map p.136 A2

One of the best of the many choices along International Drive, this is a vast, sprawling and at times confounding place, yet it's also surprisingly quiet, with plesant swimming pools and more than 1,000 spacious rooms.

Above: a garden guardian from The Courtyard at Lake Lucerne.

Downtown Orlando and Loch Haven Park

The Courtyard at Lake Lucerne
211 North Lucerne Circle East, Orlando; tel: 407-648-5188; www.orlandohistoricinn.com; $$$; map p.135 C2

This is actually four B&Bs located alongside each other in Downtown Orlando. Three are fully restored historic houses, including a sprawling old plantation home; the fourth is Orlando's finest surviving Art Deco building. In all of the houses, the rooms are well appointed and have a welcoming air that you will never find in a hotel. Breakfast is, of course, included, as is a free cocktail in the evening.

Eō Inn & Spa
227 North Eola Drive, Orlando; tel: 407-481-8485; www.eoinn. com; $$$; map p.135 C2

This historic inn was built in 1923 and overlooks Lake Eola in the prestigious Thornton Park area. It was converted into a fine boutique hotel in 1999. With only 17 rooms, the service is always personable, and the decor is chic and spacious. With the **Urban Spa** on site, this hotel feels as much a retreat as a place to stay.

SEE ALSO PAMPERING, P.97

Grand Bohemian Hotel Orlando
325 South Orange Avenue, Orlando; tel: 407-313-9000; www.grandbohemianhotel.com; $$–$$$; map p.135 C2

This high-style, Bohemian-themed hotel, across from City Hall, calls itself 'An Experience in Art and Music.' More than 100 pieces of rare artwork, including drawings by Gustav Klimt and Egon Schiele, are displayed. The **Bohemian Lounge** offers entertainment on one of only two Imperial Grand Bösendorfer pianos in the world. The 247 guest rooms and suites are dramatically furnished in dark Java wood tones, soft red and purple

Below: the old-fashioned elegance of The Courtyard at Lake Lucerne.

47

Above: the rough and ready exterior of the Veranda B&B.

velvet fabrics, silver paint, Tiffany-style lamps, and the luxurious all-white Heavenly Bed. All rooms have high-speed internet access, three telephones (two with data ports), and interactive TV. The intimate and elegant four-star **Boheme** Restaurant attracts Downtown's business and arts community. Other amenities include a Starbucks coffee shop, heated outdoor pool, spa, massage room, workout room, and guest privileges at nearby Citrus Athletic Club.

SEE ALSO RESTAURANTS, P.109

The Veranda Bed & Breakfast

707 East Washington Street, Orlando; tel: 407-849-0321 or 800-420-6822; www.theveranda bandb.com; $$; map p.135 C2

What's this, a personalized retreat on a vacation in Orlando? Five cozy 1920s homes in downtown Orlando have been turned into this delightful B&B. All the rooms have hardwood floors and period furnishings. You couldn't find an experience further away from the anonymous chain hotels lining US 192 and I-Drive.

Winter Park and Maitland

Park Plaza Hotel

307 Park Avenue South, Winter Park; tel: 407-647-1072; www.parkplazahotel.com; $$; map p.135 D4

This luxurious hotel is a bit off the beaten track for a Disney vacation, but exactly where you want to be to get away from a Disney vacation. Outside your door all the shopping and dining of Winter Park's Park Avenue awaits. Indoors, rooms are decorated in deep southern style and there is a garden restaurant.

Thurston House Bed and Breakfast

851 Lake Avenue, Maitland; tel: 407-539-1911 or 800-843-2721; www.thurstonhouse.com; $$; Link 9; map p.30

Set on the shores of Lake Eucalia, this Victorian farmhouse is a reminder of days long gone in central Florida.

One thing that hasn't changed is that you can still sit in a rocking chair on the veranda and watch the osprey dive for fish in the lake. The rooms have all the modern amenities you'd expect in a small hotel as well as some you wouldn't, such as original fireplaces filled with candles.

Space Coast

The Inn at Cocoa Beach

4300 Ocean Beach Blvd, Cocoa Beach; tel: 321-799-3460 or 800-343-5307; www.theinnat cocoabeach.com; $$

This delightful hotel is right by the beach and though from the outside it looks nothing special, inside it oozes charm and character. It's won all kinds of accolades for its hospitality, location, view and general level of comfort. The 50 rooms all have sea views, the breakfasts are generous and include home-baked muffins, and there's an honor bar, new fitness center, and an outdoor pool. Although there's no restaurant, there are plenty of choices within a 5-minute walk.

Ron Jon Cape Caribe Resort

1000 Shorewood Drive, Cape Canaveral; tel: 321-799-4900; www.ronjonresort.com; $$

Ron Jon has two quirky advantages: it is the closest oceanfront resort to most Orlando attractions and is the nearest place outside the Kennedy Space Center to watch a launch. This property is primarily for timeshare owners, but its unique locations makes it well worth

There is hardly a hotel or motel in all of central Florida that does not list 'free transportation to Disney' as one of its amenities, but the services most provide are very limited, with one departure and one return from each park each day, hardly the way to a flexible vacation, especially with children.

Prices for a standard double room:
$ under $100
$$ $100–$200
$$$ over $200

Above: some vacation rentals can have as many as seven bedrooms, making them ideal for extended families to share.

checking out for a night or two on the coast. Kids will love the elaborate pools, lazy river and water slide. The suites aren't big, but remain comfortable enough to accommodate a night or two.

Vacation Homes

You can hardly enter a shopping center along I-Drive or US 192 without encountering an office selling or renting vacation homes. Though similar, these should not be confused with timeshares.

Vaction homes are individually owned, but when owners' vacations do not require these houses or condos, the homes are offered through agencies to rent out to holidaymakers, hopefully at a profit for agency and home-owner alike.

Not only does this provide them with income, but it also means their property is regularly maintained while they are away.

For guests this is an excellent opportunity to relax in a more welcoming environment than a hotel, and for bigger families this can mean big savings, as prices aren't much more expensive than the price for two hotel rooms.

Generally speaking these homes are located around US 192 in gated communities that have decent amenities themselves – from communal pools and tennis courts to internet services and tikki

bars. Most homes will also have a private pool.

There is a downside to vacation rentals, in that it is difficult to know who you are dealing with and there can be a very large difference between the standards in properties. Do not make any arrangements without seeing pictures of the property and be very careful who you book your stay through.

VillaDirect Florida

8132 West Irlo Bronson Highway (US 192), Kissimmee; tel: 407-397-1210; www.villadirect.com
VillaDirect is a reliable, mainly internet-based company that has been providing vacation home rentals for several years. In addition to their local business, they also operate in Spain. Their service is unique in that they attempt to provide hotel-style services. Guests arrive at their main office to check in and receive their keys. VillaDirect's maintanence teams keep all their properties clean, and all are inspected prior to a customer's arrival. Their concierge service arranges cots, high-chairs and any other items you may need, including groceries. Prices vary according to property sizes, which are anything from two-bed condos to six-bed houses.

Below: all vacation homes in Florida will have access to a pool.

Bars and Cafés

O rlando and the Disney resorts are hardly the first place that springs to mind when thinking of sophisticated drinking spots around the world, but there are still unique places to sit back and enjoy a drink. Disney and Universal's efforts tend to be highly themed, though the California Grill is a sophisticated retreat. British expats will find several 'genuine' English pubs along I-Drive and US 192, but we've only listed the better ones here. If you want trendier options, head Downtown to places like the Monkey Bar or Stardust Lounge. Wherever you go, remember to take a picture ID.

Disney Resorts

Big River Grille & Brewing Works
Disney's BoardWalk
Beer-lovers can sample a selection of handcrafted suds at Disney's first brew-pub. The pub grub is nothing to write home about, but the outdoor seating is a good spot to sip a brew and watch the crowd pass by.

California Grill
Contemporary Resort
In many ways the luxuries of the Contemporary Resort have become dated, but one attraction that will never expire is its location; the California Grill's bar is a great place to have a drink during the fireworks at the Magic Kingdom.

Downtown Disney

Raglan Road Irish Pub and Restaurant
Pleasure Island; map p.92
Irish-owned and operated, this bar attempts an authentic re-creation of an Irish pub. They've succeeded if you're looking for the atmosphere of Dublin's Temple Bar during a tour group party; in other words it looks much like any other 'authentic' Irish pub in America. Many shades of stout and ale are on offer alongside a fine selection of whiskey, and live Irish folk music takes you through the night. May the road rise to meet you.

Universal Studios

Finnegan's Bar and Grill
New York; map p.20
This full-service restaurant also has a cozy Irish-style bar with Guinness and other Irish favorites on offer. Sports events are televised here if you need a distraction from the theme park. There is even

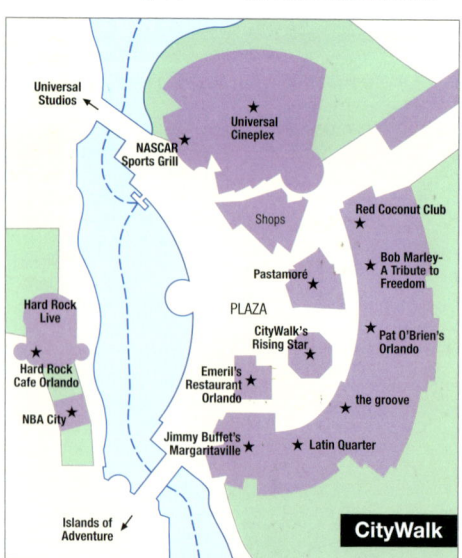

Universal Studios

Universal Cineplex

NASCAR Sports Grill

Shops

Red Coconut Club

Pastamoré

Bob Marley-A Tribute to Freedom

PLAZA

Hard Rock Live

CityWalk's Rising Star

Pat O'Brien's Orlando

Hard Rock Cafe Orlando

Emeril's Restaurant Orlando

NBA City

the groove

Jimmy Buffet's Margaritaville

Latin Quarter

Islands of Adventure

CityWalk

Left: Finnegan's Bar and Grill at Universal Studios.

Pat O'Brien's Orlando
www.patobriens.com; daily daily 4pm–2am; map p.50
An older crowd inhabits this replica of a landmark New Orleans watering hole. The singalong crowd loves the dueling pianos, and foodies enjoy jambalaya, muffeletta, and other Big Easy specialties. Wash it down with a Hurricane, O'Brien's signature rum drink.

International Drive and Lake Buena Vista
Best of British Pub
8324 International Drive, Orlando; tel: 407-264-9189; www.bestofbritishpub.com; daily 8am–late; I-Ride: mainline; map p.136 A2
People come here for one reason: the simple expat desire to watch European football and enjoy a decent pint. Though the faux pub interior is not as good as some other expat crawls, you'll have no problem getting a pie and chips to watch the match and Stella, Carlsberg, and Guinness are all on tap.

Cricketers Arms
Festival Bay Mall, 5250 International Drive, Orlando; tel: 407-354-0686; www.cricketersarms pub.com; daily noon–2am; I-

a happy hour, something you'd never find at Disney.

Universal Studios Resorts
The Velvet Bar
Hard Rock Hotel; 5800 Universal Boulevard, Orlando; tel: 407-503-2000; daily from 5pm; map p.136 A3
Music, whether it's a rocking soundtrack or live at the reservation-only Velvet Sessions, plays an unsurprisingly large part of the atmosphere at this chic cocktail bar. Chilled martinis are their signature drink, and appetizers are on offer to help line the stomach.

CityWalk
Jimmy Buffet's Margaritaville
www.margaritavilleorlando.com; daily 11.30am–2am; map p.50
There are plenty of places to get wasted at this musical watering hole. The three bars include the Volcano Bar, which erupts with Margaritas from time to time, an outdoor lounge and tiki bar beside Jimmy's seaplane, and the Porch of Indecision where a guitarist plays each evening. There are live bands nightly and the restaurant features a 'Floribbean' menu of Key West and Caribbean dishes.

Below: The Velvet Bar at the Hard Rock Hotel.

Ride: mainline, Link: 8, 24, 42; map p.136 B3

The epicenter of English expats and visitors caters to them with traditional ales and live football (known as soccer in these parts). Bar snacks include a chip butty and a cheese and Branston's pickle sandwich.

Downtown and Loch Haven Park

The Celt Irish Pub

25 South Magnolia Avenue, Orlando; tel: 407-481-2928; www.harpandcelt.com; daily 11am–2am; map p.135 C2

Of course, any Irish pub is measured in the quality of its Guinness, and you can get a decent one here. Attached to **The Harp** restaurant, they also serve good-quality pub grub here, with a selection of pies, Scotch eggs, and an Irish breakfast every Sunday from 11am–2pm. They show as much live rugby and soccer as they can, and on Saturday, fans of Notre Dame fill the pub during the college football season.

SEE ALSO RESTAURANTS, P.110

Church Street Bars

33 West Church Street, Orlando; tel: 407-649-4270; www.churchstreetbars.com; map p.134 C2

This is one building but includes three bars or a club to choose from. **Chillers** is undoubtedly the least inviting. Its cold atmosphere matches its frozen concoctions perfectly, and it's usually rather empty. Upstairs, **Latitudes** is a beach-themed rooftop bar inspired by Key West. The **Big Belly Brewery** believes in beer, beer, and more beer, though they do have spirits to wash it down with. Its comical wall hangings depict the effects of 'Big Belly' syndrome on everyone from Captain Kirk to Bruce Springsteen. All of these places are meant for a drink with friends; go next door to **Antigua** when you're ready to rave.

SEE ALSO NIGHTLIFE, P.94

Downtown Pourhouse

20 South Orange Avenue; tel: 407-425-7687; www.downtownpourhouse.com; daily 11am–2am; Link: 3, 7, 11, 18; map p.135 C2

This popular sports bar and restaurant offers a wide selection of specialty cocktails, wines, draft and bottled beers. There is outdoor seating on the patio, five 50-inch HD TVs for watching sporting events, plus video games and electronic darts. Although they have live entertainment from bands to DJs several nights a week, there's never a cover charge.

The Loaded Hog

19 North Orange Avenue, Wall Street Plaza, Orlando; tel: 407-420-1515; www.wallstplaza.net/loadedhog; Thur–Sat 9pm–2am; Link: 6, 7, 11, 13, 18, 51; map p.135 C2

This self-labeled watering hole has a cozier atmosphere than some of the more pretentious bars in the Wall Street Plaza complex. Happy-hour specials on margaritas and bottled beers.

The Monkey Bar

26 Wall Street Plaza, Orlando; tel: 407-481-1199; www.wallstplaza.net/monkeybar; Tue–Fri 5pm–2am, Sat 9pm–2am; Link: 6, 7, 11, 13, 18, 51; map p.135 C2

This might just be the classiest drinking den in the Wall Street Plaza, with a sedate interior and a balcony overlooking the hectic scene below. Oversized martinis are their specialty – drink with caution. Happy-hour specials on cocktails.

One Eyed Jack's

15 North Orange Avenue, Wall Street Plaza, Orlando; tel: 407-420-1515; www.wallstplaza.net/oneeyedjacks; daily 11am–2am; Link: 6, 7, 11, 13, 18, 51; map p.135 C2

This dark little bar aims itself at serious drinkers. Spin its drink wheel and slurp what you're given. Happy-hour specials on margaritas and bottled beers.

Stardust Lounge

431 East Central Boulevard, Orlando; tel: 407-839-0080; daily 2pm–2am; Link 5; map p.135 C2

Swanky retro decor and the occasional burlesque show give this underground bar a kitschy Vegas feel. Relax on the huge stuffed sofas with

Below: real ale and real football are frequently served.

Above: Fiddler's Green's courtyard.

one of their signature martinis, shoot some pool or strut your stuff on the dance floor.

The Tuk Tuk Room

25 Wall Street Plaza, Orlando; tel: 407-849-0471; www.wallstplaza.net/tuktukroom; Fri–Sat 9pm–2am; Link: 6, 7, 11, 13, 18, 51; map p.135 C2

The tiny bar's decor is based on an Indonesian beach bar, and the happy-hour specials include sushi rolls.

WaiTiki

26 Wall Street Plaza, Orlando; tel: 407-481-1199; www.wallstplaza.net/waitiki; daily 11am–2am; Link: 6, 7, 11, 13, 18, 51; map p.135 C2

This retro tiki lounge has mojitos in 10 different flavors, a few frozen drinks and other alcoholic concoctions consistent with its Caribbean holiday theme. Seafood snacks and sandwiches are served until 11pm. Happy-hour specials make the mojitos so cheap you could dare to try them all.

Wall Street Cantina

11 North Orange Avenue, Wall Street Plaza, Orlando; tel: 407-420-1515; www.wallstplaza.net/cantina; daily 11am–2am; Link: 6, 7, 11, 13, 18, 51; map p.135 C2

Known for their notorious collection of margaritas (one comes with a strict two-per-person limit), the Cantina also serves a good selection of Tex-Mex food that can be accompanied by a bucket of beer if you choose. Happy-hour specials on margaritas and Corona beer.

Winter Park

Austin's Coffee

929 West Fairbanks Avenue, Winter Park; tel: 407-975-3364; www.austinscoffee.com; Mon–Thur 7am–11pm, Fri and Sat 7am–1am, Sun 8am–

> Prepare to be flattered when ordering a drink in Orlando. You could be collecting your retirement pension and still be 'carded' at the bar, as many bars will ask to see everyone's ID before allowing them an alcoholic drink no matter what your age. They may even refuse you service if you are unable to produce proof you are over 21.

midnight; Link: 1, 9, 13; map p.135 D4

Walk into Austin's on a weekday and their prime customer becomes immediately obvious: studious college kids from Rollins take over entire booths with laptops, books, and coffee. At night the mood relaxes, with events including poetry slams, live bands and open mic comedy nights. In addition to organic, fair-trade coffee they sell beer, wine, and various teas.

Fiddler's Green

544 West Fairbanks Avenue, Winter Park; tel: 407-645-2050; www.fiddlersgreenorlando.com; Mon–Sat 11.30am–2am, Sun 11am–midnight; Link: 1, 9; map p.135 D4

Though Fiddler's Green is a healthy walk away from Rollins College, that doesn't keep the students away from its traditional Irish fare. In addition to the standard drinks of Guinness, Murphy's and Harp, there are several imported European beers on tap. Hearty food such as bangers and mash are available for lunch and dinner.

Behind the Scenes

Disney and SeaWorld offer some unique opportunities to get 'backstage' and see the inner workings of these enormous theme parks. The chance to interact with the dolphins and whales at SeaWorld and Epcot are once-in-a-lifetime affairs. The other tours offer access to areas of the park off limits to most guests and provide an insight into their creation and operation. The prices given below are for the tours only and do not include the cost of the day's ticket unless stated. Bookings for all of these tours must be made well in advance of arrival as their numbers are strictly limited.

Magic Kingdom
Family Magic
One to three hours; $34; must be three or older
This tour amounts to not much more than an elaborate scavenger hunt at the Magic Kingdom. Before booking, consider whether your kids are really going to want to maintain this gimmick for over two hours when all around them thrill rides and shows are waiting. No special access included.
Keys to the Kingdom
Five hours; $74; must be 16 or older
There is so much to do at the Magic Kingdom that it is easy to forget what a novelty it was at the time of creation. This tour takes visitors to significant sights, both in the park and backstage, to tell the story of Walt's original vision and includes numerous, humor-

ous anecdotes about the park's creation.
The Magic Behind Our Steam Trains
Three hours; $49; must be 10 or older
Prior to the park opening, you are given access to the backstage roundhouse where Disney stores its vintage steam trains and get the chance to go along with the engineers as they prepare them for the day ahead. A unique opportunity for trainspotters.

Epcot
Around the World at Epcot
Two hours; $99; must be 16 or older
Tour the World Showcase on a two-wheel Segway Personal Transporter and learn some of the fascinating stories behind the international pavilions. Segway training is included, and you'll learn to navigate various terrain.
Backstage Magic
Seven hours; $224; must be 16 or older; lunch at Whispering Canyon Cafe included
Though this tour begins at Epcot, you also visit Holly-

wood Studios and the Magic Kingdom to discover just how Disney's special effects are created.
Behind the Seeds
One hour; $16 for over tens, $12 for nine and under; must be three or older
For budding gardeners of any age, this tour explores in further detail the hydroponic gardens you briefly see on the Living with the Land ride.
DiveQuest
Three hours, water time is only 40 minutes; $175; must be 10 or older and in possession of scuba certification
A more in-depth chance to explore the Nemo aquarium than the Seas Aqua Tour. The time in the water is a bit longer and full scuba equipment is provided in the cost, allowing you greater access than the snorkelers above.

> To book any of the Disney behind-the-scenes experiences, tel: 407-939-8687. Places on these excursions are limited, so you need to make your reservation well in advance to avoid disappointment.

> There are more tours available at SeaWorld than we have space to list here. For more information or to make a booking, tel: 888-800-5447.

Left: getting to know the Beluga.

A rare chance to get in the water with a Beluga whale. Only a few places are available each day, and each group is accompanied by trainers who teach you to communicate with this intelligent Arctic creature.

Marine Mammal Keeper
All day from 6.30am; $399; must be 13 or older

This experience lasts the entire day and takes you backstage to accompany trainers and carers as they prepare meals for SeaWorld's wildlife. You also get up close to the sealife during feeding times. The price includes a seven-day pass to SeaWorld.

Sharks Deep Dive
90 minutes; $149; must be 10 or older

Participants on this tour get the dubious pleasure of being locked in a cage and then submerged into an aquarium full of hungry sharks, while being watched by hungry diners at the Underwater Grille. A special helmet provides air and is equipped with a microphone so you can speak with your cohorts underwater.

Dolphins in Depth
Three hours; $194; must be 13 or older

This tour gives you a chance to have a close-up encounter in shallow water with a dolphin resident at the Nemo and Friends aquarium. Not as nice an encounter as the experience at Discovery Cove *(see p.122)*, but much cheaper.

Seas Aqua Tour
Two-and-a-half hours, water time is only 30 minutes; $140; must be eight or older

A chance to explore the aquarium at the Seas with Nemo and Friends from the inside, gaining a closer look at the 65 species of fish and dolphin who live there. Snorkeling only.

Animal Kingdom

Backstage Safari
Three hours; $72; must be 16 or older

This walking safari offers more than just special access to the animals; it also includes time with the staff who are responsible for everything from toucans to tigers. A singular opportunity to learn about the special challenges the carers face on a daily basis.

Wild by Design
Three hours; $60; must be 14 or older

Anyone who has ridden on Kilimanjaro Safaris will appreciate that Disney has created a unique 'zoo' experience that appears as natural and free as the real thing. This tour reveals just how the secrets behind this design were concealed.

SeaWorld

Beluga Interaction
Two hours; $149–199; must be 10 or older

Below: the fine design and engineering of Disney's Animal Kingdom is the subject of Backstage Safari.

Budgeting and Survival

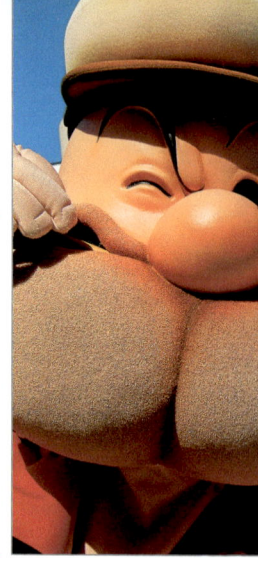

Taking on Orlando's theme parks can be a daunting prospect, especially with young children. The crowds, the heat, and the outlandish prices can sap your strength and empty your wallet before you know what's hit you. But it doesn't have to be that way. If you think things through before leaving home and arrive prepared you can save time, energy, and, most importantly, money. So, in the interest of mental and financial health, here are a few tips to prevent your dream vacation from turning into a nightmare.

Budgeting for Your Trip

HOTELS

If you're looking for a hotel with an acceptable minimum level of comfort, cleanliness, and facilities, a reasonable starting point for the price of a double room is $80 in budget-class hotels. Going up from there to around $100 should make a significant difference in quality. For between $120 and $170 a whole array of hotels opens up, ranging from bland business-traveler places to characterful establishments.

If you are staying at Disney, there is a world of difference between their budget and moderate resort categories, not to mention the deluxe options. At the budget resorts themes are high, but costs are cut; food options are poor at best and rooms cramped.

When you pay to move up a level, the facilities improve dramatically. Pools have excellent themes, slides and bars; restaurants serve tasty food, room service is good quality, kids' activities are better, and the staff are always on hand to help. If you want to enjoy the best of Disney, go deluxe or moderate.

FOOD

Food costs range from a few dollars for a bagel and coffee, through $25–40 for a 2–3-course meal at a standard (often chain) restaurant. Really special fare begins at $40 and a fine restaurant can be as pricey as you can handle.

TRANSPORTATION

Getting around by Disney transport and hotel shuttles to the park is free. Lynx buses cost $2, and taxis, due to the distance inherent in most journeys through Orlando, are expensive. Expect to spend at least $30.

Home Suite Home

Staying in a room with a kitchenette at Disney can be a costly affair, but off-resort on US 192 or I-Drive you will find many hotels that offer this valuable extra for families at a reasonable price. Not only will cooking meals at home save money in the long term, it also provides that 'normal' family downtime for kids and adults to unwind after a hectic day.

WE BEAT ALL PRICES

Left: even the best of couples can find a day at the parks a difficult affair.

Readmission

Though all theme parks sell admission for an entire day, each has its own regulations for those wishing to return to a park already visited that day. Ask a member of staff as you leave. Some will require you to have a hand stamp while others are happy simply to see your ticket again later.

Student Travelers

If you're looking to do Orlando on the cheap, you can succeed so long as you keep your expectations realistic. During the low season many budget hotels can have very affordable rates (especially if sharing), and transportation to Disney or Universal is available via Lynx, so long as you plan well. Food purchased outside the park can be inexpensive. Although there is no way to avoid paying a lot for your

Below: always collect a free map when you visit a theme park.

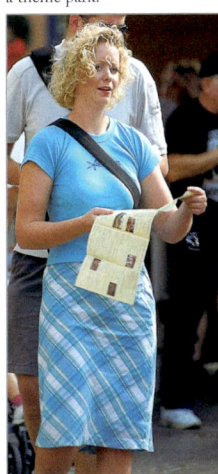

It's a rare family that tours a theme park unscathed. The ones who have the most fun, while enduring the fewest minor hassles and outright meltdowns, are those who have remember the cardinal rule of theme-park touring: slow down. This is a vacation, remember?

Another option is to rent one of the numerous vacation homes available through companies like **VillaDirect** – an ideal solution for larger families.
SEE ALSO ACCOMMODATIONS, P.49

Ticketing

There is an enormous variety of tickets offered at both Universal Studios and Walt Disney World Parks. At the time of writing, Disney guests traveling from the US or purchasing tickets on the day of arrival can buy a one-day, one-park pass for about $87, or a Park Hopper pass that allows you access to more

Left: cut-price tickets are offered everywhere, but buy with caution.

than one park and ranges in price from $145 for one day to $563 for 10 days.

Disney's Magic Your Way ticket allows you to customize your park options. The base ticket runs from 1–10 days and costs from $87 for one day to $506 for 10. You can add the Park Hopper Option for about $60 to allow you to visit more than one park in a single day. Additionally, you can add a water park option to visit Typhoon Lagoon or Blizzard Beach for $54, and if you wish to keep your tickets from expiring, you can pay $54 so that all unused days can be used on your next visit. Otherwise, they will all expire 14 days after their first use.

Universal Studios has a more straightforward approach with a one-park-per-day ticket costing from $82 for a one-day ticket to $140 for a four-day ticket. Park-to-park access tickets that allow you to visit both parks on the same day range from $112 for one-day to $175 for seven-day tickets.

Above: Universal Express eliminates waiting in line. It's free for hotel guests, but costly for those staying off-resort.

entry tickets, once inside there is no need to spend a penny. The **Palm Lakefront Hostel** is the only hostel near the parks.

SEE ALSO ACCOMMODATIONS, P.42

Curb Your Enthusiasm

It's difficult to resist the hype surrounding Orlando's theme parks, but consider the hazards of trying to do too much. Unrealistic expectations will lead only to disappointment and exhaustion. Forget about packing as much as possible into your visit, or even following some preordained schedule. Instead, select three or four 'must-dos' for each day and fill in with other attractions as time allows. Remember, if you find yourself feeling more stressed-out than at a typical day of work, you are probably missing the point.

The second most important rule is to use your time wisely. The key here is to visit the parks at the least crowded time of day, which in almost all cases is first thing in the morning.

Arrive at the parks about an hour before the posted opening. That way you can park, buy a ticket, and enter as soon as the gates swing open. Parks at Disney World and Universal Orlando usually open at least 30 minutes prior to the official time, although all attractions may not yet be running. You can often do more in the first two hours, when lines are short and temperatures are mild, than in the remainder of the afternoon. Attendance peaks between 11am and 4pm – a good time for meals, shopping, and less popular attrac-

Though it is wisest to save your theme-park purchases for the way home, if you see something you just can't resist at any Disney World shop you can ask for your purchase to be held for you at Package Pickup near City Hall at Town Square. This will keep you from lugging your purchases around all day. Additionally, you can ask for purchases to be delivered to your hotel if you are staying on-resort.

tions. If you're staying at an on-site resort, you might even sneak back to your hotel for a swim and a snooze. Keep in mind also that the Disney parks stop selling tickets when they reach capacity – another inducement to stake your claim early.

Park Opening Hours

Knowing the time a park opens is not as easy as it sounds. Opening hours at all Orlando parks are calculated on a complex matrix that attempts to maximize the use of park staff and other resources. This makes for such a complicated and unpredictable schedule that you are strongly advised to consult the parks shortly before visiting.

The easiest way is via the Web; www.disneyworld.com and www.universalorlando.com provide up-to-date information on hours and entertainment schedules. For those without Web access, telephone Disney on 407-939-6244 or Universal on 407-363-8000.

> Most visitors can expect to walk 4 to 8 miles in a typical day at a theme park.

FASTPASS

The biggest gripe people have about visiting theme parks is the long lines. Both Disney and Universal have heard your grumbles and now offer several programs that greatly reduce the amount of time you'll spend staring at the back of another person's head.

The FASTPASS system allows you to collect a timed ticket for parks' most popular attractions. As the day goes on the time between ticket issue and redemption continues to grow. Some rides, such as Space Mountain, may run out of FASTPASS tickets before lunchtime. Though it is down to the discretion of the cast member, expired FASTPASSes are usually accepted.

You are allowed to hold two 'waiting' FASTPASSes at any time so long as they are for different rides. As soon as your FASTPASS window for a particular attraction begins you are no longer considered to be 'waiting', and you can collect another FASTPASS for any attraction, even if you have yet to use your initial FASTPASS.

PhotoPass

There is little point in 'having a magical day' without photographic evidence. Disney's PhotoPass system is a mixed blessing. For those who do not feel adept at the use of a camera, and, it must be said, have a substantial amount of money to burn, purchasing this pass gives you access to dozens of professional photographers stationed throughout the park ready to take your perfect picture. Once you return home you can view all of your pictures online and receive prints, scrapbooks, and various other products.

When to Visit

Plan your visit to Orlando very carefully. Visiting during the least crowded seasons usually makes for a far more pleasant experience at the theme parks. Crowds and waiting times are daunting during the busy seasons. The obvious times to avoid are those coinciding with American school vacations. During the summer break (mid-June to late August), spring break and Easter periods (March/April), and Thanksgiving or Christmas, you will encounter the heaviest crowds and priciest hotel rooms.

From September until Thanksgiving, crowds are light, as they are in January and between the holiday weekends of Thanksgiving and Christmas.

The Sun

The Florida sun is unmerciful, so wear light-colored clothing, a hat and sunglasses, and use plenty of sunscreen. It is vital during the summer months that you retreat indoors frequently. This could even be as often as every hour. Shops and restaurants are always nice and cool, and no one will mind if you are just browsing or sitting down to drink your own bottle of water. Live shows and indoor attractions are a great escape as well.

Below: occasionally try to remind yourself you're on vacation.

Children

For Orlando, one chapter devoted to children's activities is hardly enough – you need an entire book. So we've planted tips throughout in an effort to help families on vacation. Here we try to point out some of the better attractions for various age groups. Our hope is that this will help kids, no matter what their age, get even more pleasure out of the parks, which will of course let the parents get more pleasure out of their kids. Those with children between the ages of five and 12 will have the easiest times. Under-fives are still well catered for, though teenagers may find dealing with mom and dad all day a price too high, even for Disney.

Under-5s

THEME PARKS...

The Magic Kingdom is the best theme park for the younger kids. Its dark rides, such as **Peter Pan's Flight** and **it's a small world**, are a big hit with the smallest of fans but can be a bit too tedious for those who've outgrown the characters they feature. Said characters are especially entertaining at character dining experiences held at Cinderella's Castle and Crystal Palace, amongst other locations. Check times when entering parks.

Islands of Adventures' **Seuss Landing** and Universal Studios' **Woody Woodpecker's Kidzone** are both brilliant jungle gyms by any other name.

Unexpectedly, many tots find most of the 3-D attractions in Orlando a bit too terrifying, as some sort of bug

Most thrill rides at all parks now have parent swap stations so that couples with children can all wait in the line for a ride and then take turns riding it.

Above: a hug worth waiting for.

scampering up your legs is a standard gag. Plus, the graphics can be so realistic they may forget that it's just a film. The one possible exception to this is **Mickey's PhilharMagic** in the Magic Kingdom, which is just as entertaining as other films, but suitable for all ages.
SEE ALSO MAGIC KINGDOM, P.6–9; UNIVERSAL STUDIOS, P.21; ISLANDS OF ADVENTURE, P.23

...AND BEYOND

If seeing animatronic animals or those in captivity leaves your child wanting more, the

Green Meadows Petting Farm gives kids the chance to milk a cow, ride a pony, go on a hay ride, and get up close to over 200 animals.
SEE ALSO NATURAL WORLD, P.90

5–12

THEME PARKS...

Hollywood Studios and **Animal Kingdom** are the most appealing Disney Parks for those young children who want to relive the adventures of movies and see wildlife, but are still a bit too timid for thrill rides.

Don't forget to take along an autograph book and pen to gather lasting memories of character greetings. The compulsion to collect can also be quenched by trading pins at stalls located throughout the Disney resort.

Stunt shows such as **Indiana Jones Epic Stunt Spectacular** at Hollywood Studios are great for those too big to be scared by noise but not big enough to see through the stunts' illusions (and they are performed in shaded pavilions and last long enough for you to get a bit of a rest).

Left: superheroes in the making.

Test Track and **Mission: SPACE**, but the other exhibits are likely to bore even the most inquisitive adolescent.

As far as nightlife goes, **CityWalk** and **Downtown Disney** both provide a safe environment for teens to mingle (and get away from their parents).

Though entrance is expensive, the amusements at **DisneyQuest** could entertain a teen for the entire day (or evening) and there are plenty of places nearby (**House of Blues** just across the street) that could allow adults the comfort of mind and the relaxing beverages needed after a long day at the parks.
SEE ALSO EPCOT, P.10–3; HOLLYWOOD STUDIOS, P.16–7; ISLANDS OF ADVENTURE, P.22–3; NIGHTLIFE, P.92–3; THEMED ATTRACTIONS, P.120

...AND BEYOND
For those desperate to get behind the wheel of a car, **Fun Spot Action Park** provides bumper cars and four multilevel tracks for go-cart racing.
SEE ALSO THEMED ATTRACTIONS, P.119

Below: even younger children still find Disney a magical place.

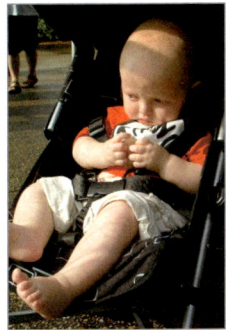

All hotels will provide cots and other items needed for childen, often at no extra cost. Disney Resorts also offer childcare for when parents want to have a night away and many hotels off-resort offer affordable suites designed for young families.

It may be impossible to pull kids away from **Discovery Cove**, where you get a handshake and a kiss from a dolphin before it swims you back to shore. It's something most children could only dream of. The park is exceptionally expensive, but travel agents often offer specials and the memory is irreplaceable.
SEE ALSO ANIMAL KINGDOM, P.14–5; HOLLYWOOD STUDIOS, P.16–7; THEMED ATTRACTIONS, P.122

...AND BEYOND
If you've got a young one whose taste for the disgusting and bizarre seems insatiable, **Ripley's Believe It or Not! Odditorium** may be just the place for them. Exhibits include a two-headed calf, among other oddities.

Really for all ages, the

Orlando Science Center is a must-see, with interactive exhibits covering everything from life in zero gravity to a journey through the human body.
SEE ALSO MUSEUMS AND GALLERIES, P.84; THEMED ATTRACTIONS, P.118

Teens

THEME PARKS...
Assuming your teen wants to push the limits of motion sickness, Universal's Islands of Adventure with the **Incredible Hulk** and **Dueling Dragons** roller coasters, plus the **Amazing Adventures of Spider Man** and other disorientating rides should be top of their list. Hollywood Studios, thanks to the **Twilight Zone Tower of Terror** and the **Rock 'n' Roller Coaster**, is the next best stop. Epcot has two fantastic thrill rides in

In the parks, walking distances are quite long, but strollers are available for rent. The sun, heat, and humidity can take their toll, especially during long waits for popular attractions.

Essentials

Orlando and the theme parks are easy to negotiate. Disney especially makes travel carefree. You could in theory be taken from airport to resort and back again and never leave Disney's safe hands. For those wanting a bit more independence, here is all the practical information you need on how to get yourself into the country, what to do in an emergency, how to understand the currency, and where to find the tourist offices. There are also details on health care, telecommunications, and where to leave your dog. For additional information, visit the useful websites listed on *pp.65–6*.

Business Hours

Off-resort, most businesses are open 9am–5pm, with many of the shopping malls open as late as 10pm. Many large supermarkets and numerous restaurants stay open 24 hours.

Banks usually remain open until at least 4pm from Monday through Thursday, and until 6pm on Friday. Some banks are open for a short time on Saturday.

Below: as beautiful as it is, Florida leads the US in the frequency of lightning storms.

During some public holidays, some or all state, local, and federal agencies may be closed. Local banks, businesses, stores, and attractions may also stop operating during some public holidays.

Climate Hazards

TORNADOES

Florida ranks eighth in the list of US states with the most tornadoes per year, but they're not nearly as bad as the awesome twisters that assail the Midwest. Trailer parks are particularly vulnerable.

LIGHTNING

Florida is unofficially dubbed the 'lightning capital of the country.' This is attributed to the hot, wet air that lies close to the ground, and unstable atmospheric conditions that exist mainly from May until September.

If you see dark clouds and flashes of lightning approaching, take cover. If in a car, stay inside until the storm passes. If in a building, don't 'make a run for it.' Many lightning victims are killed when getting into or out of their cars.

Walt Disney World is in a state of its own. It administers its own planning, has the power to build roads and water systems, and runs its own police and fire-fighting forces. It even has the approval to construct a nuclear power plant, should it ever find this a necessity.

Boaters should head for the nearest place they can tie up and evacuate the boat. During any nearby lightning storm, parks will close their outdoor attractions.

Customs Regulations

You will be given a form to complete en route to the US that requires basic identification information. When landed, you must go to an inspection area where a CBP (Customs and Border Protection) Officer will determine why you are coming to the US, if you have the necessary documents, and how long you intend to stay. If you are allowed to proceed, your passport and customs declaration form will be stamped.

Left: pack a raincoat in autumn, as sudden downpours are frequent.

from your nearest US Embassy or Consulate or on the US Customs website: see above. Other useful links are listed below.

US Department of Homeland Security
www.dhs.gov/trip
Transportation Security Administration
www.tsa.gov/travelers

CUSTOMS ALLOWANCES
Articles brought into the United States are subject to duty or internal revenue tax. Visitors, however, are given an allowance of exempted goods. These include:

Money. There is no limit on the amount of money – US or foreign traveler's checks or money orders – that you may bring into or take out of the US. But you must declare amounts exceeding $10,000 or the foreign currency equivalent.

Alcohol. Visitors over the age of 21 are permitted to bring in 34fl oz of alcohol for their personal use. Excess quantities are subject to duty and tax.

Cigars and cigarettes. Visitors may bring in up to 200 cigarettes (one carton), 50

Hand in the return part (departure record) of the form filled out en route to US when you leave the country (the cbp officer should have attached it to your passport on arrival. Failure to do so will cause you problems with the CBP in the future.

US Customs and Border Protection
www.cbp.gov

PROHIBITED GOODS
Articles which visitors are forbidden to take into the United States include: liquor-filled chocolates or candy, dangerous drugs, obscene publications, hazardous articles (e.g. fireworks) and narcotics.

Travelers using medicines containing narcotics (such as tranquilizers or cough medicine) should carry a prescription and/or a note from their doctor, and should take only the quantity required for a short stay. The medicine must be in its original, clearly labelled container. The medication must also be able to be legally prescribed in the US.

Meat and poultry, fruit and veg, most dairy, absinthe, more than 250 grams caviar, and Cuban cigars are all prohibited.

Any liquids, gels, and aerosols in carry-on luggage must be in 3oz containers or smaller. These must be placed in a quart-size, zip-top, clear plastic bag – one per traveler.

There are exceptions for prescription and over-the-counter medicines and baby formula. Put larger amounts (e.g. shampoo) in luggage.

Full details of customs requirements are available

Below: be patient at customs and immigration: waits are common.

Above: machine-readable passports are compulsory if issued after 26 October 2006.

cigars (as long as they are not Cuban), or 3lbs of smoking tobacco, or proportionate amounts of each. An additional 100 cigars may be brought in under your gift exemption.

Gifts. As a visitor to the US, you can claim on entry up to $100 worth of merchandise, free of duty and tax, as gifts for other people. Such articles may have to be inspected, so do not gift-wrap them until after you have entered the country.

Disabled Travelers

Accessibility and facilities are excellent at the theme parks and other attractions in Orlando. Special parking is available near the entrances to each park, the hotels, and other facilities.

Wheelchairs are available for rent in limited numbers in several locations, usually outside or just inside the entrance. For some attractions and rides, guests may remain in wheelchairs. For others, they must be able to leave the wheelchair. Regulations are clearly indicated in leaflets and at the appropriate entrance. Some motorized wheelchairs are available for rent, and nearly all buses and launches can accommodate conventional wheelchairs. Wheelchair access is available at toilets in all the theme parks.

For hearing-impaired guests there is a TDD at City Hall in Magic Kingdom, at Guest Services in Hollywood Studios, Epcot and Animal Kingdom, and at both Universal parks. Many rides and attractions have closed captioning. A sign-language interpreter is available for theater shows.

Sight-impaired guests can borrow complimentary cassettes and tape recorders at the same locations. A deposit is required.

Electricity

110–115 volts; flat two- or three-pronged plugs.

Embassies and Consulates

Few English-speaking countries have a consulate in Florida. These are the nearest ones to contact:

Australia
2103 Coral Way, Suite 108, Miami, FL 33145; tel: 305-858-7633

British Consulate
200 South Orange Avenue, Suite 2110, Orlando, FL 32801; tel: 407-254-3300; map p.132 C2

Canada Consulate General
200 South Biscayne Boulevard, Suite 1600, Miami, Florida 33131; tel: 305-579-1600

New Zealand
Embassy, 37 Observatory Circle, NW, Washington DC 20008; tel: 202-328-4800

Republic of Ireland
345 Park Avenue, 17th Floor, New York, NY 10022; tel: 212-319-2555

South Africa
333 East 38th Street, 9th Floor, New York, NY 10016; tel: 212-213-4880

Entry Requirements

Most foreign visitors need a machine-readable passport (which should be valid for at least six months longer than their intended stay) and a visa to enter the United States. You should also be able to provide evidence that you intend to leave the United States after your visit is over (usually in the form of a return or onward ticket), and visitors from some countries need an international vaccination certificate.

Certain foreign nationals are exempt from the normal visa requirements. Canadian citizens with a valid Canadian passport need no visa. Nor do Mexican citizens provided

Note that immigration officials are entitled to ask for proof of solvency on your arrival in the United States. You will also be fingerprinted and have an iris scan in immigration.

they have a Mexican passport and a US Border Crossing Card (Form I-186 or I-586), and as long as they are residents of Mexico.

A special 'visa-waiver' program means that citizens of some countries do not require a visa if they are staying for less than 90 days and have a round-trip or onward ticket. These include New Zealand, Japan, the UK, and about 18 other European nations. If you travel under this program, you will need to present an e-passport if your passport was assigned on or after 26 October 2006.

Mistakes are not accepted on immigration forms you fill in during the flight. So don't cross anything out – ask for a new form.

Those requiring a visa or visa information can apply by mail or by personal application to their local US Embassy or Consulate.

Vaccination certificate requirements vary, but proof of immunization against smallpox or cholera may be necessary.

Etiquette

LIQUOR LAWS
The legal drinking age in Florida is 21. Liquor can be purchased on any day of the week, but note that some municipalities do not permit retail stores to sell liquor until after 1pm on Sundays.

SMOKING
Smoking is not permitted on any attraction, ride, or in any waiting area in theme parks. Furthermore, smoking is banned in all public places in Florida. This includes bars, restaurants and cafés. Some hotels still offer smoking

rooms, but the number is dwindling.

Health and Medical Care
You should never leave home without travel insurance to cover both yourself and your belongings. Your own insurance company or travel agent can advise you on policies, but shop around, since rates vary. Make sure you are covered for accidental death, emergency medical care, trip cancelation, and baggage or document loss.

MEDICAL CARE
In the event you need medical assistance, ask the reception staff at your hotel. The larger resort hotels may well have a resident doctor.

There is nothing cheap about being sick in the US, whether it involves a simple visit to the doctor or a spell in a hospital. The initial ER fee charged by a good hospital might be $250, and that's before the additional cost of X-rays, medicines, and so on have been added. It is therefore essential to be armed with adequate medical insurance, and to carry an identification card or policy number at all times.

Right: kennels at parks help keep 'best friends' happy.

Above: it's the law.

HEALTH HAZARDS
The two most common health hazards in Orlando are sunburn and heat exhaustion; both are easily avoided.

The heat alone can be a danger, especially for the elderly or those with a pre-existing medical condition. Dehydration and salt deficiency can lead to heat exhaustion. The main symptoms are headache, weakness, lightheadedness, muscle aches, cramps, and agitation. Make a point of drinking plenty of non-alcoholic fluids (before you get thirsty), and take periodic breaks in the shade or an air-conditioned environment.

If untreated, heat exhaustion can escalate to a far more serious case of heatstroke, which means that the body's temperature rises to dangerous levels. In addition to the symptoms listed above, people suffering from heatstroke may exhibit confusion, strange behavior, and even seizures. If you suspect a companion is suffering from heatstroke, get them to a cool place, apply cold damp cloths, and call for a doctor immediately.

Internet
Walt Disney World
http://disneyworld.disney.go.com
Universal Studios
www.universalorlando.com

Above: the US is slowly doing away with its one size and color fits all denominations.

SeaWorld
www.seaworld.com
Busch Gardens
www.buschgardens.com
Orlando Visitors Bureau
www.orlandoinfo.com
Florida Tourist Board
www.visitflorida.com
Golf in Orlando
www.golforlando.com
Hotel Discounts
www.orlandohotels.com
Restaurants in Orlando
http://orlando.diningguide.net
Orlando Nightlife
www.orlando.nightguide.com
Kennedy Space Center
www.kennedyspacecenter.com

Kennels

All theme parks provide kennels for those guests who are traveling with canine companions – sorry, no dogs on Space Mountain.

Money

Foreign visitors are advised to take US dollar travelers' checks or cash to Orlando, since exchanging foreign currency – whether as cash or checks – can prove problematic. An increasing number of banks, including the First Union National Bank, Nations Bank, and Sun Bank chains, offer foreign exchange facilities, but this practice is not universal. Some department stores offer foreign currency exchange.

Most shops and restaurants accept travelers' checks in US dollars and will give change in cash. Alternatively, checks can be converted into cash at the bank.

Credit cards are very much part of daily life in Orlando and can be used to pay for pretty much anything, and it is also common for car rental firms and hotels to take an imprint of your card as a deposit. Rental companies may oblige you to pay a large deposit in cash if you do not have a card.

You can also use your credit or bank cards to withdraw cash from ATMs. Before you leave home, make sure you know your PIN number and find out which ATM system will accept your card. The most widely accepted cards are Visa, American Express, MasterCard, Diners Club, Japanese Credit Bureau, and Discover. Maestro cards are often not accepted.

Be sure to check the rate of exchange and any other charges your financial institution may levy before using your card abroad. Some charge prohibitive rates.

Most theme parks have locker rental at the entrance. Charges vary but they are invariably useful.

TIPPING

Service personnel expect tips in Orlando. The accepted rate for baggage handlers in airports is at least $1 per bag. For others, including taxi drivers and waiters, 15–20 percent is the going rate, depending on the level and quality of service. Sometimes tips are included in restaurant bills when dining in groups.

Moderate hotel tipping is around 50 cents per bag or suitcase handled by porters or bellboys. You should tip a doorman if he holds your car or performs other services. It is not necessary to tip chamber staff unless you stay several days.

Postal Services
POST OFFICES

The opening hours of post offices vary between central, big-city branches and those in smaller towns or suburbs, but all open Monday to Friday and some open on Saturday mornings.

Drugstores and hotels usually have a small selection of stamps, and there are stamp-vending machines in some transport terminals.

DELIVERY SERVICES

For the best service, you should pay for Express Mail

via the US postal service, which guarantees next-day delivery within the US and delivery within two to three days to foreign destinations. Privately owned courier services, which offer next-day delivery to most places, are also very popular.

Telephone numbers for the main courier services are:
FedEx: 800-463-3339
DHL: 800-225-5345
UPS: 800-742-5877

Tourist Information Offices

Below is a list of tourist information offices in and around Orlando.

ORLANDO
Orlando/Orange County Convention and Visitors Bureau
8723 International Drive, Suite 101, Orlando 32819; tel: 407-363-5872; www.orlando info.com; I-Ride: mainline; map p.136 A1
Walt Disney World Co
1800 Epcot Resort Boulevard, Lake Buena Vista, 32830; tel: 407-939-6244; http://disneyworld.disney.go.com/
Universal Studios
1000 Universal Studios Plaza, Orlando, 32819; tel: 407-363-8000

SPACE COAST
Titusville Area Chamber of Commerce
2000 South Washington Avenue, Titusville, 32780; tel: 321-267-3036; www.titusville.org
Cocoa Beach Area Chamber of Commerce
8501 Astronaut Boulevard, Suite 4, Cape Canaveral, 32920; tel: 321-454-2022; www.visitcocoabeach.com
Melbourne Chamber of Commerce
1005 East Strawbridge Avenue, Melbourne 32901;

tel: 321-724-5400; www.themelbournecoast.com
Palm Bay Area Chamber of Commerce
4100 Dixie Highway, Palm Bay, 32905; tel: 321-951 9998; http://greaterpalmbaychamber.com

Useful Numbers

Police, ambulance or fire service: 911
Local directory inquiries: 411
International directory inquiries: 00
Local operator: 0
International operator: 00
International direct-dial calls: dial 011 + the code of the country, followed by the area or city code minus the first 0. Some country codes:

Australia: 61
Ireland: 353
New Zealand: 64
United Kingdom: 44

Wheelchairs and Electric Scooters

All theme parks make special considerations for guests requiring the use of wheelchairs or electric scooters. Some rides allow them to be strapped securely in place, whereas assistants at other rides are happy to help transfer guests from their wheelchair to any ride. The wheelchairs are then moved to the ride's exit and assistants will help the guest back into the chair – unless, of course, they want to ride again.

Below: tourist information is easy to find.

Food and Drink

It is unfortunate that for most tourists Orlando's food memories are more likely to be a muddled medley of themed restaurants than a cornucopia of subtropical delights. After all, Florida is one of America's most important agricultural states and should be proud of its citrus industry – one of the world's finest. There are also cattle farms and two bodies of fish-filled water providing local produce. Still, you're more likely to be proudly offered Alaskan King Crab than any fresh Floridian fish by your waiter. But if you explore farmers' markets and choose more independent restaurants, you may just find a budding Floridian cuisine.

A Bountiful Harvest

Florida is a major producer of beef, fish, shellfish, and vegetables, and is a world leader in growing citrus fruit. Fierce competition means you'll usually get good value for your money, especially in the type of food America does well: steaks, barbecues, and anything fried.

In the past, theme parks were accused of dishing up only fast food laced with fat and sugar. Now, in response to the adverse publicity, the choice is more varied. The old faithfuls are still available, but the overall style is more

healthy, with plenty of salads, fresh fruit, and frozen yogurt as well as ice cream. Buffets and full-service restaurants in the theme parks and hotels cater to mainstream tastes but have become more adventurous. And, especially in Disney territory, the decor and theming are half the fun.

The problem for most foodies visiting Orlando from abroad will be the lack of fresh produce. Though oranges are usually delicious when in season, there is no emphasis on locally pro-duced fruit and vegetables at the supermarkets. For most

Americans if it's grown in the US, it is local, but the food miles involved in eating a Washington apple in Florida means that your fruit can often be pulpy and tasteless.

We list a few farmers' markets below, but for a city of this size they are depress-ingly thin on the ground. A happy exception is **Eli's Orange World** on Highway 192 in Kissimmee (tel: 407-239-6031, www.orange world192.com). Here you can buy fresh Indian River oranges, grapefruits and tangerines, or order them online for shipping anywhere in the continental US.

Farmers' Markets

Celebration
Town Center; Sun 9am–2pm
Fruit and veg stalls open each Sunday, and as this is Disney's hometown there are plenty of arts and crafts activities for kids.

Farmers' Market of Downtown Kissimmee
Toho Square, corner of Darling-ton and Pleasant Street; Thur 7am–1pm; Link: 4
This more functional market

Below: Florida produces much of America's fresh fruit and veg.

Left: Florida is known the world over for its citrus crops.

Deli

Antonio's
611 South Orlando Avenue, Maitland; tel: 407-645-1043; www.antoniosonline.com; Mon–Sat 11am–10pm, Sun noon–9pm; Link: 39; map p.30
This downstairs deli and wine shop is a gourmet's dream: bread is baked daily, several imported Italian cheeses and sausages are sold, as are handmade pastas, sauces, and other Italian extras such as artichokes and sun-dried tomatoes. There is a wide selection of Italian wines and spirits. The coffee is as good as in any café in Italy, and the lunch menu has extensive options, much more than you'd expect from a small café, with pizzas cooked in their wood-burning oven.

Supermarkets

You may find that stocking a villa's cupboards is more of a challenge than you'd expect. Good supermarkets are hard to find, unlike the rundown versions stocking their aisles with Coca-Cola, beer, and pool toys. Below are the details for Orlando's two best chains.

Goodings
Lake Buena Vista: SR 535 and I-4; tel: 407-827-1200; www.goodings.com; Link: 300; map p.139 D3
This store is a favorite for visitors. They also have an online shopping facility and will deliver to your door for an extra $20.

Publix
www.publix.com
This is a much bigger chain than Goodings, and there are locations all over central Florida. Go to their website to find the one nearest you.

offers local produce during the week in Kissimmee's historical downtown setting.

G S Produce Market
1111 South Orlando Avenue; tel: 407-623-3377; Mon–Fri 8.30am–7.30pm, Sat until 7pm, Sun 9am–5pm; Link: 39; map p.135 C4
This local farmers' shop is a rare, permanent fresh produce shop. Its business card, which says 'next to Krispy Kreme' sums up Orlando's overall attitude to food.

Orlando Farmers' Market
Lake Eola Park; www.orlando farmersmarket.com; Sun 10am–4pm; Link: 5, 6, 15, 36; map p.135 C2
In addition to fresh produce there is gourmet food available from all around the world, and art and craft stalls.

Winter Park Farmers' Market
The old train depot, 200 West New England Avenue; Sat 7am–1pm; Link: 1, 9, 23; map p.135 D4
Considered one of the best farmers' markets in central Florida, its setting in the old train depot adds atmosphere, and there are plenty of fresh baked goods.

Wine

Lakeridge Wine Company
19239 US 27 North, Clermont; tel: 800-768-9463; www.lake ridgewinery.com; Mon–Sat 10am–5pm, Sun 11am–5pm
Florida is never going to compete with its west coast rivals for winemaking in the US, but the Lakeridge Wine Company provides an insight into this industry with tours of its production facilities and tastings of its latest vintage. They have won many awards for their wines, especially their whites.

The Wine Room on Park Avenue
270 Park Avenue South, Winter Park; tel: 407-696-9463; www.thewineroomonline.com; Mon–Thur 3pm–midnight, Fri and Sat 11.30am–1.30am, Sun 1pm–9pm; map p.135 D4
A theme park for wine-lovers. There are over 200 wines being served or sold here, and you can taste about 150 of them in quantities as small as 1oz. The cosy leather chairs and well-stocked champagne bar make it worth staying for a while, and there are artisan cheeses and charcuterie to accompany your selections.

Golf

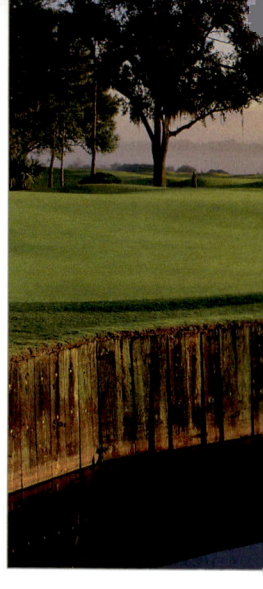

With 176 courses to choose from, you can build an entire vacation around golf in Orlando. Disney World has five championship courses and 15 golf pros. Two courses near Disney, ultramodern Grand Cypress Resort, with a 45-hole course designed by Jack Nicklaus, and Bay Hill Club and Lodge, with its famed Arnold Palmer Golf Academy, are top-rated. Nick Faldo put his stamp on two courses at Marriott's Grand Vista Resort, also on I-Drive. For a complete list of courses, order a copy of the *Golfer's Guide* (www.golfersguide.com), or go to www.orlandogolfer.com.

Disney Golf

Walt Disney World resort has five championship golf courses, four of which feature regularly on the Professional Golfer's Association tour. There are lessons by PGA pros available at all courses, and Disney transportation will take you there, if you are staying on-resort.

Lake Buena Vista

This relatively short course, only 6,819 yards, is a par 72 and set among lighthouses, and enough canals and lakes to create a water hazard for every hole.

Magnolia

Designed by Joe Lee, the course is named after the magnolia trees that surround it and lend the course a unique scent when in blossom. The course is 7,190 yards long.

Oak Trail

This nine-hole course is a bargain compared to other courses at Disney and offers a 50 percent discount on replays. Holes range from 132 to 517 yards, and the design makes it a favorite with developing golfers.

Above: caddie service at the Ritz Carlton Grande Lakes.

Osprey Ridge

Designed by Tom Fazio, this course is 7,101 yards long. The scenery is calmly Floridian, with cypress and bay trees surrounding the course. GPS guidance systems are available, and the clubhouse overlooks a lake and serves food and drink.

Palm

This is one of Disney's most challenging courses. Designed by Joe Lee, the course is surrounded by native Florida woodlands, but it's the strategically placed palm trees that challenge most golfers. The course is 6,957 yards long.

Golf Resorts

Arnold Palmer's Bay Hill Club and Lodge

9000 Bay Hill Boulevard, Orlando; tel: 888-422-9445; www.bayhill.com

There is so much here other than the golf. Amenities include tennis courts, a spa and salon, a pool, fitness center and restaurants, leaving any golf widows with more than enough to fill their day. The 18-hole course is consistently rated one of the best in Florida by readers of *Golf Digest*. Tuition is provided by the Arnold Palmer Golf Academy.

ChampionsGate Golf Resort

1400 Masters Boulevard, ChampionsGate; tel: 407-787-4653; www.champions gategolf.com

Greg Norman designed these two 18-hole courses attached to the Omni International Hotel. The National course is a traditional

World Center Drive, Orlando; tel: 800-380-7931; www.marriottworldcenter.com; map p.139 D2

Just outside the sprawling, convention-oriented Marriott World Center, Hawk's Landing is a favourite with visiting businessmen. The par 71 championsip course is 6,600 yards, and facilities include a pro shop and the Bill Madonna Golf Academy.

Marriott's Grande Vista Resort

5925 Avenida Vista, Orlando; tel: 888-463-2536; http://golf-instruction.marriott-vacations.com; map p.139 E3

Marriott built this resort around the golf. Home to the Nick Faldo Golf Institute, guests arrive here for everything from a three-day to three-hour session. The course is only nine holes, measures 2,300 yards, and is par 32. The unique design challenges golfers to practice and refine a wide variety of shots.

Mystic Dunes Resort and Golf Club

7850 Shadow Tree Lane, Celebration; tel: 407-787-5678; www.mysticdunesgolf.com

Though not a championship course, Mystic Dunes is just

Orlando has become the capital of Florida's, if not the nation's golf trade. In addition to the 176 golf courses in and around Orlando, the city is also home to the Golf Channel, *Golf Week* magazine, and the site for the annual PGA Merchandise Show. Unsurprisingly, professionals such as Tiger Woods, Arnold Palmer and Ernie Els call the area home.

American layout, while the International course recalls the feel of play in Scotland or Ireland.

Grand Cypress Golf Resort

One North Jacaranda, Orlando; tel: 877-330-7377; www.grandcypress.com; map p.139 C4

There are two options available here, the North, South and East Nines or the New Course. The former comprises three nine-hole courses. Golfers combine two of the three to create a full 18-hole round. The original course, a combination of the North and South courses, is very demanding,

the East Nine, added a couple of years later, provides a bit more respite for the less accomplished. The New Course pays homage to St Andrews in Scotland, complete with stone walls and bridges. It is the most challenging of them all. All four courses were designed by Jack Nicklaus.

The Grand Cypress Golf Academy makes the most of these resourceful courses, from short lessons to five day courses.

Hawk's Landing Golf Club

Orlando World Center, 8701

Below: morning at Mystic Dunes.

as challenging, but is a bit more capable of accommodating novices, with instruction available and the integration of five sets of tees for golfers of different levels to use. The par 71 course was designed by Gary Koch and stretches 7,012 yards. The Par View GPS system is in use, and there is a 60,000sq-ft (5574 sq m) clubhouse and a pro shop.

Orange County National Golf Center and Lodge

16301 Phil Ritson Way, Winter Garden; tel: 407-656-2626; www.ocngolf.com

Featuring two 18-hole courses and an award-winning quick nine-hole short course, Orange County makes the most of its natural environment and has yet to be fringed by development – a rarity in any Florida golf course. The prices here are quite steep for a 'public' course, and the design and features are not as elite as other area courses.

Orange Lake Resort

8505 West Irlo Bronson Memorial Highway (US 192), Kissimmee; tel: 407-239-0000 or 800-877-6522; www.orangelake.com; map p.138 A2

The Orange Lake resort has four courses: The Legends, designed by Arnold Palmer, and The Reserve are their premier, 18-hole courses with special pricing for resort guests. The nine-hole Legend's Walk, also designed by Arnold Palmer, and Crane's Bend are priced much lower, with more or less equal fees for the public as for the guests.

Orlando hosts two annual PGA tournaments. The Arnold Palmer Invitational in March is at the Bay Hill Club and the Children's Miracle Network Classic in October is at the Walt Disney Resort.

Reunion Resort and Club

7593 Gathering Drive, Reunion; tel: 888-418-9611 or 407-662-1000; www.reunionresort.com

The Reunion's three courses have a substantial pedigree: The Legacy, designed by Arnold Palmer, is 6,916 yards and features dramatic elevation changes. The Tradition, designed by Jack Nicklaus, is a more flowing course. The 7,257-yard Independence was designed by Tom Watson, who obviously has a fascination with sand – the last hole is surrounded by 16 bunkers. Also on site is the ANNIKA academy.

Ritz Carlton Golf Club Grande Lakes

4012 Central Florida Parkway, Orlando; tel: 407-206-2400; www.ritzcarlton.com

Two courses are available for guests and the public. The resort's course was designed by Greg Norman, and every golfer is provided with a caddie concierge to assist them on their round. Only five minutes away, Grande Pines is a more challenging course and was designed by Nick Faldo and Steve Smyers. It incorporates the surrounding wetlands into its smart layout.

Shingle Creek Golf Club

9939 Universal Boulevard, Orlando; tel: 866-996-9933 or 407-996-9933; www.shinglecreekgolf.com; map p.136 B1

Shingle Creek meanders through this recently opened course, which does all it can

Below: a bird's-eye view of the Reunion Resort.

Above: caddies provide expert guidance on how to play their courses.

to incorporate the native flora that existed here before the course's development.

Public Golf Courses

Falcon's Fire Golf Club

3200 Seralago Boulevard, Kissimmee; tel: 407-239-5445; www.falconsfire.com; map p.139 D1

Often cited as one of the best golf courses in Orlando, it is also one of the few not joined to a resort or hotel. The course is well designed, but playable. Even novices are likely to get around without too much frustration. The clubhouse restaurant's menu is available on the golfer's GPS systems, allowing them to deliver food directly to you if you fancy a bite.

MetroWest Golf Club

2100 South Hiawassee Road, Orlando; tel: 407-299-1099; www.metrowestgolf.com

Used as a qualifying course for the Champions Tour and US Open, MetroWest has often been named amongst the best public golf courses in the country. It has teamed up with Universal Studios to offer resort residents special packages. This meticulously maintained course features wide, error-accommodating fairways and spring-fed lakes.

Supplies

Edwin Watts Golf

I-Drive 1: 8330 South International Drive, Orlando; tel: 407-351-1444; www.edwinwattsgolf.com; Mon–Sat 10am–6pm, Sun 11am–5pm; map p.136 A2
I-Drive 2: 7024 International Drive, Orlando; tel: 407-352-2535; Mon–Fri 9.30am–8pm, Sat 9.30am–6pm, Sun 11am–5pm; map p.136 A2
Kissimmee: 2956 Vineland Road; tel: 407-397-4600; Mon–Fri 9am–7pm, Sat 9am–6pm, Sun 11am–5pm map p.139 E1
Airport: 7149 North Frontage Road, Orlando; tel: 407-812-7080; Mon–Fri 10am–7pm, Sat 10am–6pm, Sun 11am–5pm
Turkey Lake Road: 7501 Turkey Lake Road, Orlando; tel: 407-345-8451; Mon–Fri

9.30am–8pm, Sat 9.30am–6pm, Sun 11am–5pm; map p.136 A2

With stores stretching over the southeast and Massachusetts, Edwin Watts has five branches in the Orlando area. All of them offer cut-price savings in true 'outlet mall' fashion, making it easy to stock up on gear while on your golfing vacation.

Travel Agency

GolfOrlando

483 Montgomery Place, Altamonte Springs; tel: 866-342-4782; www.golforlando.com

Specializing in getting people to the land of the Mouse to play golf is a tricky business, but if your trip here has a single focus, GolfOrlando will be happy to oblige.

Below: hole number 18, a destination in itself.

History

15,000–7500 BC
Paleo-Indian hunters – Florida's first 'snowbirds' – flee Ice Age glaciers in the north and begin living on the Florida peninsula.

7500–5000 BC
Archaic hunter-gatherers occupy Florida. Archeologists later uncover the first human burials in North America near Cape Canaveral.

1497–1514
French and Spanish claim discovery of Florida. The peninsula appears on a Spanish map in 1510, and Peter Martyr writes in 1514 of a land near the Bahamas with water of eternal youth. Spanish explorers are shipwrecked off Cape Canaveral. Rescued by Timucuans, they marry into the villages and act as interpreters for later Spanish arrivals.

1513
Ponce de León lands in Cape Canaveral area in search of gold, treasure, and the Fountain of Youth. He claims the territory for Spain, naming it *La Florida* – the Land of Flowers. He is killed in 1521 by an Indian arrow.

MID-1700S
Creek Indians – dubbed Seminoles – and runaway African-American slaves, driven south by American settlers, enter Florida.

1764–83
Britain rules Florida.

1774
Quaker naturalist William Bartram of Philadelphia tours Florida. His account inspires many travelers to come to the region.

1783
Britain returns Florida to Spain.

1818

First Seminole War. Future US President Andrew Jackson campaigns against Indians and African-Americans.

1824
The territorial government creates Mosquito County, a vast area extending from near St Augustine to south of Cape Canaveral and west to Alachua County.

1835
The Second Seminole War begins.

1837
Osceola, a half-English, half-Upper Creek Indian fighting with the Seminoles, is imprisoned after entering an American camp under a flag of truce and dies a martyr in 1838.

1842
The Second Seminole War ends with 3,824 Indians and African-Americans being relocated to Arkansas. The federal government offers land to anyone willing to settle near Fort Gatlin, south of Orlando, and act as a citizen-soldier.

1843
Aaron and Isaac Jernigan migrate from Georgia to settle near Fort Gatlin, naming their settlement Jernigan.

1845
Florida becomes a state, with 57,921 residents. Mosquito County changes its name to Orange County in an effort to lure settlers.

1857
Jernigan is renamed Orlando.

1875
Orlando is incorporated (pop. 85) and becomes the seat of Orange County.

1880

Henry Plant's South Florida Railroad is extended to central Florida, allowing expansion of Orlando's agricultural markets.

1884

Fire destroys most of Orlando's downtown business district.

1887

The first African-American township in the United States, Eatonville, is built north of Orlando.

1891

The African-American writer Zora Neale Hurston is born in Eatonville.

1894–9

Severe frosts kill 95 percent of Orange County's citrus groves.

1903

The first automobile is sold in Orlando; the speed limit is 5 miles per hour.

1910–25

A land boom hits Florida. 'Tin can tourists' motor to Florida for the winter.

1929

Mediterranean fruit flies devastate the citrus industry. Bok Tower Gardens in Lake Wales are opened by President Calvin Coolidge. African-American physician W.M. Wells opens the Wells' Built Hotel in Orlando as a lodging for jazz musicians.

1949

Gatorland opens.

1950S

Postwar automobile tourism skyrockets.

1957

The Glenn L. Martin Company of Baltimore relocates to Orlando, starting a population boom.

1964

Walt Disney quietly buys more than 28,000 acres of central Florida farmland.

1965

Disney announces plans to build Walt Disney World in Orlando. Interstate 4 opens.

1966

Walt Disney dies.

1971

The Magic Kingdom opens.

1973

SeaWorld Orlando opens.

1990

Universal Studios opens in Florida.

2001

September 11 attacks depress Florida's tourist industry. The effects have yet to fade.

2003

Space Shuttle *Columbia* explodes on re-entry. All seven astronauts die.

2003

Roy Disney, the family's last representative on the board, resigns over disagreements with CEO Michael Eisner.

2005

Eisner resigns amid controversy, but after making Disney one of the world's leading entertainment companies.

2007

Universal Studios announces plans to build the Wizarding World of Harry Potter, a theme park within their Islands of Adventure theme park.

2010

The Wizarding World of Harry Potter, with thrill rides and themed attractions, such as Hogsmeade and Hogwarts, based on the popular children's series by JK Rowling, opens within Universal Studios' Islands of Adventure theme park.

Live Shows, Parades, and Fireworks

Theme parks offer more than thrill rides. They produce some fine and some not-so-fine live productions, from the shortened version of *The Lion King* to the unique water shows at SeaWorld. On top of this, Disney's parks come to a standstill each day for a parade of characters and end most nights with fireworks. Dinner theater shows dominate the entertainment menu outside the parks.

Magic Kingdom

LIVE SHOWS
Dream-Along with Mickey
Cinderella's Castle stage; see Times Guide

This show features Mickey and Minnie, and promises that dreams do come true. The royal couple confront a host of other characters, from cynical Donald Duck to the Wicked Witch. Unlike other shows, this provides no respite for sore feet or hot children, as it is performed outside the castle to a standing crowd, where little shade is available.

PARADES
Celebrate A Dream Come True Parade

Parade starts at Frontierland, travels through Liberty Square and around the hub in front of Cinderella's Castle, and then down Main Street, U.S.A. before its conclusion in Town Square; afternoons daily, usually 3pm, see Times Guide

The lesser of the Magic Kingdom's two parades *(see Main Street Electrical Parade)* still brings the park to a standstill and is a big hit with younger children who can't get

Above: Mickey at Main Street Electrical Parade.

enough of waving at famous characters. Unlike Main Street Electrical Parade, this parade is not worth planning for; in fact, if you have teens this would be the perfect time to take advantage of short waiting times and take a couple of spins on Space Mountain *(see Thrill Rides, p.124)*.

Main Street Electrical Parade

Parade starts at the park's entrance, Town Square, and continues down Main Street, U.S.A. around the right of the hub and on to Liberty Square, and then ends at Frontierland; it usually starts at 8pm, see Times Guide for days

The Magic Kingdom's nighttime parade only happens a few nights a week, but it is worth planning for, especially as it is always followed by Wishes, the park's fireworks show *(see below)*. In addition to standard-issue characters and music, this show employs spectacular lighting technology on the floats – the Magic Kingdom is even plunged into darkness to heighten its effects. If you are planning to see Wishes afterwards, try to claim a patch on the right side of the hub facing Cinderella's Castle before the parade starts: this will provide excellent viewing for both the parade and the fireworks without you needing to navigate the crowds again.

FIREWORKS
Wishes

Fireworks display is behind Cinderella's Castle; most evenings at closing time, see Times Guide

This is one of the most spectacular fireworks displays you will ever see, and the choreography of live action, music,

Left: amazing animal tricks at SeaWorld.

see Times Guide

The park's finest show and a great place to cool off. The Festival features animatronic characters from *The Lion King* film as a backdrop, but the main attractions are the performers who include dozens of costumed dancers, singers, gymnasts, ballet dancers, and a fire-eater. The music and performances are based on African culture and are of the highest caliber.

Finding Nemo – The Musical
DinoLand U.S.A.; see Times Guide

This is the Animal Kingdom's weakest production and it's poor, poor, poor. The overly emotive script condenses the killing, and there is hardly a scene that is free from fishy slaughter. The technique of using live actors carrying

and explosions is faultless – even Disney cynics are likely to be converted by its finale. To get the full effect you must have a clear view of the front of Cinderella's Castle. This makes the hub and the Plaza Restaurant very popular as showtime approaches.

Epcot
IllumiNations: Reflections on Earth
Showcase Lagoon; most evenings at closing time, see Times Guide

The centerpiece of this pyrotechnic spectacular is an enormous Earth globe created from round LED screens, which hover over the lagoon. Though visible from anywhere in World Showcase (Future World is usually closed prior to the performance), the best viewing area is in the Showcase Plaza – the small promontory of land separating Epcot's two lands. The show itself feels a bit long at 15 minutes, much of

which consists of no more than a soundtrack playing as the globe slowly rotates.

Animal Kingdom
LIVE SHOWS
Festival of the Lion King
Camp Minnie Mickey;

Right: Disney's fireworks displays are likely to be the best you've ever seen.

77

Above: Cirque du Soleil at Downtown Disney.

puppets is also confusing, and at times this seems more of a college theater workshop than the highly accomplished production that is the norm for Disney.

Flights of Wonder
Asia; see Times Guide

This show brings together several exotic bird species to show off their skills, from hunting and diving to uncanny comic timing.

PARADES

Mickey's Jammin' Jungle Parade
Parade begins in Africa, makes a loop around Discovery Island to Asia and then ends in Africa; daily, see Times Guide

This parade features all the usual characters kitted out in their jungle and safari gear. Dancers from *The Lion King* also make a special appearance.

Hollywood Studios

LIVE SHOWS

Beauty and the Beast – Live on Stage
Sunset Boulevard; see Times Guide

This condensed version of the Disney film is a big hit with children. It lacks the wow factor and air conditioning of other live shows, but often fills up prior to showtimes.

Disney Channel Rocks
Hollywood Boulevard; see Times Guide

The outdoor stage set has both the cast and the audience dancing in the street. The opening number is an energetic boys vs girls dance challenge, followed by a concert of hits from Hannah Montana, StarStruck, Camp Rock 2 and other tween favorites from the Disney Channel. A few budding pop stars join the cast onstage to learn all the right moves.

Indiana Jones Epic Stunt Spectacular
Echo Lake; see Times Guide

This 30-minute live show re-creates some of the famous scenes from the Indiana Jones movies. This stunt show is much more accessible and humorous than Lights, Motors, Action! and is a bit less noisy.

Lights, Motors, Action! Extreme Stunt Show
Streets of America; daily, see Times Guide

This must be the loudest show in Orlando! Who'd have thought that such teeny tiny cars could be made to make such an enormous amount of racket. Of course, fans of cars spinning around and making noise will love this type of thing, but for anyone else, this show is a complete

waste of time. The Indiana Jones stunt show is much better.

Playhouse Disney – Live on Stage
Animation Courtyard; see Times Guide

Playhouse Disney, the popular children's show, forms the basis for this live production. Its various characters lead young guests through songs and dances.

Voyage of the Little Mermaid
Animation Courtyard; see Times Guide

Though this is one of Disney's more modest live productions, its standards are high, and its intimate setting makes for a great break from outside.

FIREWORKS

Fantasmic!
Sunset Boulevard; see Times Guide, the show is not nightly

During peak seasons, this show fills up fast – it starts seating 90 minutes before the show begins for a reason. Unlike other parks' fireworks shows, it is difficult to appreciate Fantasmic! if you are not in the stadium. The extensive use of lasers and waters to create special effects, not to mention the wide array of live characters, make this almost as much of a Broadway production as a fireworks show. It's well worth the wait to attend.

Downtown Disney

Cirque Du Soleil's La Nouba

West Side; tel: 407-939-7600; www.cirquedusoleil.com; shows Tue–Sat 6 and 9 pm; admission charge

This is the globally acclaimed Cirque's only show in Orlando, and its themes are toned down so that children, too, can appreciate the phenomenal skill of its performers.

Islands of Adventure

The Eighth Voyage of Sindbad Stunt Show

The Lost Continent; 2 shows daily, see park map for information

Sindbad's efforts to save the princess Amoura never inspire. Though the cave-like set is a perfect backdrop for a drama, the poor acting and tired script lets this production down. Still, no one comes to the Lost Continent to see shows, but to ride thrill rides, and this quixotic show may be just the answer after the shake-up of nearby Dragon Challenge.

Holy Land Experience

Behold the Lamb, Passion Drama

Holy Land Experience (see p.120); shows twice daily, see park map for information

Disney would never do this to Mickey. The crucifixion of Christ is the key biblical re-creation at this park. Though other shows are frequently performed, this is a daily occurrence and the Holy Land's longest-running spectacle. Some people, even those who come to the Holy Land Experience to learn more about their faith, may find they have problems with this production. While it may represent Jesus's sacrifice, it could be criticized for placing him alongside Santa Claus or Peter Pan by recreating it in a theme-park setting. Even if you've no problem with this, remember that the Roman soldiers who are beating the Christ actor and nailing him to a cross may also cause fear and confusion in small children.

SeaWorld

A'Lure, the Call of the Ocean

Nautilus Theater; see show times on park map

This Cirque du Soleil-style show tells the story of the Sea Sirens who have long been said to lure fisherman into their underwater caves with their mesmerizing calls. You'll be equally hypnotized by the acrobatic feats of these amazing performers. The cool, dark theater also provides a welcome respite from the heat of the day.

Believe

Shamu Stadium; see show times on park map

For many, this show is the reason they visit SeaWorld. Shamu (a fictional persona for the star whale) has served as SeaWorld's Mickey Mouse since its early days. Though the show and beast are exquisite, the recent revamp has lost its spirit and, compared to viewings a couple of years ago, it seems obvious that Shamu is not just losing steam but also having problems with his dorsal and tail fins as a result of his long confinement. His jumping has suffered, and a sappy storyline displayed on LED screens has tried to take up the slack, but much like the overly patriotic beginning, it attempts to load the audience with emotions rather than educate them about these fascinating creatures.

Right: Blue Horizons at the Whale and Dolphin Theater.

79

Above: Shamu stops for a chat.

Blue Horizons
Whale and Dolphin Theater; see show times on park map

Previously the Whale and Dolphin Theater featured a fantastic show that showcased the incredible jumping ability of not just dolphins but some smaller whale species, too, while informing the audience about the critters they were admiring. In this production, any such educational aspects have given way to human acrobats who perform for longer than the mammals you've all come to see. The dolphins' repertoire has been seriously cut as well, with the main focus on pretending to be jet skis for the trainers. The show is still an entertaining spectacle that only SeaWorld could accomplish, but its change of focus from education to acrobatics is a real disappointment.

Clyde and Seamore Take Pirate Island
Sea Lion and Otter Stadium; see show times on park map

In front of Pacific Point Preserve is the Sea Lion and Otter Stadium, home to the ridiculously goofy Clyde and Seamore Take Pirate Island show. Scripting a comedy routine around the unpredictable behavior of sea lions, otters, and a giant wal-

rus is foolhardy at best and humiliating to the animals at worst, but the human players incorporate the goofs into the 30-minute show and you'll laugh in spite of yourself. The pirate ship set is one of the park's best, and it's remarkable to see the animals sliding around the stage and into the tank in front as if Laurel or Hardy were their second names.

Pets Ahoy
Seaport Theater; see show times on park map

This endearing animal show features cats, dogs, pigs, and other animals rescued from shelters and trained to do remarkable tricks – and shtick. Kids love meeting the actors after the show.

Dinner Shows

Arabian Nights
3081 Arabian Nights Boulevard, Kissimmee; tel: 407-239-9223 or 800-553-6116; www.arabian-nights.com; call for show times; admission charge; Link: 55, 56; map p.139 C1

The most enchanting dinner show in Orlando is Arabian Nights, which stars 50 Arabian, Lippizaner, palomino, and quarter horses that are put through their paces by skilled riders in an enormous arena. The storyline involves

the wedding of a prince and princess. The finale is worth the price of admission, featuring 15 riderless horses that prance around the arena as artificial snow falls. Dinner fare includes a choice of chicken tenders, prime rib, or lasagne.

Capone's Dinner and Show
4740 West Irlo Bronson Memorial Highway (US 192), Kissimmee; tel: 407-397-2378 or 800-220-8428; www.alcapones.com; admission charge; Link: 55; map p.18

The longest-running (and weakest) of Orlando's dinner show offerings is the amateurish Capone's. Set in a cheesy 1930s speakeasy behind a fake ice cream parlor, *Guys and Dolls* this ain't, though the waiters are dressed as gun-brandishing gangsters, and you are ostensibly attending a celebration for the notorious hoodlum Al Capone. Cafeteria-style Italian fare such as lasagne, ziti, spaghetti, and baked chicken is the bill of fare.

Medieval Times Dinner and Tournament
4510 West Irlo Bronson Highway (US 192), Kissimmee; tel: 866-543-9637; call for show times; www.medievaltimes.com/orlando; admission charge; Link: 55

Medieval Times Dinner is another horsey extravaganza, this one set in the 11th century. It features a well-executed jousting tournament that pits six knights against each other while the audience cheers on their favorites. Avoid purchasing an upgrade to preferred seating; there are only five rows in the arena, and all offer good viewing.

The Outta Control Magic Comedy Dinner Show
9067 International Drive, Orlando; tel: 407-351-8800; www.wonderworksonline.com; nightly at 6 and 8pm; admission charge; I-Ride: mainline; map p.136 A1

This one-man show is located in the upside-down WonderWorks building. Food includes hand-tossed pizza and popcorn with unlimited beer, wine and soda. Entertainment is a mixture of comedy, improv, and magic that precisely promises to 'tickle your funny bone every eight seconds.'

Pirate's Dinner Adventure
6400 Carrier Drive, Orlando; tel: 407-248-0590; www.pirates dinneradventure.com; shows nightly, call for times; admission charge; map p.136 A2

A swashbuckling theme prevails at this arena dinner show that has one of Orlando's most impressive sets: a life-size pirate ship

that serves as the centerpiece for an action-packed evening of pillaging, fighting on deck, and attempts to save Princess Anita. Expect to do plenty of oohing and aahing, cheering, and singing of pirate songs. Pre-show attractions include gypsy fortune-tellers and face painting. A post-show Buccaneer Bash continues the silliness.

Sleuth's Mystery Dinner Show
8267 International Drive, Orlando; tel: 407-363-1985 or 800-393-1985; www.sleuths.com; shows change daily, call for times and program; I-Ride: mainline; admission charge; map p.136 A2

This ever-popular place has three different theaters showing original comedy mysteries. Sleuth's involves the audience in solving a crime and is perfect for fans of murder mystery weekends and whodunits. Guests are seated at round tables to watch the first act, which gets the murdering over with and includes much ad lib at the audience's expense. Each table then chooses a spokesperson who questions

the actors as you try to solve the murder.

Titanic Dinner Event
7324 International Drive, Orlando; tel: 407-248-1166; www.titanicdinnerevent.com; call for days and times; admission charge; map p. 136 A2

One of Orlando's newest dinner shows, this is part of a larger Titanic exhibition which tells the tale of the fated ocean liner. You can dress up for a more glamorous adult evening out than the usual themed show, with a re-creation of the captain's retirement party and actors in Edwardian dress visiting your table to regale you with their stories. The menu includes filet of beef, chicken breast with Lyonnaise, beer and wine.

Treasure Tavern
6400 Carrier Drive, Orlando; tel: 877-318-2469; www.treasuretavern.com; Tue–Sat, call for times; admission charge; map p.136 A2

Located in the Pirate's Dinner Adventure complex, Orlando's newest dinner show features acrobats, dancers and comedians rollicking about a Caribbean outpost. Slow-roasted prime rib is on the menu.

Below: go back in time and cheer on the knights in the jousting competition at the Medieval Times Dinner and Tournament.

81

Museums and Galleries

Due to its relative youth and its inherent associaton with theme parks, Orlando's cultural legacy is often overlooked. While it may never compete with the likes of New York or Chicago in terms of museum space, it has several fascinating institutions that record its unique roles in southern American history. Its climate has offered a welcome home to acclaimed artists in their latter years, and there are state-of-the-art museums such as the Orlando Science Center. All of these make for a great, real-world day out.

Downtown Orlando and Loch Haven Park

Cityartsfactory
29 South Orange Avenue, Orlando; tel: 407-648-7060; www.cityartsfactory.com; gallery hours vary; free; Link: 3, 6, 7, 11, 13, 18, 51; map p.135 C2
Set in the renovated Philips Theater building, the Cityartsfactory hosts nine art galleries which include photography, glassworks, and other contemporary works. The upstairs performance space in the Eola Capital Loft has a good view of the city and is home to the SAK Comedy Lab.

Grand Bohemian Gallery
Grand Bohemian Hotel, 325 South Orange Avenue, Orlando; tel: 407-581-4801; www.grand bohemiangallery.com; Link: 3, 6, 7, 11, 13, 18, 51; map p.135 C2

Set on the ground floor of the Grand Bohemian Hotel and in other public spaces, there's no problem attracting mon-eyed clients into this cramped but intriguing gallery, which is possibly one of Orlando's finest commercial galleries for contemporary American and European fine art. The collection is constantly changing, with new imports replacing purchased pieces and special exhibitions featuring single

Below: Zora Neale Hurston and a Chiuly exhibit at the Orlando Museum of Art, *see p.84 and 87.*

After the building of Henry Plant's and Henry Flagler's railroad networks in the 1880s and 1890s, central Florida was carved open to greater visitation and settlement, and towns like Winter Park and Maitland sprang up beside the tracks. Upper-class Englishmen, attracted by the idea of being plantation owners and enjoying an easy outdoor lifestyle far from home, rushed to purchase land from state and railway corporations at a dollar an acre. The new land also lured working-class Englishmen hoping to escape the strictures of home.

Left: the Orlando Science Center.

Orlando; tel: 407-836-8500; www.thehistorycenter.org; Mon–Sat 10am–5pm, Sun noon–5pm; admission charge; Link: 3, 6, 7, 11, 13, 18, 51; map p.135 C2

ORCHC now occupies the restored 1927 Orange County Courthouse in Downtown's Heritage Square, the old Orlando town center. The museum, now an affiliate of the Smithsonian Institution, features four floors of colorful exhibits covering central Florida's 12,000 years of history, from the state's first Indian residents to Spanish explorers and missionaries, British colonists, the Seminole Indian Wars, Cracker cowmen, citrus-growers, tin can tourists, aerospace engineers, and Walt Disney.

The area's little-known Indian cultures are particularly well interpreted, with dioramas showing an ancient shell midden, Timucuan chiefs in ceremonial attire, 3,000-year-old St John's pottery (proba-

artists occurring throughout the year.

Mennello Museum of American Art
900 East Princeton Street, Loch Haven Park, Orlando; tel: 407-246-4278; www.mennello museum.org; Tue–Sat 10.30am–4.30pm; Sun noon–4.30pm; admission charge; map p.135 C3
One of only a handful of American folk art museums, much of the Mennello's

collection is devoted to the colorful paintings of Earl Cunningham, a self-taught artist and former sea captain whose long friendship with the Menellos led to the founding of this museum. Special exhibitions of American folk art are always on display as well.

Orange County Regional History Center
65 East Central Boulevard,

Below: Bunk Baxter was famed for his alligator-wrestling ability.

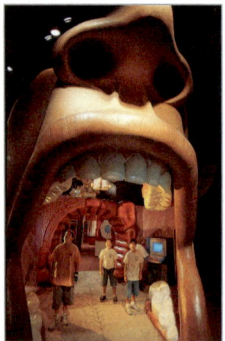

Above: so many ways to be eaten alive at the Orlando Science Center.

bly among the first to be made in North America), and contemporary Seminole culture. The latter includes a video of the Green Corn Ceremony held annually by the few hundred Seminoles still living in the Everglades.

A community museum in the best sense, ORCHC offers monthly socials and educational programs for people of all ages. Some of the best are for children. Camp-ins give them the opportunity to sleep overnight among the exhibits. Other school programs allow kids to perform mock trials of the Big Bad Wolf and other fairy-tale characters in the original courtroom where, less innocently, mass murderer

Ted Bundy was tried and sentenced to death.

Orlando Museum of Art
2416 North Mills Avenue, Loch Haven Park, Orlando; tel: 407-896-4231; www.omart.org; Tue–Fri 10am–4pm, Sat and Sun noon–4pm; admission charge; map p.135 C3
Founded in 1924 and recently expanded, OMA's well-regarded collections include ancient artifacts from the American southwest, Mexico, and Central and South America, works by 18th- to 20th-century American painters such as John Singer Sargent, Thomas Moran, Georgia O'Keeffe, and Robert Rauschenberg, and African

art. The museum also hosts temporary exhibitions, which tend to focus on art of the Americas.

Orlando Science Center
777 East Princeton Street, Loch Haven Park, Orlando; tel: 407-514-2000; www.osc.org; museum Thur–Tue 10am–5pm, observatory Sat 6–10pm; admission charge; map p.135 C3
Ten interactive exhibit halls cover everything from Florida's famous limestone sinkholes to its dinosaurs (courtesy of Disney World), an astronaut's life in zero gravity, and a journey through the human body. An eight-story CineDome shows giant-screen films, and daily sky shows are presented in the Planetarium, including one on Orlando's night sky, which can be viewed through a giant telescope in the Crosby Observatory.

Wells' Built Museum
511 West South Street, Orlando; tel: 407-245-7535; www.pastinc.org; Mon–Fri 9am–5pm; admission charge; Link: 39; map p.134 C2
This museum has the best story of any cultural institution in Orlando. Set in the old Wells' Built Hotel, this was the center of African American culture in Orlando from

Below: the Crosby Observatory at the Science Center.

84

1926 until the end of segregation. It housed legends from every walk of life, including Ella Fitzgerald, Thurgood Marshall, and Jackie Robinson. A casino nightclub stood next door at the time and hosted such big-name acts as Ray Charles and B.B. King.

The museum has recently been done up, providing a better display area for the photographs, artifacts and other memorabilia detailing this very important slice of Orlando history which resonates throughout the South.

Above: the Charles Hosmer Morse Museum.

Winter Park and Maitland

Albin Polasek Museum and Sculpture Gardens

633 Osceola Avenue, Winter Park; tel: 407-647-6294; www.polasek.org; Tue–Sat 10am–4pm, Sun 1am–4pm; admission charge; Link: 23; map p.135 D4

Listed in the National Register of Historic Places, the home of late Czech-American sculptor Albin Polasek is a peaceful 3-acre retreat with a studio, private chapel, gardens, and galleries. The collection of some 200 pieces are dominated by Polasek's works, many of them artfully displayed on the manicured grounds. The museum also exhibits sculpture by Ameri-

can masters such as Augustus Saint-Gaudens.

Charles Hosmer Morse Museum of American Art

445 North Park Avenue, Winter Park; tel: 407-645-5311; www.morsemuseum.org; Tue–Sat 9.30am–4pm; Sun 1–4pm; admission charge; map p.135 D4

Featuring the world's most comprehensive collection of late-19th-century stained glass by Louis Comfort Tiffany, the centerpiece of the collection is the reconstructed Tiffany Chapel, designed for the 1893 World's Columbian Exposition in Chicago. The museum was founded in 1942 by Jeannette Genius McKean and named for her industrialist grandfather, a Winter Park benefactor. The collections were assembled

over 50 years by Mrs McKean and her husband Hugh McKean, president of Rollins College in Winter Park, and include significant holdings of Arts and Crafts-style Rookwood pottery and American painting.

Cornell Fine Arts Museum

Rollins College, 1000 Holt Avenue, Winter Park; tel: 407-646-2000; www.rollins.edu/cfam; Tue–Fri 10am–4pm, Sat and Sun noon–5pm; admission charge; Link: 23; map p.135 D4

Though quite small, the Cornell Museum of Fine Arts, on the gracious Mediterranean-style campus of Rollins College, is one of the finest and oldest art museums in the southeast. Each year, the Cornell stages six to eight exhibitions drawn from its holdings of more than 6,000 European and American

Below: fine examples of Morse's work with the Tiffany Chapel in the middle.

works of art. The collection encompasses paintings, drawings, and sculpture from the 1450s to the 1990s. At the start of the school year, one gallery is dedicated to exhibiting work by contemporary local artists.

Holocaust Memorial Resource and Education Center
815 North Maitland Avenue, Maitland; tel: 407-628-0555; www.holocaustedu.org; Mon–Thur 9am–4pm, Fri 9am–1pm, Sun 1–4pm

A somber experience awaits visitors here. One room chronicles the history of the Holocaust with multimedia displays. Another room offers changing exhibits on aspects of the Nazi campaign to exterminate Jews, homosexuals, gypsies, and other minorities. A library holds 4,000 volumes dedicated exclusively to Holocaust history. Special events include a Kristallnacht Commemoration in November.

Maitland Art Center
231 West Packwood Avenue, Maitland; tel: 407-539-2181; Tue–Sun 11am–4pm; www.maitlandartcenter.org; free; Link: 39; map p.30

Tranquil grounds and artworks are the features of this sprawling, 6-acre art studio complex on a quiet side street. It was built in the 1930s by artist Jules Andre Smith. A formed concrete building decorated with an unusual Aztec-Mayan frieze, it is considered one of the best surviving examples of fantasy architecture. Smith, a friend of Annie Russell, the New York actress who was professor of Theater Arts at Rollins College *(see Annie Russell Theatre, p.89)*, moved to Maitland in the early 1930s and designed sets for productions at the quaint Annie Russell Theatre. In 1937, a donation from the wife of Edward Bok, the Dutch-born former editor of *Ladies' Home Journal*, allowed Smith to build a 'laboratory studio to be devoted to research in modern art.' Now managed by the Maitland Historical Society, the little museum's

Below: the Aztec-inspired building of the Maitland Art Center.

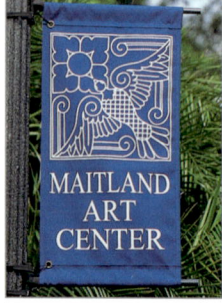

820 Lake Lily Drive, Maitland; tel: 407-644-2451; www.maitlandhistory.org; Thur–Sun noon–4pm; Link: 1, 9; map p.30

When William H. Waterhouse settled in Maitland at the end of the 19th century, he was a pioneer. By the time he'd completed his home here, he had become one of the area's most in-demand builders. This house has been fully restored to show how he and his family would have lived on the shores of Lake Lily. Waterhouse built this house himself using basic tools like those found in the Carpentry Shop Museum. Staff hold demonstrations and workshops that let you try the tools out for yourself. The house is viewed by tour only, but the tour guide is a very enjoyable chap who brings the house and the community alive with his insight. There is also a self-guided tour through a traditional Victorian herb garden.

Eatonville

Millenia Fine Art Gallery
555 South Lake Destiny Drive,

Orlando; tel: 407-304-8100 or 866-655-8655; Mon–Fri 9am–5pm; free; Link: 24, 40, 305; map p.136 B3

This 30,000sq-ft gallery is part of the Millenia art chain that exhibits contemporary art for sale across the country. The artists on their roster include Dale Chihuly, Henry Moore, and Marc Chagall, among others. Artists change regularly.

Zora Neale Hurston National Museum of Fine Arts
227 East Kennedy Boulevard, Eatonville; tel: 407-647-3307; www.zoranealehurstonmuseum.com; Mon–Fri 9am–4pm, Sat 11am–1pm; donations suggested; Link: 1, 9

Devoted to African-American culture, this tiny museum in Eatonville, the first black township in the United States, is named for Hurston, the noted Harlem Renaissance writer, anthropologist, and folklorist, who was born in Eatonville in 1891. She celebrated rural Florida life in such books as *Their Eyes Were Watching God* and *Of Men and Mules*. Revolving exhibitions feature African-American art. Each January, Eatonville holds a festival in Hurston's honor.

galleries and grounds (reputed to be haunted by Smith's ghost) still retain an aging charm. Changing exhibitions are devoted to art representing many different ethnic traditions within the community.

Maitland Historical Museum and Telephone Museum
221 West Packwood Avenue, Maitland; tel: 407-644-1364; http://maitlandhistory.org; Thur–Sun noon–4pm; Link: 39; map p.30

The Maitland Historical Museum displays old pictures, artifacts, and other items that tell the story of Maitland's development from the pioneer days to the development of lumber and citrus industries. The Telephone Museum has a collection of early phones from the Winter Park Telephone Company, which was founded in 1910 to improve the custom at a local grocery.

The Waterhouse Residence and Carpentry Shop Museums

Below: the Waterhouse Residence Museum.

Music, Dance, and Theater

Suffering the same fate as Orlando's museums, the performing arts outside of the theme parks are too often ignored by visitors. What a shame. The Annie Russell Theatre is one of the longest established theaters in the state: set on the lovely campus of Rollins College, it has a wide range of productions. The accomplished Shakespeare Theater and eccentric Mad Cow round off the drama. Orlando maintains professional philharmonic and ballet companies, which perform mostly at the Bob Carr Performing Arts Center.

Music

CLASSICAL MUSIC COMPANIES

Orlando Philharmonic
812 East Rollins Street, Suite 300, Orlando; tel: 407-770-0071; www.orlandophil.org

Established in the early 1990s, the Orlando Phil performs at several venues around the city. Its main series is the Super Series, featuring the best of classic and pop music performed at the Bob Carr Performing Arts Center; its concert opera series is also performed here. The Philharmonic presents the Sounds of Summer chamber music series and a four-concert Focus Series, as well as free outdoor community pop concerts in the spring and autumn involving the full orchestra.

VENUES

Bob Carr Performing Arts Center
401 Livingston Street, Orlando; tel: 407-849-2000;

www.orlandovenues.net; Link: 8; map p.134 C2
A year-round community auditorium that hosts regional and national musical, theater and dance performances.

Dance

Central Florida Ballet
3306 Maggie Boulevard, Suite B, Orlando; tel: 407-849-9948; www.centralfloridaballet.com; map p.136 B4
This academy for dance holds a few productions each year in its intimate Studio Theater. Its *Nutcracker* has become a Christmas tradition. Other shows include the original *9/11 An American Moment* as well as traditional favorites.

Orlando Ballet
1111 North Orange Avenue; tel: 407-426-1739; www.orlandoballet.org; map p.134 C2
Central Florida's only fully professional ballet company, its season runs from October to May and includes a Christmas *Nutcracker* as well as other light-hearted productions such as *The Pirates of Penzance*. Performances are all held at the Bob Carr Performing Arts Center.

Right: backstage getting hair and make-up done before a performance.

Left: the accomplished Orlando Shakespeare Theater.

The Rep pays special attention to providing affordable productions suitable for a younger audience and the entire family by transferring classic fairy tales and children's books to the stage. Weekend matinees are especially popular.

Annie Russell Theatre
Rollins College, 1000 Holt Avenue, Winter Park; tel: 407-646-2145; www.rollins.edu/annierussell; map p.135 D4
Seating over 300, the Annie is no simple college theater. It is at the heart of the oldest theater program in Florida and has a reputation as one of the most prestigious small theaters in America. Its program is eclectic and includes everything from rep plays by Oscar Wilde to new material and murder mystery productions. It also hosts the Rollins Dance series.

Theater

Broadway Across America
Bob Carr Performing Arts Center; tel: 407-849-2000; www.broadwayacrossamerica.com/orlando; map p.134 C2
Broadway blockbusters come to Orlando with this national touring company. The season runs from December through June, and there are several productions each year featuring some of the hottest musicals and rising stars.

Mad Cow Theatre
105 South Magnolia Avenue, Orlando; tel: 407-297-8788; www.madcowtheatre.com; map p.135 C2
Founded in 1997 as a two-show project the Mad Cow has since established itself as a key player in the Downtown arts scene. The work provides a platform for up-and-coming American talent while staging established theater from around the world and occasional rep pieces.

Orlando Shakespeare Theater
812 East Rollins Street, Loch Haven Park, Orlando; tel: 407-447-1700; www.orlando shakes.org; map p.135 C3
The Orlando Shakespeare Theater began over 20 years ago as a month-long festival and has since grown into a year-round theater. It is now partnered by the University of Central Florida, which provides further educational resources. Of course, the season is dominated by the Bard's works, but there is room for modern playwrights, too.

The Pointe Performing Arts Center
Pointe Orlando; 9101 International Drive, Orlando; tel: 407-374-3587; www.pointearts.org; map p.136 A1
Having returned to Florida after producing Off-Broadway shows in New York City, Fantasyland Theatrical Productions puts on high-quality theater throughout the year, ranging from holiday family shows to summer-stock comedy to thoughtful and provoking dramatic plays.

The Rep
1001 East Princeton Street, Loch Haven Park, Orlando; tel: 407-896-7365; www.orlando rep.com; map p.135 C3

Several seasonal productions add variety to Orlando's cultural scene. Winter Park's **Bach Festival** (www.bach festivalflorida.org), in February and March, highlights the region's talents in classical music. **ArtsFest** (www.artsfestfl.com) is a week of free arts events from ballet to opera and more, held in February at various locations. The **Festival of Orchestras** (www.festivaloforchestras.com) brings acclaimed international orchestras from as far away as Russia to Orlando for a series of concerts each winter. In May, the **Orlando International Fringe Festival** brings over 500 performances of theater, music and comedy to Downtown Orlando for 10 days. It's the oldest non-juried fringe festival in the United States.

Natural World

When Juan Ponce de León landed at Cape Canaveral in 1513, he found a unique blend of savagery and beauty. What would later become Florida was already populated by over 150,000 peoples who were creating some of the most sophisticated pottery in the Americas at the time. On the other hand, the boggy land gave way under your feet, man-eating alligators inhabited every body of water, and the air was infested with malaria-carrying mosquitoes. Still, he chose the name La Florida (Land of Flowers). The beauty that so impressed him is remarkably well preserved if you know where to look.

Animal Interaction

Green Meadows Petting Farm

1368 South Poinciana Boulevard, Kissimmee; tel: 407-846-0770; www.greenmeadowsfarm.com; daily 9.30am–4pm; admission charge; map p.18

It wasn't long ago that this area supplied cattle that made Kissimmee the center of the ranching industry in Florida. The animals are here now more to provide fun and education for local children. Train rides and traditional hay rides are also available, and guests are welcome to milk the cows.

Parks and Gardens

Audubon Center for Birds of Prey

1101 Audubon Way, Maitland; tel: 407-644-0190; http://fl.audubon.org; Tue–Sun 10am–4pm; admission charge

The Birds of Prey Center is hidden in a residential area near Lake Sibelia between Maitland and Eatonville. But don't let this dissuade you. The recently refurbished raptor rescue center offers an unforgettable experience. Audubon takes in about 600 injured birds a year and releases 40 percent of them. You won't see recuperating birds here – they are isolated to improve their odds of survival in the wild – but you will see members of some 32 raptor species whose injuries are so extensive they can only survive in captivity. Ospreys, tiny screech owls, vultures, bald eagles, red-tailed hawks, kites, and other birds of prey live in aviaries. A program also allows you to adopt a particular bird (they all have names) to help the center with its work. Guided tours for groups of 10 or more are available by reservation.

Canaveral National Seashore

map p.32

Adjacent to the Merritt Island Wildlife Refuge is the 57,000-acre Canaveral National Seashore, whose miles of barrier dunes and sea-swept beaches are a haven for beachcombers and nature-lovers. Two of the beaches, Apollo and Playalinda, at the northern and southern tips of the seashore, have restrooms, boardwalks, and, from May 30 to September 1, lifeguards. In between, the

Below: don't be fooled by the charming smile.

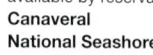

Left: exotic plants dominate the Leu Gardens.

Merritt Island National Wildlife Refuge
map p.32

At the 140,000-acre Merritt Island National Wildlife Refuge, adjacent to Kennedy Space Center, endangered West Indian manatees loll peacefully in brackish lagoons, sea turtles waddle ashore to lay eggs on pristine beaches, and alligators bask in the sun on creek banks. The refuge lies along a prime migratory flyway, and the sky is filled in early spring with warblers and shorebirds while, on the ground, egrets and herons are in breeding plumage, wood storks and ospreys build nests, and bald eaglets test their wings.

The mild climate and varied environment of marshes, hardwood hammocks, pine forest, scrub, and coastal dunes sustain more than 500 species of wildlife, including more than 20 on the Endangered or Threatened Species List. This is one of the most important nesting areas in the country for loggerhead, green, and leatherback turtles.

Much of the wildlife can be spotted along the 7-mile, one-way **Black Point Wildlife Drive**, a self-guided auto tour through salt- and freshwater marshes. The entrance is on SR 406, a mile east of the intersection with SR 402. Manatees, most prevalent in the spring and fall, can be best viewed from the observation area near Haulover Canal Bridge on SR 3.

The best time to visit is during the off-season, when wildlife populations are at their highest, and mosquitoes, high temperatures and thunderstorms are least likely to present a problem.

> Walt Disney World Resort has only ever closed once – when Hurricane Andrew threatened in 1992.

landscape has been left untouched. Portions of the seashore may be closed for days before shuttle launches or when parking lots are full.

Harry P. Leu Gardens
1920 North Forest Avenue, Orlando; tel: 407-246-2620; www.leugardens.org; daily 9am–5pm; admission charge; map p.135 D3

After days at chaotic theme parks, your sanity deserves a break at a quiet retreat like Leu Gardens. The grounds are made for gentle strolls and spending the day. The gardens were founded to inspire visitors to appreciate the plantlife of central Florida and the **Native Wetland Garden** supports a lot of native wildlife and birds, including alligators.

Other tropical environments are recreated here as well as more domestic features such as a rose, vegetable, herb, and butterfly gardens.

In the center of the grounds stands the original **Leu House,** which can be viewed by guided tour only and illustrates what life in Florida was like at the beginning of the 20th century.

If you want to delve a bit deeper into Florida's natural world, the gardens offer regular courses ranging from birdwatching to rose gardening. The gardens also show films on their Date Nights on the first Friday of each month in addition to staging other events.

Below: a hatchling begins its solitary journey.

Nightlife

Orlando's theme parks do an excellent job of keeping their clientele after hours, which is a shame, as Downtown (Orlando's not Disney's) is worth the excursion. Downtown Disney and CityWalk, on the other hand, have restaurants, bars and clubs all centrally located with transportation back to resort hotels until late evening, so you need not worry about drink-driving. Downtown Orlando is exactly what you'd expect from a modern city: a mixture of stylish clubs and bars, some characterful watering holes, and a large variety of independent restaurants. The choice is yours.

Downtown Disney

LIVE MUSIC

Bongos Cuban Cafe

Westside; tel: 407-828-0999; www.bongoscubancafe.com; Fri–Sat 11.30pm–2am; map below

Owned by superstar Gloria Estefan and her husband Emilio, this Old Havana-themed restaurant becomes a hot Latin dance club on the weekends. Party beneath the giant pineapple to Latin rhythms on a superb sound system and a mesmerizing light show.

House of Blues

Westside; tel: 407-934-2583; www.houseofblues.com; map below

Though the venue of this chain bar provides little character, and Downtown Disney could not possibly be any further away from the Bayou in terms of attitude, the House of Blues does still attract some fine artists.

Disney's Boardwalk

Atlantic Dance Hall

Boardwalk Resort

This mock pier is the only nightclub in the Boardwalk area. The Art Deco interior plays on coastal themes, but the crowd (this is Disney) is tame when the DJ

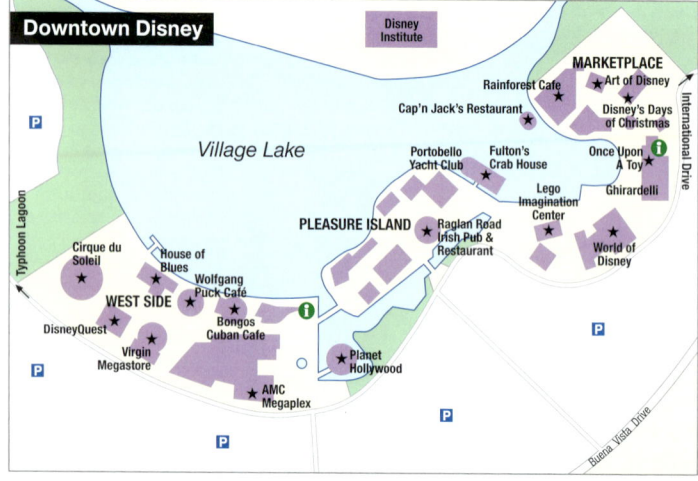

Downtown Disney

Disney Institute

Village Lake

Typhoon Lagoon

MARKETPLACE

Rainforest Cafe · Art of Disney

Cap'n Jack's Restaurant · Disney's Days of Christmas

Portobello Yacht Club · Fulton's Crab House · Once Upon A Toy

Lego Imagination Center · Ghirardelli

PLEASURE ISLAND · Raglan Road Irish Pub & Restaurant · World of Disney

Cirque du Soleil · House of Blues · Wolfgang Puck Cafe

WEST SIDE · Bongos Cuban Cafe

DisneyQuest · Virgin Megastore · Planet Hollywood

AMC Megaplex

International Drive

Buena Vista Drive

Left: Rising Star.

serving up Latin rhythms. DJs get you in the party mood with salsa, merengue and reggae music.

Red Coconut Club
Sun–Thur 8pm–2am and Fri–Sat 6pm–2am; map p.50
The Red Coconut sits on CityWalk's upper level, affording a view of the throngs below and the quiet lagoon beyond. If you are looking for a bit of peace and quiet, the indoor tables are the best bet; the area around the bar is better suited for those wanting to take in the live music or DJs.

Kissimmee and Celebration

Sun on the Beach
Old Town, 5770 West Irlo Bronson Memorial Highway (US 192); tel: 407-397-1980; www.sunonthebeachclub.com; daily 9pm–2am; Link 55; map p.139 D1
If the Old Town shopping center does anything well it's this: raucous nightlife. This is the best nightclub on the US 192 stretch. Entertainment changes nightly, and there is a regular Pride Night on Thursdays with no cover that features a midnight burlesque show by the Diamond Divas.

attempts to kick it up every night.
Jellyrolls
Boardwalk Resort
This old-time piano bar is full of merry-making, with two musical maestros tickling the ivories and trumping each other in a game of dueling pianos. Their repertoire seems to know no bounds, and audience members sing along to their favourite tunes and even dance in the aisles.

CityWalk

Bob Marley – A Tribute to Freedom

Most nightclubs have a cover charge for live bands and special events, usually ranging from $5–$10, or more for big-name acts. But most also offer specials on various nights of the week, from ladies' nights with free admission and/or drinks, to special drink prices and other themed promotions. Check their website calendars for the latest events. And wherever you go, no matter your age, be sure to take a photo ID.

Nightly 9pm–2am; map p.50
Bob Marley's home in Kingston, Jamaica has been re-created here around an open-air veranda and courtyard, with videos, photos and artifacts along with the Jamaican cuisine. Live reggae bands play most nights in the courtyard. Don't miss Jammin' Thursdays, with special prices on beer and drinks from 4pm.
CityWalk's Rising Star
Nightly 8pm–2am; Tue–Sat; map p.50
Take karaoke to a new level at this 440-seat nightclub, where you can take to the stage with a live band and back-up singers. Whether you're into country, pop or rock 'n' roll, there's a huge number of song titles to choose from and the host keeps the show lively. The bar serves a range of Karaoke Cocktails, such as the Liquid Courage martini.
Latin Quarter
Mon–Sat 10pm–2am; map p.50
The restaurant serves Latin American dishes and after dining hours it transforms itself into a vibrant nightclub

Below: the lively piano bar Jellyrolls.

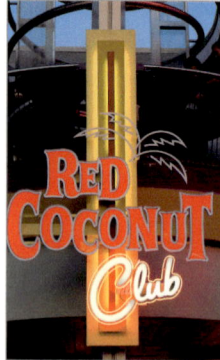

Above: enjoy live music or DJs at this CityWalk Club.

International Drive and Lake Buena Vista

Backstage
Rosen Plaza Hotel, 9700 International Drive, Orlando; tel: 407-996-9700, ext. 1719; www.rosenplaza.com/backstage; Wed–Sun; I-Ride: mainline; map p.136 A1

Orlando's 'original' nightclub is newly restored, with a tri-level stage, huge dance floor and sports bar area. Wednesdays are Latin Night, with the rest of the week featuring a mixture of DJs playing Top 40 hits and live bands.

B.B. King's Blues Club
Pointe Orlando, 9101 International Drive, Suite 2230, Orlando; tel: 407-370-4550; www.bbkingclubs.com; Sun–Thu 7.30–11.30pm, Fri–Sat 7.30pm–1.30am; I-Ride: mainline; map p.136 A1

A nightly helping of blues accompanies the Southern comfort food at the Orlando branch of this famous restaurant and music club chain. Two house bands – B.B. King's All-Star Band and Pure Blues Band – will get you on the dance floor with the greatest Motown, blues, funk and soul hits. Check the online calendar for guest performances.

ICEBAR
8967 International Drive, Orlando; tel: 407-426-7555; www.icebarorlando.com; Sun–Thu 7pm–12am, Fri–Sat 7pm–2am; admission charge; I-Ride: mainline; map p.136 A1

With everything from the seats to the bar itself made of ice, this could quite literally be the coolest bar in the country. Thermal capes and gloves are provided to help you adjust to the frosty temperature, but the beautiful ice sculptures will warm your heart. As visitors can only stay in the ICEBAR for 45 minutes, work up a sweat on the dance floor afterwards to Top 40 hits, house and trance music in the Fire Lounge.

Downtown and Loch Haven Park

Antigua
41 West Church Street, Orlando; www.churchstreetbars.com; Tue–Wed, Fri–Sat; map p.135 C2

A 20ft (6 metre) cascading waterfall and two 500-gallon fish tanks set the tone in this sleek, seductively lit nightclub. The sound system makes all audio contact impossible, but the multi-level layout makes finding your niche in the night no problem. The four bars also ensure less queuing.

Club 57 West
57 West Pine Street, Orlando; tel: 407-872-0084; www.club57west.com; daily 3pm–3am; Link 3, 7, 11, 18; map p.135 C2

Mondays are Soul of the City open mic nights featuring performances from poetry to R&B to hip hop. The rest of the week offers a mix of local DJs and live bands, with some late night comedy shows on Fridays.

Firestone Live
578 North Orange Avenue, Orlando; tel: 407-872-0066; www.firestonelive.net; Thur–Sun; Link: 3, 6, 7, 11, 13, 18, 51; map p.135 C2

The daddy of all Orlando clubs. On the scene now for over 15 years, it has been praised by everyone from MTV to Univision for its promotion of underground music – mostly hip-hop and electronica. An accomplished institution.

Roxy Nightclub
740 Bennett Road, Orlando; tel: 407-898-4004; www.roxyorlando.com; Tue–Sun; map p.135 C2

The only problem with the Roxy is that it is tucked away beyond even Thornton Park, with nothing else going on around it. Otherwise it's an accomplished club night every night, with

Below: several bars in Orlando brag about their signature martinis and margaritas.

Right: the revamped Backstage club, with pool tables in its sports bar area.

a large dance floor and heavy sound system.

Slingapour's
17 Wall Street Plaza, Orlando; tel: 407-849-0471; www.wallst plaza.net/slingapours; Thur–Sat 9pm–2am; Link: 3, 6, 7, 11, 13, 18, 51; map p.135 C2
Located in the busy Wall Street Plaza area, this late-opening club takes in the revelers as they leave the bars and restaurants – expect a few wrinkled suits to appear after a hard day at the office. Offers happy-hour specials on martinis.

Tabu
46 North Orange Avenue, Orlando; tel: 407-648-8363; www.tabunightclub.com; Wed–Sun; Link: 3, 6, 7, 11, 13, 18, 51; map p.135 C2
This club doesn't open its doors without getting crammed. It's an oldie on Orlando's scene and has developed a reputation for top DJs and wild nights.

Vintage Lounge
114 South Orange Avenue; Orlando; tel: 877-386-7346; www.vintagelounge.com; Tue–Sat 9pm–2am; Link 3, 7, 11, 18; map p.135 C2
Dress up and dance beneath the sparkling chandeliers at this upscale lounge, a see-and-be-seen place with nightly music ranging from Top 40 hits to house to dance and more.

Unless you limit yourself to resort nightclubs at CityWalk or Downtown Disney, getting back after a night out is not an easy task. Public transport in the later hours is non-existent. A taxi is your only option, and taking one, even a short distance, is very expensive.

LIVE MUSIC
Independent Bar
70 North Orange Avenue, Orlando; tel: 407-839-0457; www.independentbar.net; Tue–Sun; Link: 3, 6, 7, 11, 13, 18, 51; map p.135 C2
The main attractions at the Independent Bar are the live acts, but even on a non-concert night it still has two floors of dancing, each with their own music and an outdoor café area to unwind in. Indie and alternative music rules on Friday and Sunday, with a mixture of rock, electro and 80s new wave on the remaining nights.

The Social
54 North Orange Avenue, Orlando; tel: 407-246-1419; www.thesocial.org; open nightly, hours vary; Link: 3, 6, 7, 11, 13, 18, 51; map p.135 C2
The premier place in the Orlando area to catch live music acts, from indie rockers to electronica. The cav-

ernous club was once the only place in Orlando for touring acts to perform. Now with competition from larger venues at the amusement parks its importance has been reduced, but nothing can destroy its history.

COMEDY
SAK Comedy Lab
Eola Capital Loft, CityArts Factory; 29 South Orange Avenue, Orlando; tel: 407-648-0001; www.sak.com; Tue–Sat; Link 3, 7, 11, 18; map p.135 C2
The clever improv team at SAK don't just make their audience laugh, they train students to make their audience laugh, too. The key production is performed by the Ensemble, a professional improv team. Less expensive productions are performed by the Lab Rats. As the name suggests, these are students still learning the trade.

Pampering

After a hard day at the park you need to put your feet up. After an entire week of it, serious therapy may be needed to restore both body and soul. Though resorts are yet to examine their customers' heads, they have begun to appoint some of the finest spa facilities available in the southeast US. Big-name operators like Mandara Spa have opened local outlets, Disney's Grand Floridian has gone so far as to create its own line of beauty products, and there is no shortage of fine establishments in the larger resort hotels which cater to conventioners and vacationers alike.

Grand Floridian Spa and Health Club

Grand Floridian Resort and Spa, 4111 Grand Floridian Way, Lake Buena Vista; tel: 407-824-2332; www.relaxedyet.com; daily 6am–9pm; map p.138 A4

Run by the Niki Bryan Spa company, this is one of two full-service spas available at Disney World. Set in the lush surrounds of the Grand Floridian Resort, this lavish spa offers complete massage therapies, and special treatments for couples and young children.

Mandara Spa at Portofino

Loews Portofino Bay Hotel, 5601 Universal Boulevard, Orlando; tel: 407-503-1244; www. mandaraspa.com; fitness center 6am–8pm, spa and salon 7am–8pm; map p.136 A3

With 14 treatment rooms, separate saunas for men and women, a fitness center and full-service hair and nail salon, this spa has all the bases covered. Treatments include the Javanese Lulur, a traditional body cleansing that utilizes turmeric, red rice, fenugreek, jasmine and ylang ylang.

Mandara Spa Swan and Dolphin

Walt Disney World Swan & Dolphin, 1500 Epcot Resorts Boulevard, Lake Buena Vista; tel: 407-934-4772; www.mandaraspa.com; daily 8am–9pm; map p.138 B2

At 12,000sq ft (1114 sq m), this retreat inspired by ancient Asian architecture features two interior gardens that make tranquil resting places before and after your treatment. Elemis aromatherapy products are used exclusively.

Relâche Spa at Gaylord Palms

6000 West Osceola Parkway, Kissimmee; tel: 407-586-4772; www.gaylordpalms.com; map p.139 C1

This brand-new, full-service spa offers traditional treatments, plus full nutrition and wellness counseling and fitness training. Its specialty is the Relâche Signature Mas-

Above: a tranquil retreat at the Urban Spa.

sage, a Swedish-style massage that aims to treat all the major muscle groups in your body.

Ritz-Carlton Spa

Grand Lakes Orlando, 4012 Central Florida Parkway, Orlando; tel: 407-206-2400; www.ritzcarlton.com

The citrus-based treatments at the Ritz sound good enough to eat. Their East Indian Lime Body and Scalp Treatment uses avocado, macadamia, hazelnut oil, wild lime blossom, and other exotic Indian

> The Grand Floridian Health Spa has created its own line of grapefruit-flavored skin products.

Left: the perfect antidote to a walk in the parks.

offers fittingly rustic treatments such as the Maple Sugar Body Polish. A host of massages and facials are also available.

Spa at Rosen Shingle Creek

Shingle Creek Resort, 9939 Universal Boulevard, Orlando; tel: 407-996-9772; www.spaat shinglecreek.com; Link: 58; map p.136 B1

Just like its resort, this spa takes its cue from the natural world around it. The Ocoee Body Mask and Calusa Cacoon use the essences of Florida's indigenous plants.

Urban Spa

Eō Inn, 227 North Eola Drive, Orlando; tel: 407-481-8485; www.eoinn.com; Mon–Fri 7.30am–7pm, Sat–Sun 8am–4pm; map p.135 C2

This European-style spa comes as a bit of a surprise in Downtown Orlando. It has an extensive list of à la carte services and packages that can be tailored to fill an entire day and include lunch.

spices to create a balm that is rubbed into your skin to improve circulation. The spa's treatments also include ones specifically geared towards men, pregnant women, and children and teenagers.

Shala Salon & Spa

Shala Salon & Spa; 7226 West Sand Lake Road, Orlando; tel: 407-248-8828; www.shala salon.com; Mon–Sat 9am–8pm, Sun 10am–6pm; Link: 43; map p.136 A2

The Shala Salon and Spa offers extensive beauty treatments from haircuts to pedicures. The shorter menu of spa treatments is still enough to help you relax after meetings or a day spent trekking round the theme parks, including everything from day packages to facials.

The Spa at Buena Vista Palace

1900 Buena Vista Drive, Lake Buena Vista; tel: 866-397-6516; www.buenavista palace.com; daily 8am–10pm; map p.139 D2

Measuring over 10,000sq ft (929 sq m), this is more than your average resort spa. The menu is equally impressive, with a Pineapple Body Scrub, a full selection of massage techniques, and the unmissable Themed Park Leg Relief Wrap.

Spa at Disney's Saratoga Springs

Saratoga Spring Resort and Spa; tel: 407-827-4455; map p.139 C2

Resembling a late-19th-century country retreat in upstate New York, the spa

Below: relaxing hard at the Portofino Spa.

Restaurants

Thankfully Orlando's restaurant scene has perked up in recent years, largely due to a crop of hot young chefs who are staking a claim to North America's top tourist market. The bad news – and this pertains mostly to the theme parks, especially Disney – is that food is overpriced and often of poor quality. It's not to say quality can't be had in theme parks. Some places, like Cinderella's Royal Table and the Coral Reef Restaurant, take unique advantage of their park's features to create unforgettable experiences. Here we highlight only the full-service options that are available.

Magic Kingdom

Cinderella's Royal Table
Cinderella's Castle; tel: 407-939-3463; daily B, L, D; $$$
Though the food at this restaurant is far below the standard you'd expect at this price, its setting at the heart of Cinderella's Castle cannot be beaten. Children are also given the opportunity to have their picture taken with Cinderella before lunch, and other fairytale princesses pay them a personal visit while they are eating – a better interaction than most of the meet-and-greet opportunities in the park. In addition to the Fairytale Lunch, there is a Once Upon a Time Breakfast Buffett. The dinner sitting does not include characters. Reservations must be made far in advance.

Tony's Town Square Restaurant
Main Street, U.S.A.;

Prices for an average three-course meal with wine:
$ under $25
$$ $25–35
$$$ over $35

tel: 407-939-3463; daily L, D; $$
With decor inspired by the classic film *Lady and the Tramp*, this restaurant serves up standard Italian fare in a light and airy environment. Be warned of Disney's tomato sauce. This oregano-laden concoction is definitely not to everyone's taste but is served throughout the park, finding its way onto everything from the posh pasta here to kiddie's spaghetti meals in other restaurants.

Epcot

Akershus Royal Banquet Hall
Norway Pavillion; daily B, L, D; $$$
In addition to its character breakfast featuring Disney princesses in a Norwegian castle setting, this restaurant offers a fine lunch and dinner menu. Guests can choose their main course from a list of Norwegian specialties that include several good fish dishes. Additionally, the smorgasbord of cheeses, pickled fish, and rustic breads is open to all.

Above: Epcot's Italian food is as convincing as its surroundings.

Biergarten Restaurant
Germany Pavilion; daily L, D; $$
This buffet-style restaurant set in a dimly lit mock-timber house pays a typically German homage to bratwurst and other stodgy fare. There is, of course, a healthy selection of beers to wash it down with, and the accordion player will catch up with you eventually.

Bistro de Paris
France Pavilion; D daily; $$$
The signature restaurant for France is poorly appointed, with a dining area that feels not unlike a convention lunch-

Left: the dramatic backdrop in the Coral Reef Restaurant.

Les Chefs de France
France Pavilion; daily L, D; $$

The more accessible of France's two restaurants, there is nothing pretentious in this restaurant's decor – a faithful re-creation of a typical Parisian café. The cooking may not be up to Michelin-star status, but it is very good, and you get the opportunity to dine under a faux Eiffel Tower.

L'Originale Alfredo di Roma Ristorante
Italy Pavilion; daily L, D; $$

Colorful, festive offshoot of the famous Roman restaurant. The specialty is fettuccine Alfredo. All pastas are made fresh. Strolling musicians entertain guests.

Nine Dragons Restaurant
China Pavilion; daily L, D; $$

Most will be pleased by the cuisine from different Chinese regions, including Mongolia and Szechuan. The menu also features a range of Chinese beers, and the setting is a re-creation of a Chinese palace.

Restaurant Marrakesh
Morocco Pavilion; daily L, D; $$$

After experiencing the fantastic warren-like architecture of the Morocco pavilion, you can't help but be disappointed by the lack of authenticity once you enter Restaurant

If there is a particular restaurant you'd like to experience at Disney World, book far in advance. There's a reason that Disney takes reservations over a year in advance; during peak season demand easily outweighs supply, and Disney visitors are notorious for their obsessive forward planning. To make a booking, tel: 407-939-3463.

looking scenic ecosystems and boat ride, its menu includes salads and vegetables grown in The Land greenhouses. The 'Full Country Breakfast' stars Mickey, Minnie, and Chip 'n' Dale.

Le Cellier Steakhouse
Canada Pavilion; daily L, D; $$$

Americans like their steak as much as their northern neighbors, and if you plan on having dinner here you must book in advance even during the slow periods. The wine cellar could make a romantic setting if you are lucky enough to get a table in a quiet corner.

eon setting. The lengthy wine list and fine view could help you forget this, but you'd expect more from a Disney restaurant charging this much.

Coral Reef Restaurant
The Seas with Nemo and Friends Pavilion; daily L, D; $$$

This seafood restaurant is situated alongside the aquarium at The Seas with Nemo and Friends, providing dreamy views into the largest inland saltwater environment ever built, which contains 85 different species of tropical fish. The food is fine dining at Disney's best.

Garden Grill
The Land Pavilion; daily D; $$

A revolving restaurant over-

Below: soon to be seen served at the Garden Grill.

Above: just like an old-fashioned drive-in, only in-car activities are much changed.

Marrakesh. The interior beyond the guest services desk seems bare, and although some of the food excels, most of it is a poor Americanized version of Middle Eastern food. This must be the only Moroccan restaurant in the world without a standard tagine dish. On a more positive note, the live music and belly dancing add a touch of Moroccan flare.

San Angel Inn Restaurante
Mexico Pavillion; daily L, D; $$–$$$
Authentic Mexican food served in a very faux environment – under the shadow of a Mayan temple and a smoldering volcano. The dim lighting makes a good option for couples hoping for a bit of romance – an aspect of human experience Disney has yet to turn into a theme park.

Teppan Edo
Japan Pavilion; L, D daily; $$
Reservations for most meals are necessary to get a seat

Prices for an average three-course meal with wine:
$ under $25
$$ $25–35
$$$ over $35

around one of the five teppan-yaki grills. Diners encircle the chef as he creates various stir-fry creations which are shared around the table.

Tutto Italia Ristorante
Italy Pavilion; daily L, D; $$–$$$
Elegant but casual, this restaurant features dishes from different regions of Italy, with handmade pasta and mozzarella, and freshly baked breads and desserts.

Animal Kingdom

Rainforest Café
Tel: 407-939-3463; www.rainforestcafe.com; daily B, L & D; $$; map p.14
This is one of the most highly themed restaurants in Disney. Many will be familiar with this chain and its reliance on animatronic animals and faux decor to re-create a rainforest canopy. Unfortunately, the theme stops at the food. Instead of an iguana burger and plantains, expect typical American food with large portions, and a dessert called the Volcano that is surely a health risk in itself. If you were in any doubt about the chain's true motives, its shop is as large as the restaurant. Waits of an hour or more are not uncommon without reservations.

Hollywood Studios

50s Prime Time Café
Hollywood Boulevard; daily L, D; $; map p.16
This reincarnation of mom's kitchen has a certain fetish appeal. Waiters discipline anyone who does not clean their plate, or is caught with elbows on the table. And at times they behave like mom's children, too, becoming tattle tales and pests just the same. The food is just what you'd expect from mom and includes meatloaf, peas, and indulgent deserts you choose from a retro Viewmaster toy.

The Hollywood Brown Derby
Hollywood Boulevard; daily L, D; $$$; map p.16
This re-creation of the legendary Hollywood restaurants features fine food at fine prices. Of course, the only celebrities you are likely to see here are in photographs that adorn the walls.

Mama Melrose's Ristorante Italiano
Backlot; daily L, D; $$; map p.16
This cozy Italian restaurant serves child-friendly favorites such as pizza and lasagne.

Sci-Fi Dine-In Theater
Backlot; daily L, D; $$; map p.16
This is Hollywood Studio's

best dining experience. Every party gets to take a seat in an old Chevy or other vintage car and watch classic sci-fi films on the drive-in screen. The food plays second fiddle to this theme and features burgers, sandwiches, and pasta dishes. Nevertheless, reservations are essential here, even during the slow seasons.

Downtown Disney

Bongos Cuban Café
Westside; tel: 407-828-0999; www.bongoscubancafe.com; daily L,D; $$; map p.92
The brainchild of pop star Gloria Estefan and her husband Emilio. A giant pineapple sprouting from the roof sets the tone of the place, which throbs with Latin music and brilliant colors. Aficionados of Cuban cuisine may have better luck elsewhere.

Cap'n Jack's Restaurant
Marketplace; daily L, D; $$; map p.92
This pier-house restaurant features crab, lobster, clams, and oysters, plus plenty of 'land lubber' specials. Pleasant views of the lake.

Fulton's Crab House
Marketplace; daily L, D; $$$; map p.92
Downtown Disney's lagoon provides berth for this replica of a Mississippi riverboat. Inside is one of Disney's finer fine-dining restaurants. Unsurprisingly, the menu offers a bounty of seafood with a few beef, poultry, and pasta dishes to keep everyone in the party happy. The Alaskan king crab claws are bigger than most men's hands, and there is a decent wine list and a wine selector to help choose the best accompaniment to your meal.

House of Blues
Westside; daily L, D; $$; map p.92
Founded by actor, comedian, and original Blues Brother Dan Aykroyd and others, and done up like the kind of ramshackle wharfside warehouse you might find in the Mississippi Delta. The food is surprisingly good for a chain operation, with spicy southern favorites like fried catfish, seafood gumbo, jambalaya, and bread pudding dribbled

> The lakeside patio at Bongos Cuban Café is a pleasant place to sip a fancy tropical drink.

with brandy sauce. If you're traveling with kids, consider booking a table for the **Sunday Gospel Brunch**. You'll jump up for Jesus and chow down on all the southern vittles you can eat. It's a soulful way to finish your week at Disney.

Planet Hollywood
Westside; tel: 407-939-3463; daily L, D; $$; map p.92
The worldwide restaurant chain launched by Arnold Schwarzenegger, Bruce Willis, Sylvester Stallone, and entrepreneur Robert Earl. Every inch of the dome-shaped dining room is jammed with movie props, memorabilia, and other eye candy. The good news is that the food has improved since the company's brush with bankruptcy in 1999. The bad news? The wait can be terribly long, especially when the theaters let out, so it's sensible to make reservations well in advance.

Below: Bongos Cuban Café gives Downtown Disney a fruity skyline.

About: if visiting from abroad, don't leave Orlando without sampling some Mexican favourites.

Portobello

Marketplace; daily L, D; $$$; map p.92

First-rate northern Italian cuisine and seafood specialties fill the menu here, while diners cram the floor in a restaurant that could be a fine-dining experience if the spacing wasn't so similar to sitting in a cafeteria.

Rainforest Café

Marketplace; tel: 407-939-3463; daily L, D; $$; map p.92

The smoke you've been seeing billowing in the distance is from a smoldering volcano that sits atop the Rainforest Café, a cavernous restaurant with an extravagant jungle setting. Even with priority seating, you'll have a good long wait. Management hopes you'll spend the time (and at least a few extra dollars) in the adjoining gift shop.

T-REX Café

Marketplace; tel: 407-828-8739; daily L, D; $$

This dinosaur-themed café is naturally very popular with families, with its animatronic creations to entertain the kids while they eat. The menu is themed too, so you can tuck into dishes such as Layers of the Earth Lasagna or the Chocolate Extinction dessert. Book ahead to be sure of a table.

Wolfgang Puck Café

Westside; daily L, D; $$–$$$; map p.92

The cavernous rooms aren't exactly conducive to an intimate conversation; the atmosphere is all color and energy, with open kitchens, video monitors showing chefs at work, and a bustling wait staff. The menu runs the gamut from sushi and gourmet pizza to lamb chops and seafood, all prepared with the celebrity chef's Californian flair (except perhaps the Wiener schnitzel). The upstairs dining room is quite expensive, but the downstairs café is cheaper and more casual.

Disney Resort Dining

MAGIC KINGDOM RESORTS
Artist's Point

Wilderness Lodge, 901 Timberline Drive, Lake Buena Vista; daily D; $$$; map p.138 B4

Don't forget to leave a tip when dining out in the United States; servers are paid very little in actual wages, on the assumption that tips will keep them afloat. For large parties and at a few more expensive restaurants, gratuities or a service charge will be added to the bill. If not, leave an additional 15–20 percent tip for good service.

Inspired by America's national-park lodges, this hotel restaurant features salmon, rainbow trout, elk chops, venison, bison, and other hearty dishes associated with the American west. The wine list features labels from the Pacific northwest.

California Grill

Contemporary Resort, 4600 North World Drive; daily D; $$$; map 138 B4

Views of the Magic Kingdom are spectacular from this refined restaurant on the 15th floor of the Contemporary Resort. The menu changes seasonally but usually includes entrées like oak-roasted chicken and pork tenderloin prepared with a light California touch. Don't pass up the appetizers, an eclectic mix of sushi, salads, and pasta. Ask to be seated in time for the fireworks.

Citricos

Grand Floridian Resort and Spa; 4401 Grand Floridian Way, Lake Buena Vista; daily D; $$$; map p.138 A4

Citricos brings a bit of Mediterranean warmth to the Grand Floridian with a selection of food sourced from French, Italian and Spanish cuisines.

Narcoossee's

Grand Floridian Resort and Spa, 4401 Grand Floridian Way, Lake

Prices for an average three-course meal with wine:
$ under $25
$$ $25–35
$$$ over $35

Buena Vista; daily D; $$$; map p.138 A4

With a sweeping lakeside setting, this is the Grand Floridian's 'casual' offering. Its inventive cuisine uses fresh ingredients and lots of seafood. Soft-shell crabs and Prince Edward Island mussels in white wine and garlic are signature dishes.

Victoria and Albert's
Grand Floridian Resort and Spa; 4401 Grand Floridian Way, Lake Buena Vista; daily D; $$$; map p.138 A4

Disney spins a Victorian fantasy at this prix-fixe restaurant. The seven-course meal is served by a white-gloved butler and maid (Albert and Victoria) in a romantic, domed dining room. The menu features some of the finest Continental cuisine in town. Very expensive but, fans say, worth the money.

EPCOT RESORTS
ESPN Club
Disney's BoardWalk; daily L, D; $$; map p.138 B2

Jocks will love this theme restaurant crammed with all things sporty, including more than 70 television screens; there's even one in the restroom, lest you miss a minute of the big game. Bring a big appetite. Entrées, including hamburgers, hot dogs, sirloin, and grilled chicken, are oversized.

Flying Fish Café
Disney's BoardWalk; daily D; $$$; map p.138 B2

One of Disney's best restaurants, in a whimsical setting with a busy stage kitchen. It serves potato-wrapped yellowtail snapper and other creative dishes. There's chocolate lava cake for dessert.

Il Mulino New York Trattoria
Swan Resort, 1200 Epcot Resorts Boulevard; daily D; $$$; map p.138 B2

Is this the classiest restaurant at Disney World? The illuminated wine bar is tops for sure, and it has a good selection of fine wines. Food features recipes based on classic Italian bistro recipes. The seafood dishes stand out the most.

Kimonos
Swan Resort, 1200 Epcot Resorts Boulevard; daily D; $$; map p.138 B2

As much a retreat as a restaurant, the sushi chefs here are not shy and are happy to prepare their beautiful creations in front of your eyes. For those who prefer their fish cooked, there are hot dishes and tempura available as well. The class doesn't last all night – karaoke begins in the evening.

Todd English's bluezoo
Dolphin Resort, 1500 Epcot Resorts Boulevard; daily D; $$$; map p.138 B2

Presentation is king at this fine-dining restaurant, from the sleek backlit bar and minimalist design to the simply decorous plates of seafood with a wedge of lemon. There is a kids' menu here, but do yourself a favor and leave the little ones behind so you can enjoy this very grown-up restaurant.

ANIMAL KINGDOM RESORTS
Jiko – The Cooking Place
Animal Kingdom Lodge, 2901 Osceola Parkway, Lake Buena Vista; daily D; $$$; map p.138 A1

An African sunset sets the color scheme for this romantic restaurant, but the cuisine takes its tone more from Europe and India than the African savannah.

Celebration and Kissimmee
Azteca's Restaurant
809 North Main Street, Kissimmee; tel: 407-933-8155; www.aztecasmexrestaurant.com; Mon–Thur 11am–9.30pm, Fri and Sat 11am–10.30pm, Sun 11am–8pm; $$; Link: 4

There's nothing pretentious about this local favorite. The walls are decorated with eclectic hangings, and the menu includes Mexican standards such as burritos, enchiladas, and nachos for starters. All Mexican beers are available.

Below: a Spanish paella from Columbia Restaurant, *see p.104.*

Above: the classy interior of Celebration's Columbia Restaurant.

Bohemian Bar and Grill
Bohemian Hotel Celebration, 700 Bloom St. Celebration; tel: 407-566-6000; www.celebrationhotel.com; Mon–Fri 7–10.30am, Sat–Sun 7–11am, daily L and 6–10pm D; $$$

One of the best places to eat in Celebration is in the Bohemian hotel where their grill has been winning awards and merits a 4-Diamond rating from AAA. There's naturally a wide range of steaks, with lobster, jumbo shrimp and scallops also on the menu.

Café D'Antonio Ristorante Celebration
691 Front Street, Suite 110, Celebration; tel: 407-566-2233; www.antoniosonline.com; Mon–Fri 11.30am–3pm, 5–10pm, Sat 11.30am–10pm, Sun 11.30am–9pm L, D; $$$

This upscale Italian serves an extensive selection of pastas but an even wider selection of meat and chicken dishes, with several veal selections. Its wine list includes fine Italian wines and a healthy selection from California. There is also a location in Maitland that includes a deli and café (see p.69).

Columbia Restaurant
649 Front Street, Celebration; tel: 407-566-1505; www.columbiarestaurant.com; daily 11.30am–10.30pm; $$$

The Columbia restaurant chain dates back to 1905 when its original outlet opened in Tampa's Ybor City. This classy restaurant serves Spanish cuisine that has amalgamated Cuban and Mexican influences while in Florida. The result for anyone who likes a bit of spice is a winner. There is flamenco dancing in the evening.

Garibaldi Mexican Cuisine
1804 W Vine St, Kissimmee; tel: 407-933-0774; www.garibaldicuisinetasteofmexico.com; Mon–Fri 11am–3pm, D daily; $$

Garibaldi's rates highly among the locals for its authentic Mexican cooking, with fajitas, chimichangas, flautas, burritos, quesadillas and a whole host of house specialties as well. They also have a good range of tequilas and Mexican beers, and mariachi music too.

Market Street Café
701 Front Street, Celebration; tel: 407-566-1144; daily B, L, D; $$

This classic American diner serves breakfast all day, which includes everything from a posh crab omelette to buttermilk pancakes. Dinner selections are varied and include burgers, meatloaf, and stir-fry. There is also an old-fashioned soda fountain serving ice cream treats.

Universal Studios

Finnegan's Bar and Grill
New York; tel: 407-224-3613; daily L, D; $$; map p.20

Meant to be a hometown Irish pub in New York City, Finnegan's has very friendly wait staff and serves fish and chips, corned beef, and, of course, Irish stew. Guinness is on tap.

Lombard's Seafood Grille
San Francisco/Amity; tel: 407-224-3613; daily L, D; $$; map p.20

Lombard's serves the best food at Universal Studios. The clam chowder pays homage to the east coast,

Below: a deliciously citrus concoction.

> Another thing you'll find at Universal Studios that Disney would never consider is a happy hour at Finnegan's Bar and Grill.

while the fresh seafood and tasty pastas have a more Californian feel. Either way, you're likely to leave happy.

Islands of Adventure

Confisco Grille
Port of Entry; tel: 407-224-4012; daily B, L; $$; map p.22
Decorated as an exotic wharfside tavern, Confisco Grille offers ethnic dishes ranging from fajitas and pad thai to barbecued ribs. Drinks are available at the Backwater Bar, which has a small patio perfect for people-watching. The restaurant also hosts the daily character breakfast on Thursdays and Sundays.

Mythos
Lost Continent; tel: 407-224-4012; daily L only; $$$; map p.22
The park's best restaurant is ensconced in a regally appointed cavern with sculpted walls, purple upholstery, and lagoon views. Entrées include wood-roasted lobster with wild mushroom risotto, cedar-planked salmon with orange horseradish mashed potatoes, and wood-fired pizza, plus other child-friendly dishes.

CityWalk

Bob Marley A Tribute to Freedom
Tel: 407-224-3663; daily D; $$; map p.50
You can chow down on yucca chips, jerk chicken, and plenty of Red Stripe beer while jammin' to reggae. The exterior is modeled after Marley's home in Kingston, Jamaica. Inside, photos and

Above: the world's largest Hard Rock Café.

other artifacts chronicle his life and career. Live bands perform nightly on the courtyard stage.

Bubba Gump Shrimp Company
Tel: 407-903-0044; daily L, D; $$
For many, Bubba Gump is the last character they'd like to have dinner with, having spent more than enough time with this annoying 'life is a box of chocolates' character in the film. But where there's a celluloid success in the US, a themed restaurant is not far behind. The food here is mostly shrimp-based and of the quality you'd expect from a roadside café in Mobile for at least half the price.

Emeril's Restaurant Orlando
Tel: 407-224-2424; daily L, D; $$$; map p.50

Featuring the creations of television chef Emeril Lagasse. Assertive Creole flavors bubble up through artfully prepared specialties like grilled pork chop with caramelized sweet potatoes. Wine connoisseurs can choose from more than 10,000 bottles. The desserts are equally glorious; homey favorites like root beer floats and banana cream pie become decadent masterpieces.

Hard Rock Café Orlando
Tel: 407-370-5890; daily L, D; $$; map p.50
When it comes to theme restaurants, the big daddy of 'em all is the Hard Rock Café. With seating for 600 in the restaurant and 3,000 in the concert hall, this is the largest Hard Rock in the world, and, like its humbler brethren, its walls are plas-

Below: CityWalk's most exclusive restaurant.

105

Above: sushi is popular in trendy restaurants.

tered with gold records, album covers, flashy costumes, and instruments that have been strummed and drummed by some of the rock world's biggest names. A pink Cadillac revolves over the bar; a Sistine Chapel-like mural featuring a heavenly host of dead rock stars adorns the ceiling; and stained-glass panels pay tribute to a trinity of rock legends – Elvis Presley, Chuck Berry, and Jerry Lee Lewis. It's a bit much to take in over a meal, which is why the Hard Rock offers free tours in the afternoon.

Jimmy Buffet's Margaritaville
Tel: 407-224-2155; daily L, D; $$; map p.50

For a laid-back beach bum, Jimmy Buffet is quite the entrepreneur. Decked out in beachy, tropical style, this restaurant leans toward Caribbean flavors – conch fritters, seafood chowder, grilled fish – with a sprinkling of American standards, including the inevitable 'cheeseburger in paradise.'

Latin Quarter
Tel: 407-224-3663; daily D; $$; map p.50

Both the food and the music are spicy at the Latin Quarter, dedicated to the culture and cuisine of 21 Latin American nations. After dinner, an orchestra and dance troupe take the stage. Dance instructors initiate neophytes into the wonders of merengue, salsa, and the mambo.

NASCAR Sports Grille
Tel: 407-224-7223; daily L, D; $$; map p.50

Anchoring the far end of the Plaza, near the bridge to Universal Studios, is NASCAR, a testament to the popularity of stock-car racing. Fans munch on chicken wings, chili, and burgers in a boisterous room with video games and live acts, where every square inch is plastered with racing paraphernalia. There are even a couple of racing cars suspended from the ceiling.

NBA City
Tel: 407-363-5919; daily L, D; $$; map p.50

NBA City, if you hadn't guessed, is the restaurant with the statue of a basketball player towering over the entrance. Inside is hoopster heaven, with skill games, shrines to b-ball stars, and a battery of video monitors replaying the game's greatest moments. There is grilled salmon, roasted chicken, and strip steak, as well as kid-friendly choices like burgers, pizza, and sandwiches. The milkshakes are a slam dunk; for nearly a tenner, they ought to be.

Pastamoré
Tel: 407-224-3663; daily D; $$; map p.50

Pastamoré serves up abundant portions of eggplant parmigiana, veal Marsala, and a dozen varieties of pizza and pasta. An option to dine family-style lets you taste a little bit of everything, including the *dolci assortiti*, a selection of yummy desserts.

Pat O'Brien's Orlando
Tel: 407-224-3663; daily D; $$; map p.50

An older crowd inhabits Pat O'Brien's, a replica of a landmark New Orleans watering hole. The singalong crowd loves the dueling pianos, and foodies enjoy jambalaya, muffeletta, and other Big Easy specialties. Wash it down with a Hurricane, O'Brien's signature rum drink.

Universal Studios Resorts

Bice Ristorante
Loews Portofino Bay Hotel; 5601 Universal Boulevard, Orlando; tel: 407-503-1415; daily D; $$$; map p.136 A3

The clean, simple lines of this upscale trattoria make way for a fine Italian dining experience. The Bice chain began in Milan and is famed as much for its hospitality as its food.

Prices for an average three-course meal with wine:
$ under $25
$$ $25–35
$$$ over $35

With three bars and one margarita-spewing volcano, Jimmy Buffett's Margaritaville keeps customers well oiled whether they're there to eat or not.

Emeril's Tchoup Chop
Royal Pacific Resort, 6300 Hollywood Way, Orlando; tel: 407-503-2467; Mon–Fri L, daily D; $$$; map p.136 A3

Emeril's second restaurant on Universal Orlando's property is dedicated to the delicate flavours of Asian and Polynesian cuisine. The restaurant's seductive decor is created using palm trees, bamboo, and waterfalls.

Mama Della's Ristorante
Portofino Bay Hotel; 5601 Universal Boulevard, Orlando; tel: 407-503-3463; daily D; $$$; map p.136 A3

As heavy on themes as on the stomach. The hearty Italian fare is accompanied by fine wines and strolling entertainment, including singers and guitarists. Mama herself makes an appearance, too, insisting that everyone eats up.

Palm Restaurant
Hard Rock Hotel, 5800 Universal Boulevard, tel: 407-503-7256; daily D; $$$; map p.136 A3

Carnivores can slice into slabs of beef at this knock-off of the famous New York steakhouse – a favorite with the meat and martini crowd. Like the original, there are celebrity caricatures on the wall and a whiff of testosterone in the air.

International Drive and Lake Buena Vista

Bergamo's Italian Restaurant
Festival Bay Mall, 5250 International Drive, Suite 54 Orlando; tel: 407-352-3805; www.bergamos.com; daily 5–10pm; $$$; I-Ride: mainline; map p.136 B3

Bergamo's has earned kudos for an attractive ambience and beautifully-prepared pasta, steak, and seafood (thankfully not overcooked, as is so often the case in Orlando). It also has the largest list of Italian wines in the city, and the wait staff, all talented vocalists, sing everything from operatic arias to Neopolitan folk songs.

B-Line Diner
Peabody Hotel, 9801 International Drive, Orlando; tel: 407-352-4000; www.peabodyorlando.com; 24hrs; $$; I-Ride: mainline; map p.136 B1

A cozy, 1950s-style diner that's open 24 hours a day, it features thick sandwiches, griddle cakes, and a jukebox with vintage tunes. The corned-beef hash and eggs for breakfast is about as good as slop can get.

Cala Bella
Rosen Shingle Creek, 9939 Universal Boulevard, Orlando; tel: 407-996-3663; www.calabella restaurant.com; $$; Link: 58; map p.136 B1

Located at the out-of-the-way Rosen Shingle Creek Resort, this Italian restaurant has a reputation for well-presented basic Italian dishes like risottos, fresh pastas, clams, steaks, seafood, and Tuscan bean soup.

The Capital Grille
Pointe Orlando, 9101 International Drive, Orlando; tel: 407-370-4392; www.capital grille.com; Mon–Fri 11.30am–3pm, Sun–Thur 5–10pm, Fri and Sat 5–11pm; $$$; I-Ride: mainline; map p.136 A1

Dry-aged steak is the centerpiece of the Capital Grille's menu, one that is not kind to vegetarians, but does offer a few seafood options. The wine cellar has over 5,000 bottles from around the world.

Capriccio Grill Italian Steakhouse
Peabody Orlando, 9801 International Drive, Orlando; tel: 407-352-4000; www.peabody orlando.com; $$$; I-Ride: mainline; map p.136 A1

A show kitchen is the center of attention at this upscale, marble-clad restaurant specializing in gourmet pizza, grilled meats and seafood, heaping bowls of pasta, and other Italian dishes.

Ciao Italia Ristorante Italiano
6149 Westwood Boulevard, Orlando; tel: 407-354-0770; www.ciaoitaliaonline.com; daily 5–11pm; $$$; I-Ride: mainline; map p.139 E4

This family-run restaurant has a warm, welcoming setting combined with fine food. The standard menu is basic,

Below: one of many good restaurants at Pointe Orlando.

Above: see the Peabody's famous mascots if dining at Capriccio Grill, *see p.107*.

but evening specials offer more adventurous entrées, and the wine list has a fine selection of Italian wines.

Hanamizuki Japanese Restaurant

8255 International Drive, Suite 136, Orlando; tel: 407-363-7200; www.hanamizuki.uk Mon–Sat 11.30am–2pm, daily 5–10.30pm; $$; I-Ride: mainline; map p.136 A2

Tucked away in the Goodings Plaza is this wonderful Japanese restaurant. The head chef's skills are so advanced he has even been given the honor of serving the Emperor of Japan at his summer retreat. The food and drink, from sushi to sake, is as authentic as you'll find in central Florida, and the relaxing minimalistic decor is a welcome retreat from chaotic I-Drive.

Hemingway's

Hyatt Regency Grand Cypress Resort, 1 Grand Cypress Blvd, Lake Buena Vista; tel: 407-239-3854; www.hyatt grandcypress.com; daily 6–10pm; $$$; map p.138 C4

Even if you're not staying at the Grand Cypress, it's worth booking a table for a meal here. This seafood restaurant, which has a Key West theme and photos of the eponymous author on the wall, has a relaxing and romantic atmosphere and serves up dishes

such as Florida rock shrimp chowder and herb-basted diver scallops.

A Land Remembered

Rosen Shingle Creek, 9939 Universal Boulevard, Orlando; tel: tel: 407-996-3663; www.landrememberedrestaurant.com; $$$; Link: 58; map p.136 B1

This steakhouse is named after a novel written by Patrick Smith, which focused on Florida's history and landscapes. So it should be no surprise that alligator sometimes appears on the menu. Otherwise, the fine-dining menu is varied, with several seafood options available for those not wanting steak. The wine list will leave no one disappointed.

Ming Court

9188 International Drive, Orlando; tel: 407-351-9988; www.ming-court.com; daily 11am–3pm, 4.30–11pm; $$; I-Ride: mainline; map p.136 A1

Interior koi ponds and gardens set the stage at this fine Chinese restaurant. The chefs cook up specialties of several provinces and even produce fine sushi, as well as

a delectable dim sum menu. Ask for a table near the open kitchen.

Norman's

The Ritz-Carlton Grande Lakes, 4012 Central Florida Parkway, Orlando; tel: 407-393-4333; www.normans.com; D daily; $$$

Norman Van Aken's New World Cuisine is defined by dishes created when European tradition encounters the native cultures of the Caribbean, Central America, and Florida. Sommeliers offer advice on which vintages best accompany these dishes, and the setting is elegance all the way.

The Oceanaire Seafood Room

Pointe Orlando, 9101 International Drive, Orlando; tel: 407-363-4801; www.theoceanaire.com; Sun–Thur 5–10 pm, Fri–Sat 5–11pm; $$$; I-Ride: mainline; map p.136 A1

Decorated like a 1930s ocean liner, this sleek diner serves 'ultra-fish' seafood, which means that it has arrived that day and was probably in the sea the day before. Such ideals deserve celebration, especially in a city where such sourcing of ingredients often plays second fiddle to grand themes. Hence the menu changes daily, but often includes

> Prices for an average three-course meal with wine:
> $ under $25
> $$ $25–35
> $$$ over $35

No duck is served at any of the Peabody's restaurants, in honour of the hotel's famous mascots.

oysters, simple and tasty fish entrées, and a fine wine list with stewards to guide your selection. Still, it's a pity that in the heart of Florida so much is flown in from New England and Alaska instead of making the best of the bounty of two nearby coasts.

Primo
The Ritz-Carlton Grande Lakes, 4040 Central Florida Parkway, Orlando; tel: 407-393-4444; www.primorestaurant.com; Mon–Sun 6–10pm; $$$

Chef Melissa Kelly creates this 'sensible' Italian menu based upon locally sourced ingredients, making the most of the varied citrus fruits and seafood available in Florida.

Texas de Brazil
5259 International Drive, Suite F-1; tel: 407-355-0355; www.texasdebrazil.com; L Fri–Sun, D daily; $$; map p.136 B2

Although this is a steak-house chain restaurant it's an exceptionally good one, and manages to combine a lively Brazilian atmosphere with good food at reason-

able prices. Slow-roasted cuts of various meats along with Brazilian sausages are the specialties here, and there's a huge salad bar to help yourself to, but leave room for one of their decadent desserts.

SeaWorld
Seafire Inn Restaurant
daily L, D; $$; map p.26

This sprawling restaurant serves Caribbean-style food during the daily Music Maestro lunch show. Reservations are required for the Makahiki Luau, a Polynesian-themed dinner theater.

Sharks Underwater Grill
Near Sharks Encounter; daily L, D; $$$; map p.26

Set beside the enormous Sharks Encounter aquarium: one entire wall of the Underwater Grill's dining room is exposed to the tank, letting you sit in awe of the magnificent creatures swimming past. The food here, mostly seafood, is exquisite; the restaurant can easily produce one of the best meals you'll have at a theme park.

Downtown and Loch Haven Park
The Boheme
Grand Bohemian Hotel, 325 South Orange Avenue, Orlando; tel: 407-313-9000;

www.grandbohemianhotel.com; daily 6am–2pm (until 2.30pm on Sun), D daily; $$$; Link: 3, 6, 7, 11, 13, 18, 51; map p.135 C2

This is one of Orlando's best restaurants, and as each year passes another award is received. A recent addition, the Bohemian Wine Room, allows parties of up to 14 guests to enjoy a private dining room and exclusive service for the evening.

Ceviche Tapas Bar
125 West Church Street, Orlando; tel: 321-281-8140; www.ceviche.com; L daily, D Mon–Thur; $$; map p.135 C2

With over 100 tapas to choose from, and a flamenco room open till 2am at the weekends, this is a real taste of Spain, complete with hams hanging over the bar. There's also a selection of paellas and other main course dishes, with Spanish flans among the authentic desserts.

Crooked Bayou
50 E. Central Blvd, Orlando; tel: 407-839-5852; www.crookedbayou.com; Mon–Fri 11am–2am, Sat noon–2am; $$; map p.135 C2

This lively place near the public library is incredibly popular, and always busy. There's a bar serving great cocktails and draft and bottled beers, and the mainly

Below: the Sharks Underwater Grill's infamous voyeurs.

Louisiana-style menu has simple but hearty dishes like Caijan chicken, catfish po'boys and Cuban pork.

Gargi's Lakeside Italian Ristorante
1414 North Orange Avenue, Orlando; tel: 407-894-7907; www.gargislakeside.com; Mon–Thur 11.30am–10pm, Fri until 11pm, Sat noon–11pm, Sun 3–9pm; $$; Link: 1, 2, 9; map p.135 C3

Left: trying the gastropub-style in Orlando.

Located on Lake Ivanhoe, this family-run restaurant has grown over the years from a tiny bistro. The menu features veal, steaks, and seafood, all served with fresh pasta. In addition to a sturdy wine list, there is a wide selection of martinis to choose from.

The Globe
27 Wall Street Plaza, Orlando; tel: tel: 407-849-0471; www.wallstplaza.net/globe; D daily 9–11pm; $$; Link: 3, 6, 7, 11, 13, 18, 51; map p.135 C2
As it's located in Downtown's Wall Street Plaza nightlife area, The Globe serves two purposes: a quick bite for office workers and a quick lining of pizza, sandwiches, or salads before heading on for more serious drinking elsewhere.

The Harp Restaurant
25 South Magnolia Avenue, Orlando; tel: 407-481-2928; www.harpandcelt.com; daily L & D; $$$; map p.135 C2
Could this be Orlando's first gastropub? The attached **Celt Irish Pub** has a lively atmosphere, while The Harp serves meaty entrées from a limited menu in sedate surrounds. The prices are far too high for pub grub, but neither

the atmosphere nor the food exceed those standards.
SEE ALSO BARS AND CAFÉS, P.52

HUE Restaurant
629 East Central Boulevard, Orlando; tel: 407-849-1800; www.huerestaurant.com; Sun–Wed 3–11, Thur–Sat 3pm–12am; $$$; Link: 5; map p.135 C2
HUE makes the most of local produce in creating familiarly American fare such as wood-grilled filet mignon. The designer interior has a cozy, Scandinavian vibe, with crisp lines accented by warm lighting and candles. The happy hour is very popular.

Little Saigon
1106 East Colonial Drive, Orlando; tel: 407-423-8539; www.littlesaigonrestaurant.com; daily 10am–9pm; $; Link: 28, 29; map p.135 C2
This no-nonsense family-run restaurant is a welcome addition to a town that celebrates simulation over authenticity. Traditional Vietnamese dishes range from delicate spring rolls and rice noodles to big bowls of soup and fiery stir-fries.

White Wolf Café
1829 North Orange Avenue, tel: 407-895-9911; www.whitewolf Mon–Fri 7am–9pm (10pm Fri), Sat 8am–10pm, Sun 8am–3pm; $; Link: 1, 2, 9; map p.135 C3
This tiny slice of Bohemia is a breath of fresh air in theme-crazed Orlando. The service isn't exactly snappy, but the atmosphere is friendly, and the menu – ranging from egg salad sandwiches to wild mushroom lasagne – has enough creative quirks to sustain your interest.

Below: several Vietnamese restaurants operate along East Colonial Drive.

Prices for an average three-course meal with wine:
$ under $25
$$ $25–35
$$$ over $35

We've selected some of Winter Park's best restaurants for our listings, but if you take the time to stroll Park Avenue you may discover a favorite of your own – the choice, especially for Orlando, is astounding.

Winter Park and Maitland

Antonio's la Fiamma

611 South Orlando Avenue, 2nd floor, Maitland; tel: 407-645-1035; www.antoniosonline.com; Mon–Fri 11.30–2.30, 5–10pm, Sat 5–10pm; $$$; Link: 1, 2, 9; map p.135 C4

Another branch of the fine Antonio's restaurant chain serving pastas, risottos, and authentic Italian meat and fish entrées.

Brio Tuscan Grille

480 North Orlando Avenue, Suite 108, Winter Park; tel: 407-622-5611; www.brioitalian.com; Mon–Thur 11am–10pm, Fri–Sat until 11pm, Sun 10am–10pm; $$; Link: 39; map p.135 D4

This dark-wood-lined Italian chain restaurant could make a good setting for a romantic evening, but one suspects business lunches are more common in this branch, part of the Winter Park Village shopping complex. The menu emphasis is on pork and steaks, but there are hand-tossed pizzas and other lighter touches available for vegetarians or children.

Café de France

526 Park Avenue, South Winter Park; tel: 407-647-1869; www.lecafedefrance.com; Tue–Sat 11.30am–2.30pm, 6–10pm; $$$; map p.135 D4

Start your meal with foie gras, escargot or the daily selection of pâté before enjoying a fine selection of soups and salads and entrées that include lamb, pork, and a fish of the day. A fine wine list is available to accompany your meal.

Houston's

215 South Orlando Avenue, Winter Park; tel: 407-740-4005; www.hillstone.com; $$$; Sun–Thur 11am–10pm, Fri–Sat 11am–11pm; Link: 39; map p.135 D4

You are unlikely to stumble across this restaurant, as it is tucked away from Orlando Avenue with not much else around it to draw visitors, making its setting on the edge of one of Winter Park's lakes feel even more secluded. The menu varies from five-star burgers costing an arm to gourmet steaks and seafood.

Luma on Park

290 South Park Avenue, Winter Park; tel: 407-599-4111; www.lumaonpark.com; daily from 5.30pm; $$$; map p.135 D4

This is perhaps the finest dining experience in the buzzing Park Avenue restaurant scene. The menu features a lot of seafood, from scallops to barramundi, and there are steaks and chops, too. The wine list consists of boutique winemakers, mostly from California, and there is a 'flight' available that provides samples of their bottles. Uniquely, half-glasses are available for those who would like to change wines for each course yet remain upright.

Space Coast

Cocoa Beach Pier

401 Meade Avenue, Cocoa Beach, ½ mile north of SR 520, off A1A; www.cocoabeachpier.com; daily L, D; $–$$$

You could do a lot worse than ending your trip to the Space Coast on the pier at Cocoa Beach. Walk to the end of the pier and you can see the launch pads. It's no secret that this is prime launch-viewing real estate. On the pier itself are three places to eat: the Atlantic Ocean Grille is the fanciest option, but any of the choices affords a great view of the Atlantic.

The Ravenous Pig

1234 N. Orange Ave, Winter Park; tel: 407-628-2333; www.theravenouspig.com; Tue–Sat 11.30am–2am and 5pm–late; $$$; map p.135 D4

The Pig serves up fine American gastropub cuisine and the chef-owner trained at the Culinary Institute of America. He borrowed the British gastropub style and serves everything from simple bar food to pumpkin tortellini.

Below: rough and ready restaurant with a view that can't be beat from Cocoa Beach Pier.

Shopping

In Orlando, shopping isn't merely about buying stuff, it's just as much about 'retail entertainment.' Extravagant malls anchor either end of International Drive, and become destinations in themselves in other areas of the city. Specialty shops abound here, especially along the cozy main street of Winter Park, but you'll also find factory outlets which offer enormous savings on everything from sporting goods to designer clothing. Of course, there is no shortage of shops selling themed memorabilia, but there are even a few places where you can get Disney souvenirs at a discount.

What to Buy

If you are into kitsch – plastic flamingo ashtrays, canned sunshine, orange perfume, and the like – you will find Orlando's myriad gift shops a veritable treasure house, and you won't need our help in finding one as they are on nearly every corner.

There are also homegrown souvenirs like oranges, tangerines, limes, kumquats, and grapefruits, which can be shipped home for a small fee. But if you look a little harder, Florida also has an array of quality goods to take home from a trip. There are shops worth seeking out that sell designer clothing at factory prices, fascinating examples of Art Deco and old Floridian antiques, and Native American crafts.

Theme Parks

MAGIC KINGDOM
Le Chapeau Hat Shop
Main Street, U.S.A
Located on the right side of Main Street, U.S.A. as you enter the park, this shop has a special boutique where you can Build Your Own

Ears and customize a set of Mickey Mouse ears to suite your personal style. From rhinestones to glow-in-the-dark, anything goes.

EPCOT
Mitsukoshi Department Store
Japan
You could easily forget about the rest of Epcot once you enter this shop. At least that's the case for anyone with a liking for finely finished, delicate sushi-serving sets, samurai swords, or paper lanterns.
Plaza de Los Amigos
Mexico
Beneath the Aztec Temple is a treasure trove from south of the border, with brightly painted, carved wooden animals, silver jewelry, baskets, pottery, woven blankets, toys and more.

HOLLYWOOD STUDIOS
Sid Cahuenga's One of a Kind
Hollywood Boulevard
One of the few retail spaces in any of the theme parks that sells something truly

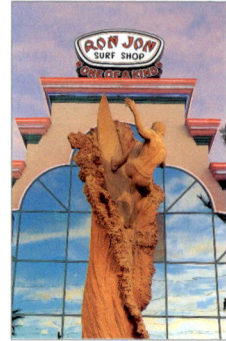

Above: Cocoa Beach's most famous store.

unique. Sid's crowded collection of motion-picture memorabilia includes everything from autographed photographs and vintage movie posters to animation stills from classic Disney pictures. A great place to browse, even if the prices are a bit steep for most wallets.

DOWNTOWN DISNEY
Art of Disney
Marketplace
This is your chance to purchase genuine original cells of Disney's animated films. The

Left: Mainstreet, U.S.A. is lined with stores selling everything from standard souvenirs to customized mouse ears.

still surprises you in this, the largest of all Disney shops. A better plan would be to ignore the park's shops and come here, once.

ISLANDS OF ADVENTURE
All the Books You Can Read
Seuss Landing

Finding every Seuss book in print, in more than one language, is a challenge, and this shop really is a one-of-a-kind for parents or collectors wanting to find the more unique Seuss creations for their child.

Comic Book Shop
Marvel Super Hero Island

For those who grew up reading about the adventures of Marvel's super heroes, this store will make a sweet walk down memory lane with action figures, vintage editions, and recent creations all on sale.

Dervish and Banges
Wizarding World of Harry Potter

Whether you want to get kitted out for Quidditch, buy a broomstick or find a sneako-scope or other magical goods, this shop sells an array of merchandise from the famous films and books.

Most Floridians do their shopping in malls, which contain the usual mix of department stores, boutiques, chain stores, and one-of-a-kind shops. Hours vary, but most shopping centers are open seven days a week.

---

price isn't cheap, but it is artwork well worth investing in.

Disney's Days of Christmas
Marketplace

This shop sells everything Christmas all year round. Few can pass up the opportunity to get a unique tree decoration to commemorate their time in Disney World.

Lego Imagination Center
Marketplace

More creative children will welcome this opportunity to build and destroy instead of purchase and unwrap. In addition to selling every conceivable Lego set, this store doubles as an enormous Lego play area, with children free to make anything they choose out of the buckets of bricks left at their disposal.

Once Upon A Toy
Marketplace

This store is devoted solely to toys, both vintage and modern. Interactive exhibits let you get more involved in making your purchase, and there are classic board games for sale here that have been given a unique Disney-fication.

World of Disney
Marketplace

If you've been spending your vacation exploring Disney World, by the time you get here you will think you've seen all there is to see in terms of memorabilia. But there may be something that

Below: gift shops, many of them of dubious quality, are ubiquitous in Orlando's main tourist areas.

Above: sunwear is available everywhere.

Ollivander's
Wizarding World of Harry Potter
The wandkeeper will let you try out the magic wands, but ultimately the wand chooses you in this interactive shopping experience for young witches and wizards.

KENNEDY SPACE CENTER
Space Shop
Most theme parks' big shops offer items you can find in any decent shopping mall, but the KSC shop is the largest store in the world devoted to NASA memorabilia. From space ice cream to souvenir shirts and space suits for children, this really is a unique place to buy great space gear.

Shopping Malls
Festival Bay
5250 International Drive, Orlando; tel: 407-351-7718; www.shopfestivalbaymall.com; Mon–Sat 10am–9pm, Sun 11am–7pm; I-Ride: mainline; map p.136 B3

Festival Bay is more than an outlet mall. It contains some of the heaviest-themed stores in the area, including **Vans Skatepark** (tel: 407-351-3881

for bookings), with a 25,000sq-ft street course, as well as a **Ron Jon Surf Shop** (tel: 407-481-2555) with an accompanying Surf Park. There is also the enormous **Bass Pro Shop** (tel: 407-563-5200) for your fishing gear and a **Sheplers** (tel: 407-563-1063) outlet for your western wear.

Florida Mall
8001 South Orange Blossom Trail, Orlando; tel: 407-851-7234; www.simon.com; Mon–Sat 10am–9pm, Sun noon–6pm, some restaurants and department stores stay open later; Link: 4, 7, 37 42, 43, 52; map p.137 D2

A destination in itself, the Florida Mall is too big to be explored in one day. For those who feel that is a challenge, be prepared to encounter, for a few minutes each, six department stores, 18 jewelry stores, 22 shore stores, over 53 clothing stores, and one hotel. Enjoy the smell of your burning plastic.

Lake Buena Vista Factory Stores
15657 South Apopka Vineland Road, Orlando; tel: 407-238-9301; www.lbvfs.com; Mon–Sat 10am–9.30pm, Sun 10am–7pm;

Link: 300; map p.139 D1

When faced with so many supermalls in Orlando, it's easy to overlook this smallish strip mall located east of I-4, but its bargains would stand out anywhere else. The Gap and Reebok outlets provide some of the best discounts in Orlando, while the S&K Men's Store has unbelievable bargains on tailor-made men's suits, shirts, and pants.

Mall at Millenia
4200 Conroy Road, Orlando; tel: 407-363-3555; www.mallat millenia.com; Mon–Fri 10am–9pm, Sat 10am–10pm, Sun 10am–8pm; Link: 24, 40, 305; map p.136 B3

Anchored by Neiman Marcus, Bloomingdale's, and Macy's department stores, this mall has over 100 other stores. There are plenty of familiar names such as Gap and Burberry to choose from, and a few unique stores to make things more interesting. In addition to the standard food court fare, there are a few more upscale chains if you'd like to have a bit of luxury with your post-shopping refreshments.

Pointe Orlando
9101 International Drive, Orlando; tel: 407-248-2838; www.pointeorlando.com; Mon–Sat noon–10pm, Sun noon–8pm, some restaurants open later; I-Ride: mainline; map p.136 A1

This is the central shopping and dining venue along International Drive. Shops range from Chico's (tel: 407-352-4780) stylish, middle-of-the

> Recently developed central Florida may not seem the place to hunt for antiques, but a surprising number of shops operate on Antique Road, otherwise known as Orange Avenue in Downtown Orlando.

road womenswear and Gray Fifth Avenue's (tel: 800-549-4497) fine male fashion, to an Armani Exchange (tel: 407-352-3311) offering cut-rate deals on designer goods, and the unique Bimini Shoes (tel: 407-354-9898) with 'fashion for your feet.'

Premium Outlets

Two branches of this mega-outlet mall anchor either end of International Drive.

4951 International Drive, Orlando; tel: 407-352-9600; www.premiumoutlets.com/orlando; Mon–Sat 10am–11pm, Sun 10am–9pm; I-Ride: mainline; map p.136 B3

With its recent expansion complete, this is now the largest outlet mall in the Southeast. There are currently some 180 stores here, including factory outlets for such favorite brands as Nike, Gap, Adidas, Reebok, Tommy Hilfiger and Neiman Marcus.

8200 Vineland Avenue, Orlando; tel: 407-238-7787; www.premiumoutlets.com/orlando; Mon–Sat 10am–11pm, Sun 10am–9pm; Link: 303; I-Ride: main and greenlines; map p.139 D3

With 110 discount stores, Premium Outlets' older mall is still one of the largest in Florida. Designer names include Polo Ralph Lauren (tel: 407-239-7656), Hugo Boss (tel: 407-465-0660), Dior (tel: 407-239-0090), Burberry (tel: 407-238-7777), Giorgio Armani (tel: 407-550-4490), Diesel (tel: 407-239-6267), Calvin Klein Men's and Women's (tel: 407-465-0030), and Gap Outlet (tel: 407-238-1514). Sportswear can be found at Nike Factory Store (tel: 407-239-2662), Adidas (tel: 407-239-2836), Reebok (tel: 407-239-8901), and Puma (tel: 407-239-6211). There is a simple food court if you need refreshment.

Winter Park Village

17–19 between Lee Road and Fairbanks Avenue, Winter Park; tel: 407-571-2700; www.shopwinterparkvillage.net; Mon–Sat 10am–9pm, Sun noon–6pm, restaurants and cinema open later; Link: 1, 2, 9; map p.135 D4

Several large anchor stores and the Regal Cinema border Winter Park Village's small, walkable 'main street', with a collection of smaller independent shops and familiar chains. Like everything else in Winter Park, the place feels spacious, calm and high-class. This town does not do discount malls. There are also several places to eat or drink here.

Independent Shops

MENSWEAR
John Craig
Winter Park: 132 Park Avenue

South; tel: 407-629-7944; www.johncraigclothier.com; Mon–Sat 10am–6pm, Sun noon–5pm

Recently named one of the top 100 independent men's retailers in the US by *Esquire* magazine, this upscale store offers everything from made-to-measure suits and shirts to off-the-rack designers such as Zanella and David Chu.

BEACHGEAR
Ron Jon Surf Shop
4151 North Atlantic Avenue, Cocoa Beach; tel: 321-799 8888; www.ronjonsurfshop.com; daily 24 hours

A neon-lit palace devoted to bikinis, boogie boards, surfboards, scuba equipment, and other beach gear. Famous surfers occasionally drop in for autograph sessions; scuba diving and surfing lessons are also available.

Below: subtle souvenirs make the best presents.

Sport

Whether you're a couch jockey or a true athlete, Orlando has more than enough sports-related activities to keep you happy, and there is hardly a hotel that doesn't offer amenities meant to keep their guests fit. Balmy year-round weather makes the area a natural choice for golfers, fishermen, tennis players and other out-doorsy types. For those desperate to catch a wave, Cocoa Beach is only about an hour's drive away. The Orlando Magic may be the only fully professional sports team in the area, but each spring brings half of the Major League baseball teams to the state for their spring training games.

Baseball

Baseball fans can cheer for the Class AA Orlando Rays (www.orlandorays.com). Tickets are about $10. Disney's Wide World of Sports is home to the Atlanta Braves' spring training camp, as well as a wide range of professional and amateur competitions. Check http://espnwwos.disney.go.com for a schedule of upcoming events.

Basketball

The Orlando Magic is the city's professional basketball team. They play at the Amway Arena. The season begins in September and runs through May. Call the box office (tel: 407-849-2255) for information and tickets. www.nba.com/magic

Boating, Canoeing and Water-skiing

The Walt Disney World Resort has a web of water-ways connecting lakes large and small, and almost all of its resorts are on a lake or canal, with their own landing places or marinas. Dozens of different types of pleasure craft can be rented.

For sailing, conditions are best at two big lakes (Seven Seas Lagoon and Bay Lake at the Magic Kingdom resorts). Single hulls and catamarans are available at several Disney resort hotels. The same locations also have speedboats, drivers, and all the equipment necessary for water-skiing.

The canals around Fort Wilderness are good for canoeing, and you can take pedal boats on the lakes. If you prefer a motor to do the work, take a mini-speedboat, a gentler motorized raft, or rubber boat.

Outside the Walt Disney World Resort, several resort hotels have lakes and water-sports opportunities, or check with your hotel guest services desk.

Fishing

Fish flourish in Florida's many lakes and canals thanks to

Golf plays such a big role in Orlando's sporting scene, we've devoted an entire chapter to it. For more information *see Golf, p.70–3.*

careful stocking and strict environmental policies. Guests at the Walt Disney World Resort are usually surprised to find that fishing is allowed from the shores at Fort Wilderness (but it is, of course, carefully controlled).

In addition, organized fishing expeditions leave daily from Bay Lake, starting at 8am and in late morning and mid-afternoon. Reservations are required and the cost is quite high, but chances are good that you'll catch sizeable bass. Tackle, bait and refreshments are provided.

Outside the Walt Disney World Resort, Florida's fresh-water lakes and rivers are abundant. Try Lake Tohopekaliga (or Toho) in Kissimmee.

Rodeo

Kissimmee Rodeo
958 South Hoagland Boulevard, Kissimmee; tel: 407-933-0020; www.ksarodeo.com; check website for events; admission charge; map p.18
Not so long ago, Kissimmee was one of the country's largest cattle-ranching areas,

Left: Kissimmee's rodeo still attracts big crowds.

a fine beach with yearly surfing championships.

Central Florida YMCA Aquatic & Family Center
8422 International Drive, Orlando; tel: 407-363-1911; www.centralfloridaymca.org; Mon–Fri 5.30am–9pm, Sat 8am–5pm, Sun noon–4pm; admission charge; I-Ride: mainline; map p.136 A2
This Olympic-standard aquatic center is handily located on I-Drive for any swimmers craving a lengthier lap than most hotel pools offer. There are also t'ai chi and yoga courses, and racquetball.

and folks around here like to celebrate the fact most weeks by taking part in a little friendly roping and riding. You'll see bareback riding, bull riding, bronco busting, and calf roping, as well as a calf scramble, in which kids from the audience chase a herd of young dogies. Concession stands sell cowboy hats and hot dogs, burgers, hot chocolate, and drinks.

If it's the real thing you're after, try to time your visit to Orlando for the Fourth of July, when the annual Silver Spurs Rodeo attracts professional rodeo riders from all over the United States.

Swimming and Surfing

Apart from the water parks, every resort and hotel in the Walt Disney World Resort has at least one pool. Many are imaginatively themed around ruined pirate forts, beached ships, grottoes, and mountains, and have fun slides for the children.

Then there are the beaches. The Walt Disney World Resort may be an hour's drive from the sea, but the lakeside resorts have fine, white sandy shores, shady trees, lounge chairs, and cabanas – and the lake water is pure and clean. Lifeguards are on duty (if not, there will be a sign notifying you of their absence). Disney hotels' pools or beaches are open only to guests staying at Disney-owned accommodations, but many other resort hotels have excellent facilities, and most budget hotels or motels will have some sort of pool.

Outside the Walt Disney World Resort, Cocoa Beach, south of Cape Canaveral, has

Tennis

More than two dozen tennis courts are scattered around the Walt Disney World Resort – at the Grand Floridian, Contemporary, and Fort Wilderness resorts; between the Walt Disney World Swan and Walt Disney World Dolphin, and at the Yacht and Beach clubs. If you want to improve your strokes, sign up for lessons with the pros at one of several Disney resorts. Outside the Walt Disney World Resort, the big hotels and country clubs all have courts.

Below: Cocoa Beach is one of the east coast's premier surfing locations.

117

Themed Attractions

When you want to get away from it all, what more could you ask for than a vacation from reality? Whether it's watching lethargic alligators suddenly jump for their lunch, seeing first-hand freakery at Ripley's Believe It or Not!, or getting consumed in a virtual world, things are not always what they seem in Orlando. And with the weather so often hot, it should be no surprise that healthy competition exists between water parks, two of which are owned by Disney, inviting guests to come in, cool off, and get soaked.

Classic Florida

Gatorland

14501 South Orange Blossom Trail, Orlando; tel: 800-393-5297; www.gatorland.com; daily 9am–5pm; admission charge; Link: 4

Opened in 1949 by Kissimmee cattle rancher Owen Godwin, this 55-acre (22-hectare) combination 'gator farm, exotic zoo, and wetlands is still the best – or at least the safest – place to have your Orlando alligator experience. This working 'gator farm sends about 1,000 'gators to market each week.

You can sample the taste of alligator meat in one of the restaurants, but don't miss classic entertainments like the **Gator Jumparoo Show**, where the critters jump for their dinner, and the **Gator Wrestling Show**, popular since Bunk Baxter first jumped astride a 'gator and opened its mouth for inspection in Downtown Orlando in the late 1800s.

These days, Gatorland uses more than half a century of experience with alligators to promote a strong conservation message (well, except when you are eating them). It also works with the University of Florida on alligator research. And the Gator Night Shine program lets you explore the swampy walkways at night with nothing but a flashlight – a chance to experience the fear Florida's first settlers must have felt come nightfall.

Ripley's Believe It or Not!

8201 International Drive, Orlando; tel: 407-345-0501; http://orlando.ripleys.com; daily 9.30am–midnight, call for seasonal closing times; admission charge; I-Ride: mainline; map p.136 A2

If you're in the mood for a walk on the weird side, head

Below: memories of Old Florida at Gatorland.

Left: this is not a stunt show, here the danger is real.

rover. One of the highlights is the state-of-the-art Simulator Station interactive area, where visitors can experience firsthand a variety of astronaut-training devices. Among them is a G-force centrifuge that creates the sensation of gravity four times that on Earth, a moon-walk simulator, and a shuttle simulator that allows visitors to test their piloting skills. Special activities are arranged for viewing shuttle launches, and astronauts occasionally drop by for a visit.

Fairground Attractions

Fun Spot Action Park
5551 Del Verde Way, Orlando; tel: 407-363-3867; www.fun-spot.com; hours vary with later opening times on Fri and Sat evenings; admission charge; I-Ride: mainline; map p.136 B2
Four twisting, multilevel tracks make this one of the best go-cart speedways in Orlando (try the 1,375ft, three-level QuadHelix for real thrills), and there are also bumper-car rides and other fairground attractions. For a change of pace, climb aboard the 101ft-high Ferris

to one of I-Drive's most memorable buildings: an ornate Italian villa sliding into a Florida sinkhole. Newspaper cartoonist Robert Ripley had a taste for natural and manmade oddities, and made a fortune collecting bizarre artifacts from 198 countries. Prepare to be equally grossed out and intrigued by such exhibits as a two-headed calf, a Mona Lisa recreated in small squares of toasted bread, and a three-quarter-scale Rolls-Royce crafted from matchsticks. The topsy-turvy theme is carried through in skewed rooms, where things seem to roll uphill, and a disorienting catwalk, which appears to be stationary but is really moving.

U.S. Astronaut Hall of Fame

6225 Vectorspace Boulevard, Titusville; tel: 321-449-4444; www.kennedyspacecenter.com daily 9am–7pm; admission charge, included in Kennedy

Space Center admission charge; map p.32
'[T]he surface was beautiful, beautiful… Magnificent desolation.' So wrote Buzz Aldrin in a 1972 letter describing how it felt to walk on the moon. The document, on exhibit here, is just one artifact among thousands in this collection that tells the story of the American experience in space. But there's a lot more here, including a Mercury trainee capsule, the command module from Apollo 14, and wheels from the moon

Right: the command module from Apollo 14.

119

Above: the upside-down eye-catcher that is WonderWorks.

wheel for panoramic views of I-Drive and Universal Orlando. There is also a 10,000sq-ft (929 sq m) video-game arcade.

Magical Midway
7001 International Drive, Orlando; tel: 407-370-5353; www.magicalmidway.com; Mon–Tue 2–10pm, Wed–Fri 2pm–midnight, Sat–Sun 10am–midnight; admission charge; I-Ride: mainline; map p.136 A2

Owned by the same company that created WonderWorks in order to compete with Ripley's Believe It or Not!, this park's obvious rival is Fun Spot, though its go-cart tracks are not nearly as well designed or unique. However, the price is nearly $10 cheaper.

Gamers' Heaven and Digital Dreams

DisneyQuest
Downtown Disney, Westside; Sun–Thur 11.30am–10pm, Fri–Sat 11.30am–11pm; admission charge; map p.139 C2

What do you get when you compress all the thrills of a theme park into a five-story building? Well, something like DisneyQuest, a high-tech pleasure dome packed with simulator rides and souped-up video games in a wavy, aquamarine building. Like a real theme park, DisneyQuest is divided into distinct areas, each spread over several levels connected by a labyrinth of elevators (known here as cyberlators), ramps, and twisting slides. Also like a real theme park, admission isn't cheap, and afternoon crowds can be extremely thick.

WonderWorks
9067 International Drive, Orlando; tel: 407-351-8800; www.wonderworksonline.com; daily 9am–midnight; admission charge; I-Ride: mainline; map p.136 A1

If illusions and tilted buildings are your thing, don't miss WonderWorks, next to Pointe Orlando. In typical Orlando one-upmanship, the three-story WonderWorks tops Ripley's by featuring a subsiding neoclassical building that is also upside down. Inside, it's a gamer's heaven, with more than 100 games, science-museum-style hands-on experiments that teach physics, and the world's largest laser tag game. Other attractions let you design and ride your own virtual roller coaster, experience an earthquake, take part in virtual-reality war or climb the new indoor ropes challenge course.

Religious Centers

Holy Land Experience
4655 Vineland Road, exit 31 on I-4, Orlando; tel: 407-872-2272; www.holylandexperience.com; Mon–Sat 10am–6pm; Link: 303; map p.136 B4

No matter where you stand on the novelty of a Christian theme park, this $16 million, 15-acre 'Living Biblical Museum' is undeniably well executed and uses effective multimedia presentations to interpret the roots of Christianity, albeit from a distinctly partial point of view.

The park reflects the combined efforts of Islands of Adventure design firm ITEC Entertainment and founder Marvin Rosenthal, a Jewish-born Baptist minister. Rosenthal's motives for creating the park have been questioned since the project

All water parks are cleverly designed and well landscaped, and their slides can be thrilling. They are also usually crowded, as they make popular places to cool off during a scorching Florida afternoon. Like the theme parks, the trick to beating the crowds is to arrive about 30–45 minutes before opening and make a beeline to the most popular slides. By noon on a hot day, the queues can be prohibitively long and the pools unpleasantly mobbed. Another option is to arrive in the late afternoon – say 4–5pm – after the early birds have pooped out and gone home. Consider, too, that frequent electrical storms in summer will cause the water parks to close. A long storm can work in your favor, however, since some guests will get discouraged and return to their hotels. Bring a towel, sunscreen, snacks, and enough cash to last you the day.

Above: an actor at Holy Land Experience.

was announced in 1993. None of this seems to bother Christian groups, though, who have made up the vast majority of visitors since the park opened in February 2001.

The core of the Holy Land Experience is a re-creation of the city of Jerusalem between 1450 BC and AD 66 that includes the world's largest scale model of the Calvary Garden Tomb, the Wilderness Tabernacle, and the Qumran Dead Sea Caves. A scriptorium houses one of the world's largest private collections of original biblical manuscripts and books. Live shows, including **Behold the Lamb, Passion Drama**, and **Celebrate Jesus – Karaoke** often take place in the Plaza of the Nations on the steps of the Temple of the Great King.

SEE ALSO LIVE SHOWS, P.79

WordSpring Discovery Center

11221 John Wycliffe Boulevard, Orlando; tel: 407-852-3626; www.wordspringdiscovery center.com; Mon–Fri 9am–4pm; admission charge

The WordSpring Discovery Center is a fascinating explanation of the work of the Wycliffe Bible Translators. Linguists, as well as those visiting for spiritual reasons, will find the exhibits on language learning and acquisition intriguing. Wycliffe's goal is to translate the Bible into every language in the world. In the process, representatives located in some of the world's remotest areas are preserving some of the world's most endangered languages, and, in some cases, they are creating written languages for people who currently only communicate via the spoken word.

Thrills and Spills

Richard Petty Driving Experience

Walt Disney World Speedway; tel: 800-237-3889; www.drive petty.com; see website for schedule; Link: 50, 56; map p.138 A3

While most attractions in Orlando appeal to the whole family, this is strictly for the big boy racers. If you've always wanted to drive a souped-up, 630-horsepower Pontiac Grand Prix at 125mph, this NASCAR-affiliated racing school is the place. Choices range from a three-lap shotgun ride with a professional driver to an intensive two-day program that includes exercises in side-by-side driving and a final duel on the speedway between student and pro.

Skyventure

6805 Visitors Circle, off International Drive, Orlando; tel: 407-903-1150; www.skyventure orlando.com; Sun–Thur 11.30am–9pm, Fri and Sat 11.30am–10pm; admission charge; I-Ride: mainline; map p.136 A2

This unique attraction uses an inverted wind tunnel to generate enough upward force to allow you to 'fly' above it. The experience lasts for an hour, but only a couple of minutes of this time is spent flying, making this one of the most expensive experiences in Orlando.

Water Parks

Aquatica

5800 Water Play Way, Orlando; tel: 407-351-3600; www.aquaticabyseaworld.com; daily 10am–5pm; admission charge; map p.139 E4

Operated by SeaWorld, Aquatica is a state-of-the-art water park with thrilling slides, a lazy river and other water rides for all ages. The unique attraction will be a clear tube slide that goes through a dolphin-filled aquarium. There is also a white-sand beach and private

Below: the WordSpring Discovery Center explores language and faith around the world.

Above: the once-in-a-lifetime experience of Discovery Cove.

cabanas for those who just want to relax.

Discovery Cove
6000 Discovery Cove Way, Orlando; tel: 877-557-7404; www.discoverycove.com; daily 9am–5.30pm; Link: 8, 43; map p.139 E4

This all-inclusive resort-style park is across the road from SeaWorld. Up to 1,000 lucky guests a day arrive at the attractive, thatch-roofed tiki entrance to register for a day of sunbathing, swimming, interacting with tropical animals, and – the highlight – swimming with a dolphin.

Imported sandy beaches, deckchairs, cabanas and refreshment stands surround the cool, saltwater Coral Reef, which has been stocked with stingrays and 6,000 tropical fish, as well as glassed-in sharks, a grouper, and a moray eel. Nervous youngsters (and adults) can enjoy the stingray experience in a baby stingray pool adjoining the Coral Reef.

But if that's too much for some – as it may well be – plan on floating around the park in the warm, freshwater Lazy River, passing waterfalls and submerged ruins. The river will lead you to the

Aviary, a hugely popular spot, where staff members answer questions and hand you cups of food for the toucans, ibises, sun conures, guinea fowl, and even a tiny muntjac deer. A substantial gourmet lunch is included in the fee.

While it's possible to enjoy all this and more by signing up for the less expensive Non-Dolphin Swim Package, you'll probably kick yourself later if you don't take the opportunity to get into the water with one of the 30 dolphins. You can't change your mind when you arrive; the park is sold to capacity almost every day, and there are few last-minute cancellations. If you haven't made reservations, you're out of luck.

Included in the **Dolphin Swim Package** is a 30-minute session interacting

> Said to be the world's highest free-fall slide and the fastest in the country, Blizzard Beach's **Summit Plummit** zips riders down a 350ft ramp at an angle of 60 degrees and speeds approaching 60mph. Needless to say, this is not an experience for the faint of heart.

> Water rides are notorious for giving wedgies and stripping off bathing suits. Tie your suit tightly and leave the teeny-weeny bikini at home.

with a dolphin and two trainers in groups of no more than six people. Dolphin swims take place at specific time slots all day. You will be given your time when you arrive at the park and assigned a special cabana, where you will receive an orientation before getting into the water. The skill of the trainers makes this a very safe experience, and great care is taken to give each guest ample one-on-one dolphin time. You'll get a chance to try out hand signals to get your dolphin to roll, wave flippers, exchange kisses, and tow you along. And that, everyone seems to agree, is an experience that is almost priceless.

Disney's Blizzard Beach
1500 West Buena Vista Boulevard, Bay Lake; daily 9am–8pm, winter 10am–5pm; map p.138 B1

This is Disney's newest and largest water park, and the one with the most bizarre concept. At its center is **Mount Gushmore**, a 90ft peak serviced by what may be the state's only ski lift (there are also stairs and a gondola for disabled guests). At the top, guests choose among an assortment of routes to ride back down. The most exciting, the **Summit Plummet**, actually begins on a platform 30ft above the mountaintop. Other attractions suit quieter pursuits such as whitewater rafting or floating down the lazy river. For kids, **Tike's Peak** and the **Ski Patrol Training Camp** have tubes, body slides, and a bungee cord slide. Blizzard Beach is also home to **Disney's Winter**

Above: I-Drive's most popular place to cool off.

Summerland Miniature Golf,
with two elaborately designed
18-hole courses.

Disney's Typhoon Lagoon
1195 East Buena Vista Drive,
Lake Buena Vista; daily
9am–8pm; map p.139 C2

Typhoon Lagoon, we are led
to believe, is the waterlogged
remains of a tropical resort
drowned by a hurricane. In
the center of the park is the
Surf Pool, which generates
waves more than 5ft tall, high
enough for the surfing com-
petitions that are held here.
Rising above this scene is the
summit of the 85ft-high
Mount Mayday, crowned
with the wreckage of *Miss
Tilly*, a washed-up trawler.

The action is a bit tamer
here than at Blizzard Beach,
but not by much. You can
lounge on a sandy beach,
frolic in the waves, and take a
relaxing 45-minute float trip
through rainforest grottoes
and waterfalls. At **Shark
Reef**, you get a brief snorkeling lesson, then fin around a
sunken tanker accompanied
by tropical fish and real
(friendly) sharks. This is one
adventure you want to do just
after the park opens. By midday, the lines are too long
and the tank too crowded to
be much fun.

There's no lack of high-
speed slides, either. Dare-
devils shoot the rapids,

careen through caves, and fly
down a trio of 214ft slides at
Humunga Kowabunga. The
thrills are toned down at
Ketchakiddee Creek,
designed especially for children aged two to six.

Wet'n Wild
6200 International Drive,
Orlando; tel: 407-351-1800;
www.wetnwildorlando.com; see
website for hours; admission
charge; I-Ride: mainline; map

p.136 A2

Near Universal Studios, a
massive tower holds three
rides: **Mach 5**, a spiraling
flume; **The Blast**, a furious
raft ride with added sound
effects and water cannons
that ensure you get soaked;
and **The Flyer**, a fast drop
with hairpin turns in a four-
person toboggan. The
Surge, in a separate tower,
offers another hairy ride, as
your raft screams down a
banked tube some five stories high. Small children have
their own fun in the sun: a
kiddie pool and a pint-size
multilevel water play area
that includes water cannons,
slides, the mini **Surf Lagoon**
wave pool, and a **Lazy River**
that takes you through
Florida's past. The water at
Wet'n Wild is heated, and
the park is open year-round,
though you'll find the winter
months quite chilly.

Below: Disney's water parks are as well crafted as their other
theme parks.

Thrill Rides

For certain tourists the accumulated miles of steel track at Orlando's theme parks are not to be feared but challenged. Below we list the best thrill rides at each park. Some, relatively speaking, are a doddle, where others will scare the life out of even the most seasoned riders. If you are a real aficionado and want to ride attractions several times, take advantage of single-rider lines and the FAST-PASS and Express options available at Disney and Universal, respectively. For families traveling with children too short to enjoy a ride, most will have a parent swap station allowing one parent to ride while the other looks after the child.

Magic Kingdom

Splash Mountain
Frontierland; height requirement: 40in; FASTPASS

This down-home log ride features characters out of the Brer Rabbit children's story. For most of the ride this seems little more than a trumped-up dark ride, and then you come to the end: a five-story drop that guarantees to get you wet.

Big Thunder Mountain Railroad
Frontierland; height requirement: 40in; FASTPASS

While no self-respecting thrill-seeker would call this a proper thrill ride, it is a good stepping stone for those who have just graduated from the kiddie coasters or are trying to gain courage for Space Mountain. The runaway train never exceeds 40mph during its twisting and turning journey.

Space Mountain
Tomorrowland; height requirement: 44in; FASTPASS

For many, this is the only true thrill ride in the Magic Kingdom, and with a maximum speed of just under 30mph, it is quite tame in comparison to more recent coasters built elsewhere. It is still a classic, though, and the FASTPASSes for this ride through the darkness of space run out by midday, so get one quick if you plan to ride it.

Epcot

Mission: SPACE
Future World; height requirement: 44in; FASTPASS

This is the most sophisticated motion simulator in Orlando. Strapped into your spaceship's cockpit, the G-forces of take-off are recreated using an enormous centrifuge which slows down just as you exit the Earth's orbit, giving you a temporary feeling of weightlessness. The views of your home planet are equally serene, but don't think the ride is over just yet – you also have to land. This ride is so intense that Disney has recently created a 'light' version that does not include the centrifugal force. To our knowledge this is still the only thrill ride in Orlando to come with a sick bag.

Below: be sure to leave your witch's broom in a locker.

Left: you'll never look at mummies the same again.

Some thrills come in small packages, and little ones may use these attractions to test their limits in preparation for riding the more serious thrill rides later.

Below are listed some remedial thrill rides, equally guaranteed to get a response of approval from under-8s and a sigh of boredom from teenagers:

High in the sky but only round and around, kids love the heights and slow comfort of hub-and-spoke classics such as the Magic Carpets of Aladdin (Adventureland, Magic Kingdom), Dumbo's Flying Elephant (Fantasyland, Magic Kingdom), Astro Orbiter (Tomorrowland, Magic Kingdom), TriceraTop Spin (DinoLand U.S.A., Animal Kingdom), and One Fish, Two Fish, Red Fish, Blue Fish (Seuss Landing, Islands of Adventure).

In Islands of Adventure, Pteranodon Flyers (Jurassic Park) and Flight of the Hippogriff (Wizarding World of Harry Potter) are also popular. Spinning until sick is another favorite little-people pastime. It's amazing how much longer a child can withstand these rides than their gullible parents: Mad Tea Party (Fantasyland, Magic Kingdom) and Storm Force Accelatron (Marvel Super Hero Island, Islands of Adventure).

And finally, little coasters are great introductions to the steel-track behemoths: Barnstormer at Goofy's Wiseacre Farm (height requirement: 35in, Mickey's Toontown Fair, Magic Kingdom), Woody Woodpecker's Nuthouse Coaster (height requirement: 36in, Woody Woodpecker's Kidzone, Universal Studios).

Test Track

Future World; height requirement: 40in; FASTPASS

For years this re-creation of automobile-testing procedures was the only thing approaching a thrill ride in Epcot. The ride does show its age now and is mild in comparison to other rides in the resort, but the finale, which includes banked turns at over 60mph, is a classic. The ride has notoriously long lines, though, so use your FASTPASS or join the single-rider queue.

Animal Kingdom

DINOSAUR

DinoLand U.S.A; height requirement: 40in; FASTPASS

What begins as a gentle dark ride ends with roller coaster-like drops and spins. This is ideal for those wanting thrills, but who may be a bit too young (or short) for Expedition Everest.

Expedition Everest

Asia; height requirement: 44in; FASTPASS

The park's high-altitude thrill ride feels like a decrepit mountain train scaling its way up the side of the world's tallest peak, and includes a steep backward drop when you come to the 'end of the track.' As if that weren't enough to frighten you, there is always the chance that the Yeti might surprise you as well.

Hollywood Studios

Rock 'n' Roller Coaster Starring Aerosmith

Sunset Boulevard; height requirement: 48in; FASTPASS

Though this coaster's design is enclosed, this is no Space Mountain. It begins with a 0–60mph acceleration that exerts over 4Gs on the riders. This is then followed by a loop, a roll, and a corkscrew. As if that were not enough, the entire ride is synchronized to a custom-made Aerosmith soundtrack. Lightweights need not apply.

The Twilight Zone Tower of Terror

Sunset Boulevard; height requirement: 40in; FASTPASS

The basis of this ride is a simple lift-and-drop amusement ride, but Disney Imagineers have done their best to make it even scarier. After

125

checking in to the decrepit hotel, Rod Sterling from the *Twilight Zone* series is your guide through a series of disorientating exhibits that precede a random series of drops and lifts.

Universal Studios

Hollywood Rip Ride Rockit
Production Central; height requirement: 51in

Universal Studio's newest thrill ride lets you pick your own music to accompany your trip on Orlando's tallest roller coaster. It climbs straight up 17 stories above the park, then comes rocketing down at 65mph through sensational loops and near-miss turns. Your high-adrenalin adventure is all captured on video, which you can edit into a music video for an additional fee.

Revenge of the Mummy
New York; height requirement: 48in; Express

Billed as a psychological thrill ride, novice riders may find that they do need therapy after this journey through haunted Egypt. Mummy uses intense special effects and terrifying voices in an attempt to play with your mind. Be careful you don't get too relaxed at the beginning of the ride, when it seems little more than a very well-executed haunted house. The ride reaches speeds of up to 45mph and includes periods of total darkness.

Islands of Adventure

The Amazing Adventures of Spider Man
Marvel Super Hero Island; height requirement: 40in; Express

This ride combines the finest elements of theme-park design. The track is classic dark-ride material enhanced by the use of 3-D technology, and the car you board is a fully maneuverable motion simulator. These elements combine to convince you that you are flying over the city, and it's impossible to believe you are standing still at the finale.

Dragon Challenge
Wizarding World of Harry Potter; height requirement: 54in; Express

Three elements make this one of the best rides in the south-

> A computer system monitors the trains in order to minimize the flyby distance between the trains – and maximize the terror.

east. First, it's an inverted coaster, meaning the cars attach to the track overhead, while your legs dangle freely below (and sometimes above). Next, it's not merely one coaster, but two. The Chinese Fireball and Hungarian Horntail ride on intertwining tracks devilishly engineered for several near misses as they do battle and race through the air. Last, the attraction is elaborately themed with Harry Potter lore, including a burning Goblet of Fire and a gleaming TriWizard Cup. Both dragons deliver multiple loops, corkscrews, rolls, and up to 5Gs. Expect an extremely long wait for all but the earliest and latest few rides; the wait is even longer if you are one of those gluttons for punishment who elect to sit in the front cars. Do yourself a favor and get a Universal Express ticket.

Right: SeaWorld's Kraken may be surrounded by cuddly animals, but it's a beast.

Flight of the Hippogriff
Wizarding World of Harry Potter; height requirement: 36in; Express

Children and others who aren't up to Dragon Challenge can take a spin on the enchanting Hippogriff. It's a much tamer, family-friendly experience.

Incredible Hulk Coaster
Marvel Super Hero Island; height requirement: 54in; Express

This is Orlando's most memorable thrill ride, and you could not call yourself a thrill-seeker without riding this at least twice. The trip begins with a 0–40mph acceleration that takes all of two seconds and is followed by seven inversions, including a unique cobra roll, and a top speed of 67mph.

SeaWorld

Journey to Atlantis
Height requirement: 42in

A unique attraction that combines a roller coaster with a water ride whose final soaking plunge is one of the steepest in the world. There's a story-line behind the ride to do with the Lost Continent of Atlantis and a battle between the gods, but once your boat gets moving it's all secondary to the action. There's a barrage of lasers and holographs, and a rapid-fire succession of drops and dips, including two 60ft dives that will have your stomach doing somersaults. Expect to get drenched, especially in the front seats. Waiting times can be as much as an hour during the busy season, so try to ride early in the morning or late in the afternoon.

Left: Universal's most daring roller coaster.

Kraken
Height requirement: 54in

This 150ft-high, floorless roller coaster, named after a legendary sea monster, will terrify the living daylights out of even seasoned riders. Raised seats allow your legs to dangle freely as this monster reaches speeds of 65mph, creating a G-force that keeps you glued to your seat during a ride involving seven inversions (including a cobra roll, vertical loop and flat spin), underground passages, and a soaking in the eel-infested monster's lair.

Manta
Height requirement: 54in

In an amazing simulation of a manta ray's 'flight' through the sea, you glide, soar and dive while strapped face down beneath a roller coaster shaped like a ray. The coaster reaches speeds of almost 60mph and goes through four inversions.

Space Coast

Shuttle Launch Experience
Minimum height: 48in

Created shortly after Epcot's Mission: SPACE, this is a much tamer ride. The concept, however, is exactly the same: to let you feel what the astronauts feel when a space shuttle is launched. The biggest difference between the two rides is that you do not feel the heavy G-forces here as there is no spinning involved. The pre-show here also pays more attention to what happens in a real launch, explaining the physics of getting into outer space. Compared to Orlando's other motion simulators, this ride is rather tame, so should be fine for visitors who are not exactly fans of thrill rides.

127

Transportation

Getting to Orlando should be no problem, nor should getting around this sprawling metropolis, so long as you know how to drive. Major airlines from all over the world serve Orlando International Airport, and it is a main stop on Amtrak's east-coast line. Once you've left the airport, the city spreads out in an orderly fashion around the Interstate-4 corridor. The sprawling layout does have its disadvantages: distances between attractions at Disney and those in Winter Park are great, and there is hardly any efficient public transportation to ease the journey.

Getting There

BY AIR
Most major US and international carriers serve Orlando. Fare prices are competitive, so shop around before buying a ticket. A variety of discount fares and 'package deals,' which can significantly cut round-trip rates, are also available. Many scheduled services are supplemented by charter flights.

Orlando International Airport (code MCO) is 9 miles south of Downtown Orlando and about 25 miles from Walt Disney World Resort. Spacious, glittering, and constantly expanding, it has two terminals, with satellite gates reached by 'people-mover' shuttle trains. Disney characters often make appearances during the day.

A lot of package flights land at Orlando Sanford International Airport, about 30 miles north of Orlando. During the busy summer months this small airport is utilized to cope with the large numbers of tourists, and lines at immigration can be long. Furthermore, the extra distance can be a costly inconvenience if you plan to use taxi or shuttle buses to reach Orlando.

> Security at airports since September 11, 2001, has become a serious matter indeed. As long as you give yourself plenty of time, remain patient, and take absolutely no chances, you should be fine. Ensure that you are not taking any sharp objects onto the plane with you. Along with obvious weapons such as knives or scissors, nail clippers, jewelry with spikes on it, and even tweezers may be confiscated. Arrive early enough to deal with all the random searches. Three hours should be the norm now. Also be prepared for searches that may be embarrassing and/or offensive. Unfortunately, not all staff protecting the airports are as courteous as they might be. Remain calm and don't take it personally: they are only doing their job. Keeping your cool will also get you through quicker and with fewer hassles.

Orlando International Airport Tel: 407-825-2001
Orlando Sanford International Airport Tel: 407-585-4000

AIRLINES
Telephone numbers of major airlines serving Florida (numbers are US unless stated):
American
Tel: 800-433-7300
UK tel: 020-7365-0777
www.aa.com
British Airways
Tel: 800-247-9297
UK tel: 0870-850-9850
www.britishairways.com
Continental
Tel: 800-523-3273
UK tel: 0845-607-6760
www.continental.com
Delta
Tel: 800-241-4141
UK tel: 0845-600-0950
www.delta.com
Lufthansa
Tel: 800-645-3880
UK tel: 0871-945-9747
www.lufthansa.com
Southwest
Tel: 800-435-9792
www.southwest.com
United Airlines
Tel: 800-864-8331

Getting Around

TO/FROM THE AIRPORTS

Taxis and less expensive shuttle minibuses run between the airports and Walt Disney World locations, International Drive, Downtown Orlando, Kissimmee, and Cocoa Beach. Some hotels operate free shuttle services to and from the airports; if you are on a package tour, airport transfers may be included. There's a public bus – Lynx no. 42 – to International Drive that departs every 30 minutes (hourly on Sun) from 6am–10.30pm Monday–Saturday, 6.30am–9.30pm Sunday.

PUBLIC TRANSPORTATION

Like most cities in the United States, public transportation exists in Orlando but offers only infrequent service and only to major destinations. Luckily, this is usually along the tourist route. If you are staying along I-Drive, in Kissimmee, or in Downtown Orlando, service is adequate to other major areas only. Ask your hotel which bus takes you where, though be prepared for odd responses – most concierges are never asked

UK tel: 0845-844-4777
www.united.com
US Airways
Tel: 800-428-4322
UK tel: 0845-600-3300
www.usairways.com
Virgin Atlantic
Tel: 800-821-5438
UK tel: 0844-874-7747
www.virgin-atlantic.com

BY RAIL

Amtrak offers services from America's Midwest, northeast, and south – and connecting service from points west – to certain Florida cities. There is daily service from New York City on the Silver Service. The Sunset Limited travels from Los Angeles via New Orleans. For those who want to take their car along, too, Amtrak offers an Auto Train service from Lorton, Virginia (near Washington, DC), to Sanford, Florida, near Orlando.

Amtrak services within Florida are not extensive, being most useful for destinations along the east coast and in parts of central Florida.
Amtrak
Tel: 800-872-7245
www.amtrak.com

BY ROAD

Greyhound provides bus services to Florida and all over the state. While some intercity bus services include many stops en route, making long distances seem interminable, there are also express buses which take in fewer stops.

Many bus terminals, including the one in Downtown Orlando, are in a dodgy area of town, so take care when traveling to or from stations. The station in Kissimmee is in a better area.
Greyhound
Tel: 800-231-2222
www.greyhound.com

Below: take a nostalgic trip down International Drive.

Above: trams make the arduous journey from car to gate a bit quicker.

for bus information. Your best bet is to call the Lynx information line.

Additionally, the I-Ride Trolley goes up and down I-Drive and Universal Boulevard from 8am–10.30pm. A single fare is $1.25, but exact change is required.

Lynx
Tel: 407-841-5969
www.golynx.com
I-Ride Trolley
Tel: 866-243-7483
www.iridetrolley.com

DISNEY TRANSPORTATION

The Walt Disney World Resort transportation system is complex, as are the rules about who can use it. They include those staying at Disney accommodations, at the Plaza hotels, or those carrying four- or five-day passes. Additionally, those with Magic Kingdom tickets can use the monorail or ferry to get to its entrance.

Disney buses connect all areas within the Walt Disney World Resort. They all look the same, but have electronic destination displays in the window to identify them. Bus stops outside parks and resorts are clearly labeled. If in any doubt, ask the driver. He or she will ever-so-happily tell you where they're going, in between

wishing everyone a magical day as they board.

The Disney World Monorail links Disney's Magic Kingdom resorts with the Magic Kingdom and Epcot.

Ferries run between the Ticket & Transportation Center (TTC) and the Magic Kingdom. They also transport guests at the BoardWalk Inn, Beach Club Resort, Yacht Club Resort, Swan Hotel and Dolphin Hotel to and from Epcot and Hollywood Studios. Water taxis are available to ferry guests to the Magic Kingdom from the Grand Floridian Resort, Polynesian Resort, Fort Wilderness Resort and the Wilderness Lodge.

UNIVERSAL STUDIOS TRANSPORTATION

Like Disney, all of Universal's resorts are linked to the parks by free transportation. In this case, though, it's all boats that dock at the City-Walk lagoon.

TAXIS

Taxis are available in all the main tourist centers. They tend to be expensive, and you usually have to telephone in advance for pick-up. Your hotel should call for you; otherwise, numbers are listed in the Yellow Pages.

Don't stand by the side of the road and expect to hail a passing cab.

Driving

Driving is the most popular way to travel to and around Orlando. About three-quarters of domestic leisure visitors enter the Sunshine State by car every year. Unless you plan to remain within Disney World or Universal Orlando or along International Drive during your entire stay, a car is the most convenient way to get around. Bus, train, and taxi service is quite irregular, and slow to cover the vast distances between Disney World and the rest of Orlando.

CAR RENTAL

Renting a car is by far the easiest way to explore the Orlando area beyond Disney World and Universal, allowing you to zip quickly between the major parks, unless, of course, you encounter one of the many traffic jams that snarl the area's major roads. If possible, avoid driving the I-4 corridor during rush hour (7–10am and 4–7pm).

Most rental agencies require that you are at least 21 years old (sometimes 25), have a valid driver's license and a major credit card. Some will take a cash deposit in lieu of a credit card, but this might be as high as $500. Travelers from some foreign countries may need to produce an international driver's license from their own country.

> Florida has some of the toughest laws in the US against driving under the influence of alcohol. The maximum level permitted is so small that you are advised to drink no alcohol at all if driving.

If you happen to book your car online in another country, you must provide a foreign driver's license for the discounted fee to be honored when you pick up the car.

Visitors wishing to rent a car after arriving in Orlando will find rental offices at the airports, at Downtown locations, and even at some hotels. Rates are cheap by US and international standards, but you should shop around for the best rates and features. Local rental firms outside the airports are often less expensive than the national companies, and can be more convenient if you want a car only for a day or two. The cost of insurance is usually tacked on to the rental fee, so be sure to check insurance provisions before signing anything.

If you are traveling from overseas, it is normally cheaper to arrange car rental in advance. You should also check with your airline or travel agent for special package deals that include a car, since rental rates can be reduced by about 50 percent if you buy a so-called 'fly-drive' deal. However, be wary of offers of 'free' car rental, which do not include extras like tax and insurance.

Available rental vehicles range from modest economy cars to luxury convertibles and vans.

Be sure to check that your car-rental agreement includes Loss Damage Waiver (LDW), also known as Collision Damage Waiver (CDW). Without it, you will be liable for any damage done to your vehicle in the event of an accident, regardless of whether or not you were to blame. You are advised to pay for supplementary Liability Insurance on top of the

standard third-party insurance. Insurance and tax charges combined can add $35 to each day's rental.

CAR RENTAL AGENCIES

These rental agencies may be contacted within the US and from abroad:

Alamo
Tel: 800-462-5266
www.alamo.com

Avis
Tel: 800-331-1212
www.avis.com
UK tel: 0844-581-8181
www.avis.co.uk

Budget
Tel: 800-527-0700
UK tel: 01344-484-100
www.budget.com

Dollar
Tel: 800-800-3665
UK tel: 020-3468-7685
www.dollar.com

Hertz
Tel: 800-654-3131
www.hertz.com
UK tel: 0870-844-8844
www.hertz.co.uk

National
Tel: 800-227-7368
UK tel: 0871-384-1140
www.nationalcar.com

Thrifty
Tel: 800-847-4389
www.thrifty.com

SPEED LIMITS

American states set their own speed limits. In Florida they

are: 55–70mph on highways, 20–30mph in residential areas, 10–20mph near schools.

Limits change suddenly and for only short distances, so pay attention to signs. The Highway Patrol is good at enforcing limits, including minimum speeds: signs along interstates sometimes oblige motorists to drive at over 50mph.

MAPS

Most service stations and convenience stores sell maps. Florida tourist offices (including overseas) often distribute the Official Transportation Map of Florida, which has city plans, free of charge.

Parking

All theme parks provide extensive facilities for car parking. There is usually a charge, although at Disney parks it is free if you are staying at Disney-owned accommodations and display the card that you are given when you register. If you do have to pay a parking fee, keep the ticket, since it is valid at all parks for that day. Remember to make a careful note of the exact location where you leave your car. After a few days of parking in vast lots that all look the same, it's easy to become confused.

Below: an American classic.

131

Atlas

The following streetplan of greater Orlando makes it easy to find the attractions listed in the A–Z section. A selective index to streets and sights will help you find other locations throughout the city.

Map Legend

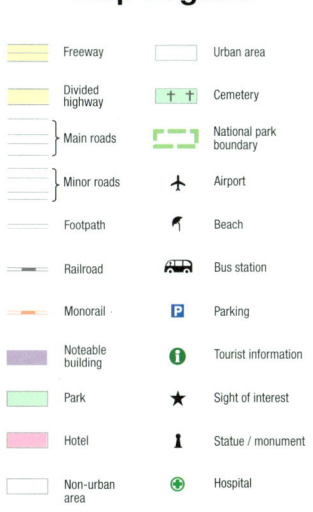

Freeway		Urban area
Divided highway		† † Cemetery
Main roads		National park boundary
Minor roads		✈ Airport
Footpath		↖ Beach
Railroad		🚌 Bus station
Monorail		P Parking
Noteable building		ⓘ Tourist information
Park		★ Sight of interest
Hotel		⚱ Statue / monument
Non-urban area		✚ Hospital

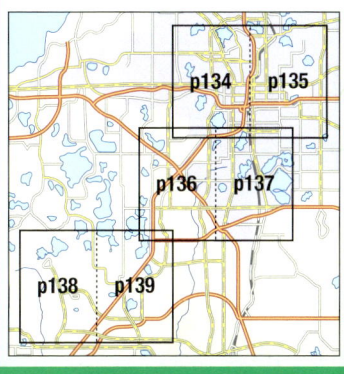

p134   p135

p136   p137

p138   p139

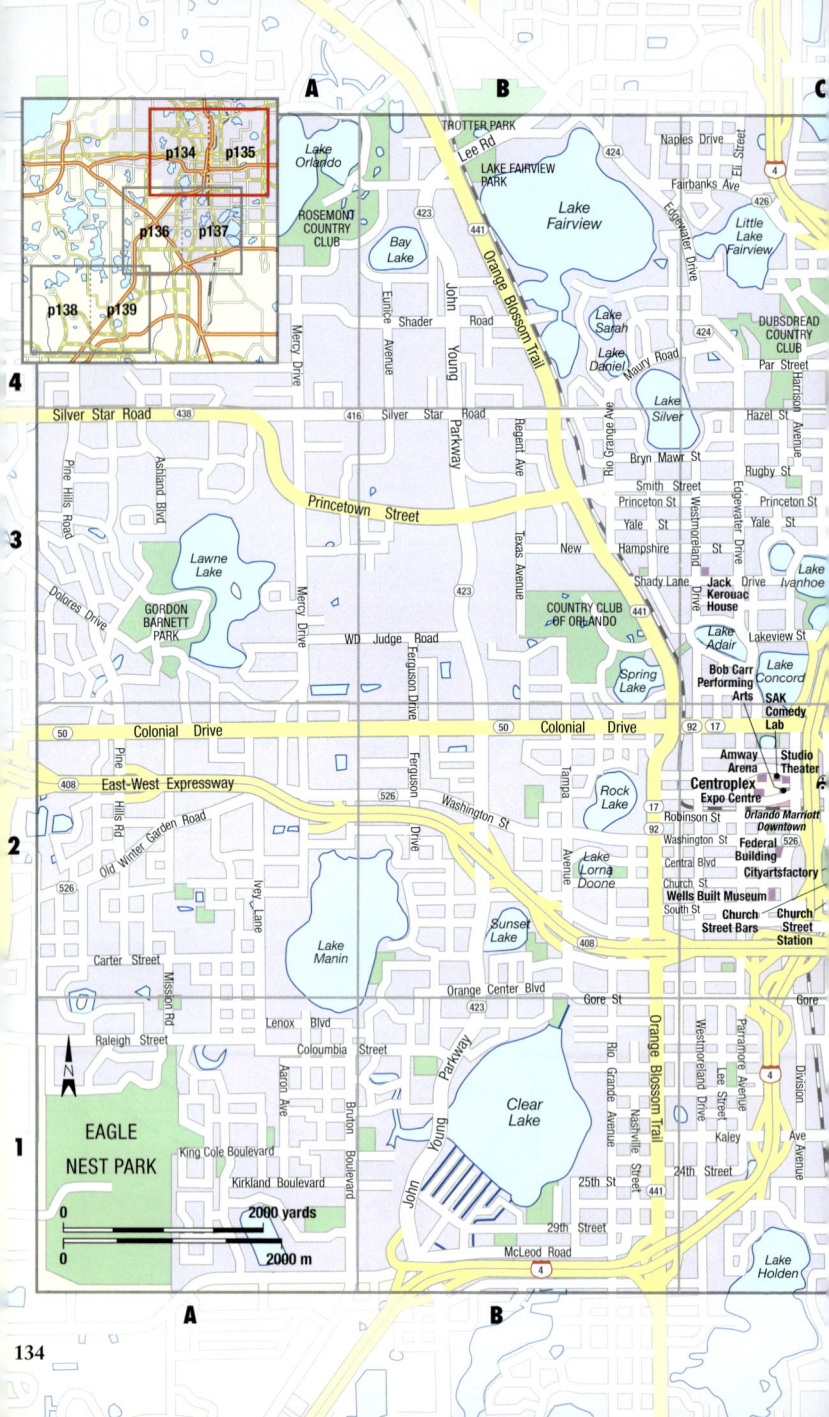

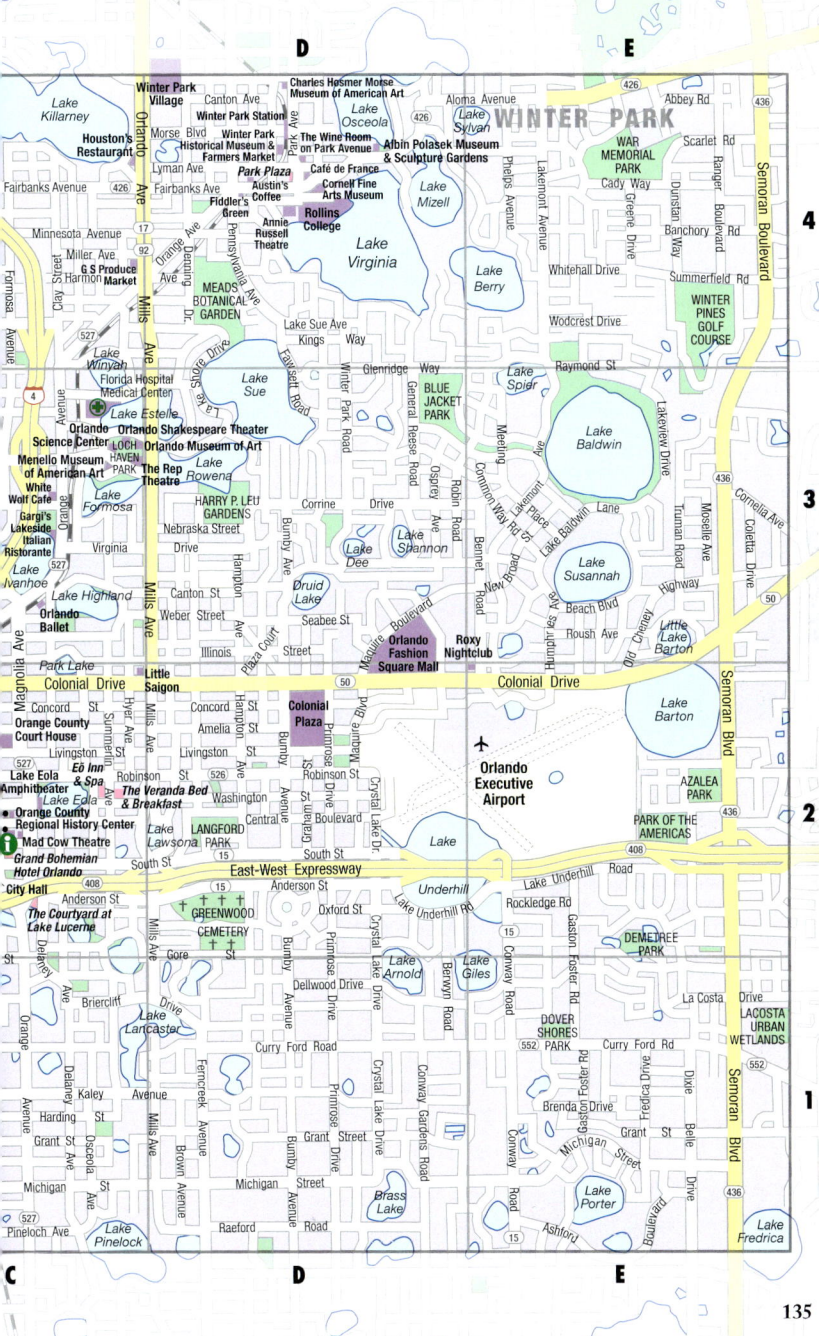

D

Lake Killarney

Winter Park Village

Canton Ave
Morse Blvd

Winter Park Station
Winter Park Historical Museum & Farmers Market

Charles Hosmer Morse Museum of American Art

Aloma Avenue

Lake Osceola

WINTER PARK

Abbey Rd

Houston's Restaurant

Lyman Ave

Park Plaza

The Wine Room on Park Avenue

Albin Polasek Museum & Sculpture Gardens

Lake Sylvan

WAR MEMORIAL PARK

Scarlet Rd

Cady Way

Banger

Dunstan Way

Fairbanks Avenue

Fairbanks Ave

Fiddler's Green

Café de France

Cornell Fine Arts Museum

Rollins College

Lake Mizell

Phelps Avenue

Lakemont Avenue

Greene Drive

Banchory Rd

Summerfield Rd

Minnesota Avenue

Austin's Coffee

Annie Russell Theatre

Lake Virginia

Whitehall Drive

WINTER PINES GOLF COURSE

Miller St

G S Produce Market

Lake Berry

Wodcrest Drive

MEADS BOTANICAL GARDEN

Lake Winyah

Lake Sue Ave

Kings Way

Glenridge Way

Lake Spicr

Raymond St

Florida Hospital Medical Center

Lake Estelle

Lake Sue

Fawsett Road

Winter Park Road

Lake Baldwin

Lakeview Drive

Cornelia Ave

Orlando Science Center

Orlando Shakespeare Theater
Orlando Museum of Art

LOCH HAVEN PARK

The Rep Theatre

BLUE JACKET PARK

General Reese Road

Meeting

Lakemont

Lake Baldwin Lane

Moselle Road

Truman Road

Coletta Drive

Menello Museum of American Art

White Wolf Cafe

Lake Rowena

Corrine

Drive

Osprey

Robin Road

Common Way Rd St

Lake Place

Highway

Gargi's Lakeside Italian Ristorante

Lake Formosa

HARRY P. LEU GARDENS

Nebraska Street

Lake Dee

Lake Shannon

Bennet Road

New Broad

Lake Susannah

Beach Blvd

Old Cheney

Little Lake Barton

Lake Ivanhoe

Lake Highland

Virginia

Drive

Canton St

Hampton

Druid Lake

Seabee St.

Roush Ave

Orlando Ballet

Weber Street

Ave

Mature Boulevard

Orlando Fashion Square Mall

Roxy Nightclub

Park Lake

Little Saigon

Illinois

Plaza Court

Street

Colonial Drive

Colonial Drive

Lake Barton

Concord St

Hyer Ave

Concord St

Hampton St

Colonial Plaza

Orange County Court House

Amelia St

Primrose

Summerlin

Livingston St

Livingston St

Eö Inn & Spa

Robinson St

Robinson St

AZALEA PARK

Lake Eola Amphitheater

Lake Eola

The Veranda Bed & Breakfast

Washington

Bumby

Crystal Lake Blvd

Boulevard

Orlando Executive Airport

PARK OF THE AMERICAS

Orange County Regional History Center

Central

Ave

Lake

Mad Cow Theatre

LANGFORD PARK

Lake Lawsona

South St

Grand Bohemian Hotel Orlando

South St

East-West Expressway

Lake Underhill

Road

City Hall

Anderson St

Anderson St

Lake Underhill Rd

Rockledge Rd

The Courtyard at Lake Lucerne

Mills Ave

Oxford St

Crystal Lake Dr

Gaston

Foster Rd

DEMETREE PARK

Delaney

Gore

GREENWOOD CEMETERY

Lake Arnold

Lake Giles

Conway Road

La Costa

Drive

LACOSTA URBAN WETLANDS

Briercliff

Dellwood Drive

Primrose

Berwyn Road

DOVER SHORES PARK

Lake Lancaster

Curry Ford Road

Curry Ford Rd

Fredica Drive

Dixie

Belle

Kaley

Avenue

Ferncreek Avenue

Brown Avenue

Bumby Avenue

Conway Gardens Road

Grant

Belle

Harding Ave

Grant Street

Brenda S Drive

Grant Ave

Osceola St

Michigan

Michigan Street

Conway

Michigan

Street

Brass Lake

Lake Porter

Boulevard

Raeford Road

Ashford

Lake Fredrica

Pineloch Ave

Lake Pinelock

Lake

C

D

E

135

EAGLE
NEST PARK

Central
Florida Ballet

Holy Land
Experience

CYPRESS
CREEK
COUNTRY
CLUB

Mall at
Millenia

THE
EAGLEWOOD
GOLF CLUB

TURKEY
LAKE
PARK

Turkey
Lake

Lake
Richmond

McLeod Road

34th Street
35th Street
36th Street

McLeod Road

Middlebrook
Road

Conroy Road

Millenia Road

Borrow
Pit

Conroy Road

Conroy Road

LAKE
CANE-
MARSHA
PARK

Lake
Cane

Lake
Marsha

Marsha Drive

Loews
Portofino
Bay Hotel

Universal
Studios

Hard Rock
Hotel

Universal
Orlando
Resort

CityWalk

Islands of
Adventure

Loews
Royal
Pacific
Resort

Four Points by Sheraton
Orlando Studio City

Skyventure

Wet'n Wild

Holiday
Inn Express

Magical Midway

Titanic
Dinner
Event

Sandy Lake
Enclave Suites
Hotel & Suites

Pirates Dinner
Adventure

Fairfield Inn
by Marriott

Skull
Kingdom

Fun Spot
Action Park

Texas de Brazil

Howard
Johnson
Universal
Gateway Inn

Orlando
Premium
Outlets

Oak Ridge Road

Festival
Bay Mall

Tropical
Lake

Major Blvd

Vanguard Street

Mandarin Street

Anzio Street

Steyr Street

Kingspointe Parkway

Major Blvd

ORANGE
TREE
COUNTRY
CLUB

Wallace

Spring
Lake

International

Carrier Drive

Sand Lake Rd

Sand Lake Road

Little
Sand
Lake

Bola Ristorante

Best of British Pub

Orlando
Metropolitan Resort

Central Florida YMCA
Aquatic & Family Center

Wyndham Resort

Ripley's Believe It or Not!

Goodings Plaza

Sleuth's Mystery
Dinner Show

Holiday Inn Resort
Orlando - The Castle

Orlando/Orange County
Convention & Visitors Bureau

Big
Sand
Lake

ICEBAR

Wonderworks

Ming Court

Rosen Plaza Hotel

The Peabody
Orlando

Convention
Center

The Outta Control Magic
Comedy Dinner Show

Pointe
Orlando

Universal Boulevard

Shingle Creek

SHINGLE CREEK

Rosen
Shingle
Creek

GOLF CLUB

Bee Line Expressway

Ritz Carlton Orlando
Grande Lakes ↓

John Young Parkway

Presidents Drive

South Park Circle

Consulate Drive

136

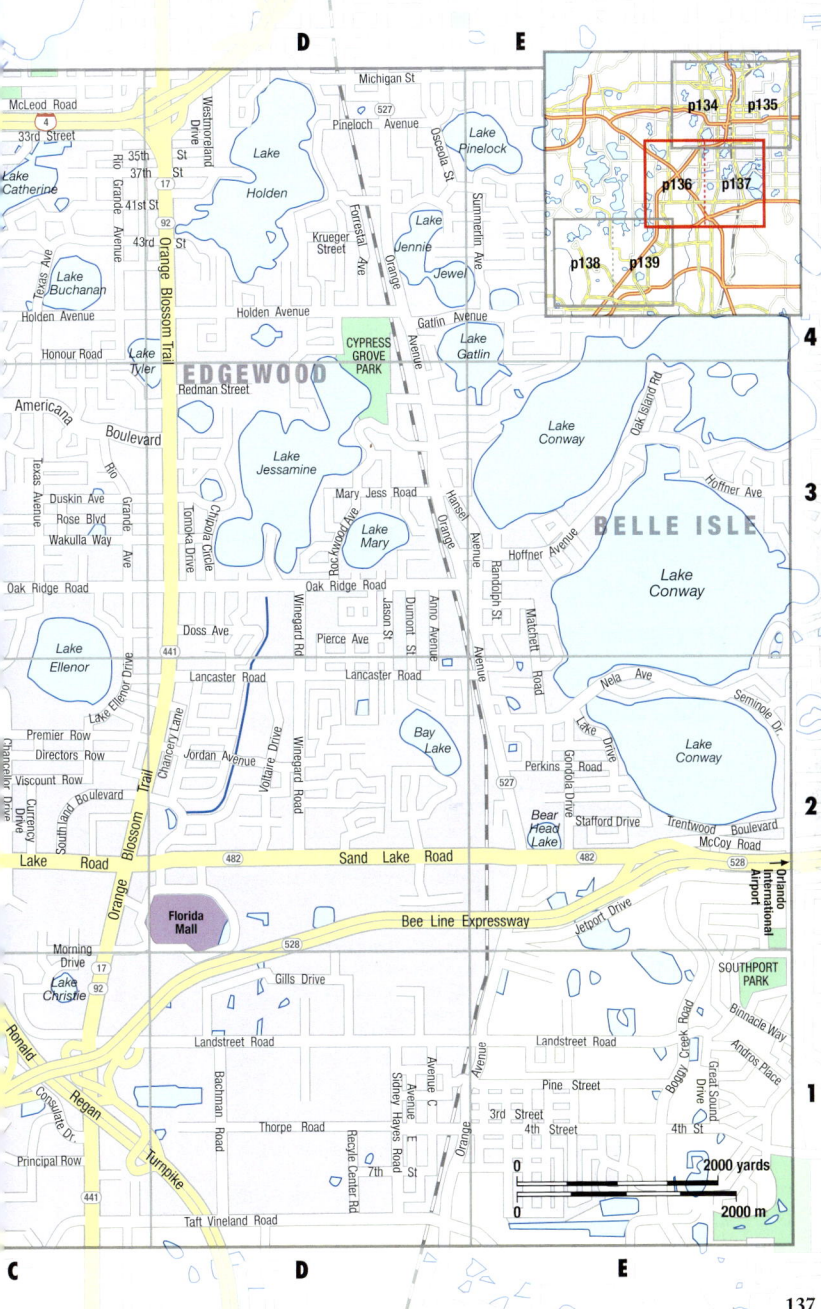

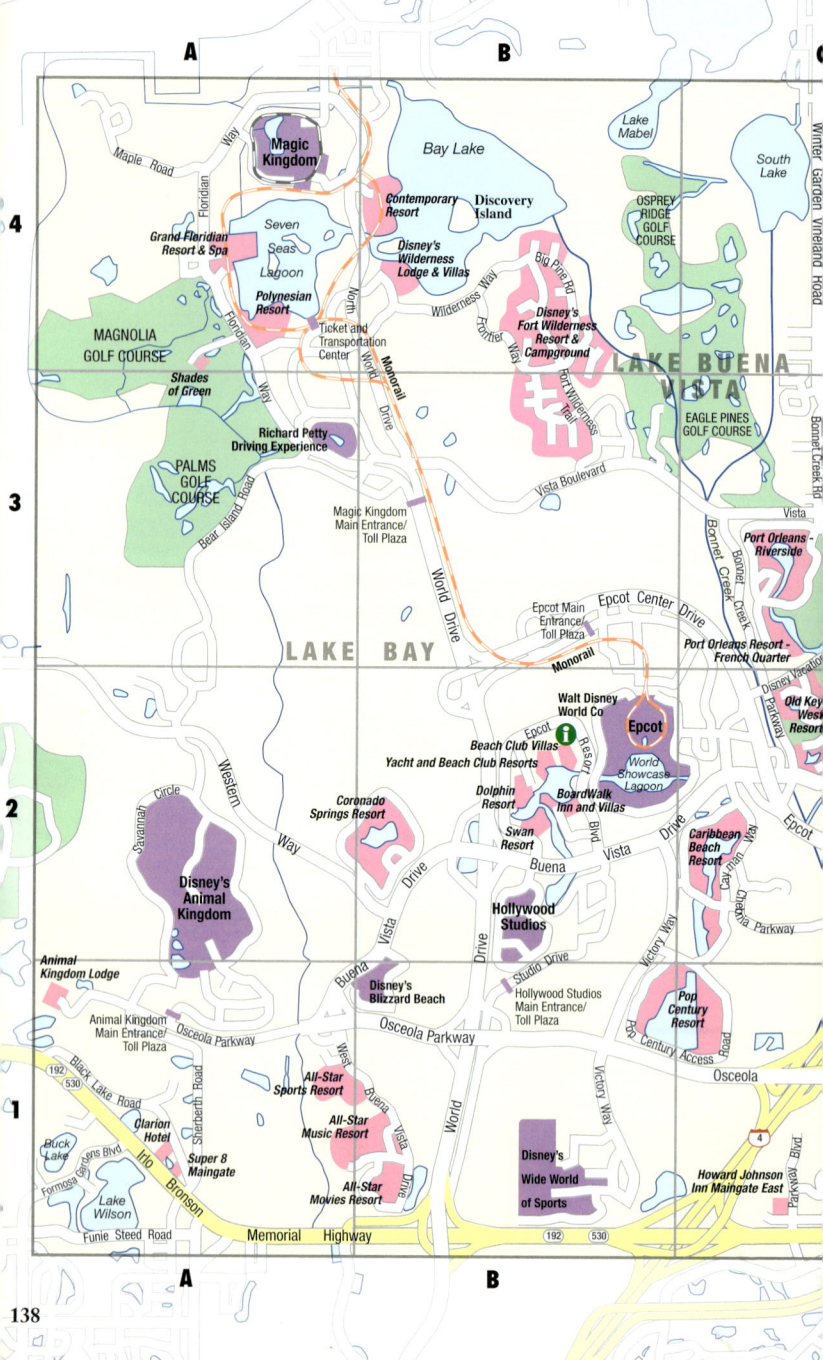

A

B

C

4

Maple Road

Floridian Way

Magic Kingdom

Bay Lake

Lake Mabel

South Lake

Contemporary Resort

Discovery Island

OSPREY RIDGE GOLF COURSE

Grand Floridian Resort & Spa

Seven Seas Lagoon

Disney's Wilderness Lodge & Villas

Big Pine Rd

Polynesian Resort

North

Wilderness Way

Disney's Fort Wilderness Resort & Campground

LAKE BUENA VISTA

Ticket and Transportation Center

World

Monorail

Frontier

Fort Wilderness Trail

Winter Garden Vineland Road

MAGNOLIA GOLF COURSE

Floridian Way

Drive

EAGLE PINES GOLF COURSE

Bonnet Creek Rd

Shades of Green

Vista Boulevard

Vista

3

Richard Petty Driving Experience

Bear Island Road

World

Bonnet Creek

Port Orleans - Riverside

PALMS GOLF COURSE

Magic Kingdom Main Entrance/ Toll Plaza

Drive

Bonnet Creek

Port Orleans Resort - French Quarter

Epcot Center Drive

Disney Vacation

Old Key West Resort

Epcot Main Entrance/ Toll Plaza

Monorail

L A K E   B A Y

Walt Disney World Co

Epcot

Resort

2

Circle

Western

Beach Club Villas

Yacht and Beach Club Resorts

World Showcase Lagoon

Coronado Springs Resort

Dolphin Resort

BoardWalk Inn and Villas

Drive

Caribbean Beach Resort

Epcot

Savannah

Way

Vista

Swan Resort

Buena   Vista   Drive

Cayman   Way

Chatham Parkway

Disney's Animal Kingdom

Drive

Hollywood Studios

Victory Way

Animal Kingdom Lodge

Buena

Studio Drive

Hollywood Studios Main Entrance/ Toll Plaza

Pop Century Resort

1

Animal Kingdom Main Entrance/ Toll Plaza

Osceola Parkway

Disney's Blizzard Beach

Osceola Parkway

Pop Century Access

Osceola

192 530

Black Lake Road

Sherberth Road

All-Star Sports Resort

West

Buena

World

Victory Way

4

Clarion Hotel

All-Star Music Resort

Vista

Drive

Disney's Wide World of Sports

Howard Johnson Inn Maingate East

Buck Lake

Irlo

Bronson

Super 8 Maingate

All-Star Movies Resort

Formosa Gardens Blvd

Lake Wilson

Funie Steed Road

Memorial   Highway

192 530

A

B

138

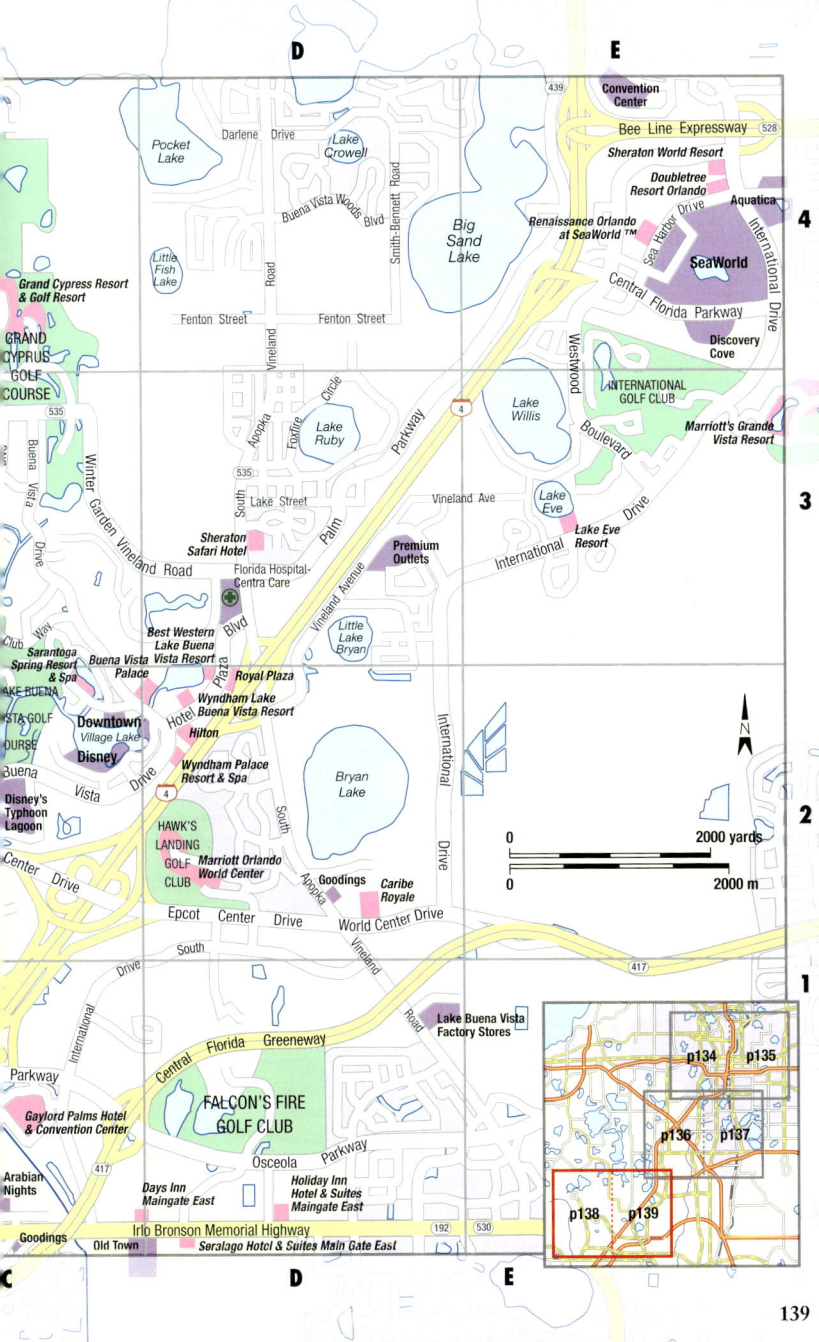

Selective Index for Street Atlas

PLACES OF INTEREST

Albin Polasek Museum & Sculpture Gardens 135 D4
Amway Arena 134 C2
Annie Russell Theatre 135 D4
Aquatica 139 E4
Arabian Nights 138 C1
Austin's Coffee 135 D4
Bob Carr Performing Arts 134 C3
Central Florida Ballet 136 B4
Central Florida YMCA Aquatic & Family Center 136 A2
Centroplex 134 C2
Charles Hosmer Morse Museum of American Art 135 D4
Church Street Station 134 C2
Cityartsfactory 134 C2
City Hall 135 C2
CityWalk 136 A3
Colonial Plaza 135 D2
Convention Center 136 A1
Cornell Fine Arts Museum 135 D4
Discovery Cove 139 E4
Disney's Animal Kingdom 138 A2
Disney's Blizzard Beach 138 B1
Disney's Typhoon Lagoon 139 C2
Disney's Wide World of Sports 138 B1
Downtown Disney 139 C2

Epcot 138 B2
Expo Centre 134 C2
Federal Building 134 C2
Festival Bay Mall 136 B3
Fiddler's Green 135 D4
Florida Mall 137 D2
Fun Spot Action Park 136 B2
Goodings Plaza 136 A2
Grand Bohemia Hotel Orlando 135 C2
G S Produce Market 135 C4
Hollywood Studios 138 B2
Holy Land Experience 136 B4
Islands of Adventure 136 A3
Jack Kerouac House 134 C3
Lake Buena Vista Factory Stores 139 D1
Lake Eola Amphitheater 135 C2
Mad Cow Theatre 135 C2
Magic Kingdom 138 A4
Magical Midway 136 A2
Mall at Millenia 136 B3
Menello Museum of American Art 135 C3
Ming Court 136 A1
Old Town 139 C1
Orange County Court House 135 C2
Orange County Regional History Center 135 C2
Orlando Ballet 135 C3

Orlando Fashion Square Mall 135 D3
Orlando Museum of Art 135 D3
Orlando Premium Outlets 136 B3
Orlando Science Center 135 C3
Orlando Shakespeare Theater 135 C3
Outta Control Magic Comedy Dinner Show, The 136 A1
Pirates Dinner Adventure 136 A2
Pointe Orlando 136 A1
Premium Outlets 139 D3
Rep Theatre, The 135 D3
Richard Petty Driving Experience 138 A3
Ripley's Believe It or Not! 136 A2
Rollins College 135 D4
SAK Comedy Lab 134 C2
SeaWorld 139 E4
Skyventure 136 A2
Sleuth's Mystery Dinner Show 136 A2
Studio Theater 134 C2
Universal Studios 136 A3
Wells Built Museum 134 C2
Wet'n Wild 136 A2
Wine Room on Park Avenue, The 135 D4
Winter Park Historical Museum & Farmers Market 135 D4
Winter Park Village 135 D4
WonderWorks 136 A1

PARKS

Azalea Park 135 E2
Blue Jacket Park 135 D3
Cypress Grove Park 137 D4–D3
Demetree Park 135 E2
Dover Shores Park 135 E1
Eagle Nest Park 134 A1
Gordon Barnett Park 134 A3
Harry P. Leu Gardens 135 D3
Lake Cane-Marsha Park 136 A4–A3
Lake Fairview Park 134 B4
Langford Park 135 D2
Loch Haven Park 135 C3
Meads Botanical Garden 135 D4
Park of the Americas 135 E2
Southport Park 137 E1
Trotter Park 134 B4
Turkey Lake Park 136 A4
War Memorial Park 135 E4
Winter Park Village 135 D4

STREETS

Amelia Street 135 D2
Americana Boulevard 137 C3
Anderson Street 135 C2–C3
Bee Line Expressway 136 A1–C1, 137 C1–D2–E2
Bennet Road 135 E3
Bonnet Creek Parkway 138 C3–C2
Bruton Boulevard 134 A1
Buena Vista Drive 139 C3–D2–C2, 138 B2–A1

Bumby Avenue 135 D3–D1
Canton Avenue 135 D4
Carrier Drive 136 A2–B2
Central Boulevard 134 B2–C2, 135 C2–E2
Central Florida Greeneway 139 C1–D2–E2
Church Street 134 B2–C2
Colonial Drive 134 A2–C2, 135 C2–E2
Columbia Street 134 A1–B2
Concord Street 135 C2–D2
Conroy Road 134 A4–B4–C3
Convention Way 136 A1
Conway Gardens Road 135 D1
Conway Road 135 E2–E1
Crystal Lake Drive 135 D2–D1
Curry Ford Road 135 D1–E1
Delaney Avenue 135 C2–C3
Division Avenue 134 C1
East-West Expressway 134 A2–C2, 135 C2–E2
Edgewater Drive 134 B1–C3
Epcot Center Drive 138 B3–C2, 139 C2–D2
Epcot Resort Boulevard 138 B2
Fairbanks Avenue 134 C4, 135 C4–D4
Ferguson Drive 134 B3–B2
Ferncreek Avenue 135 D1
Florida's Turnpike-Ronald Regan Turnpike 136 A4–C1, 137 C1–D1
Floridian Way 138 A4–A3
Gaston Foster Road 135 E2–E1
Gore Street 134 B2–C2, 135 C2–D2
Grant Street 135 C1–E1
Hampton Avenue 135 D3–D2
Harrison Avenue 134 C4–C3
Hiawassee Road 136 A4
Hoffner Avenue 137 E3
Holden Avenue 137 C4–D4
Hollywood Way 136 A3
Hotel Plaza Boulevard 139 D2–D3
Hyer Avenue 135 C2
International Drive 136 B3–B2–A2–A1, 139 E4–E3–D2
Irlo Bronson Memorial Highway 138 A1–C1, 139 C1–D1
John Young Parkway 134 B4–B1, 136 C4–C1
Kaley Avenue 134 C1, 135 C1–D1
Kirkman Road 136 B4–B2
Lake Underhill Road 135 D2–E2
Lakemont Avenue 135 E4–E3
Lakeview Street 134 C3
Lancaster Road 137 D2
Landstreet Road 137 D1–E1
Livingston Street 135 C2–D2
Magnolia Avenue 135 C3–C2
Major Boulevard 136 B3
Maquire Boulevard 135 D2–D3
McLeod Road 134 B1, 136 B4–C4, 137 C4

Mercy Drive 134 A4–A3
Michigan Street 135 C1–E1
Millenia Road 136 B3–C4
Mills Avenue 135 D4–D1
Minnesota Avenue 135 C4
Mission Road 134 A2–A1, 136 B4
Morse Boulevard 135 D4
New Hampshire Street 134 B3–C3
North World Drive 138 A4–B3
Oak Ridge Road 136 B3, 137 C3–D3
Old Winter Garden Road 134 A2
Orange Avenue 135 D4–C3–C1, 137 D2–E2–D1
Orange Blossom Trail 134 B4–B1, 137 D4–C2
Orange Center Boulevard 134 B2
Orlando Avenue 135 C4
Osceola Parkway 138 A1–C1, 139 C1–D1
Palm Parkway 139 D3
Park Avenue 135 D4
Pennsylvania Avenue 135 D4
Primrose Drive 135 D2–D1
Princetown Street 134 A3–C3
Rio Grande Avenue 134 B4–B3 & B1, 137 C1–C3
Robinson Street 134 B2–C2, 135 C2–D2
Sand Lake Road 136 A2–C2, 137 C2–D2
Sea Harbor Drive 139 E4
Semoran Boulevard 135 E4–E1
Silver Star Road 134 A3–B3
Smith Street 134 B3–C3
South Apopka Vineland Road 139 D4–D1
South Street 134 B2–C2, 135 C2–D2
Summerlin Road 135 C2
Turkey Lake Road 136 A1–A4
Universal Boulevard 136 A3–B1
Victory Way 138 B2–B1
Vineland Avenue 139 D3
Vineland Road 136 A3–B3–C4
Virginia Drive 134 C3–D3
Vista Boulevard 138 B3–C3, 139 C3
Washington Street 134 B2–C2, 135 D2
West Buena Vista Drive 138 A1–B1
Western Way 138 A2
Westmoreland Drive 134 C3–C1, 137 D4
Westwood Boulevard 139 E4–E3
Wilderness Way 138 B4
Winegard Road 137 D3–D2
Winter Garden Vineland Road 138 C4, 139 C3–D3
Winter Park Road 135 D3
World Center Drive 139 D2
World Drive 138 B3–B1
Yale Street 134 B3–C3

Index

A

accommodations 36–49, 56–7
Adventureland, Magic Kingdom 7
Africa, Animal Kingdom 15
Akershus Royal Banquet Hall,
    Epcot 12, 98
Albin Polasek Museum and
    Sculpture Gardens 31, 85
All-Star Resorts 39
All the Books You Can Read,
    Islands of Adventure 23
Amazing Adventures of Spider
    Man, Islands of Adventure
    22, 126
American Adventure, Epcot 13
American Idol Experience,
    Hollywood Studios 17
Animal Kingdom 14–5
    accommodations 39–40
    backstage tours 55
    live shows 14–15, 77–8
    parades 78
    restaurants 14, 100, 103
    thrill rides 125
Animal Kingdom Lodge 40
Animation Courtyard, Hollywood
    Studios 16–7
Annie Russell Theatre 31, 89
Aquatica water park 121
Arabian Nights 19, 80
Arnold Palmer's Bay Hill Club
    and Lodge 44, 70
Asia, Animal Kingdom 15
Audubon Center for Birds of
    Prey 31, 90

B

backstage tours 54–5
bars and cafés 50–3
Beauty and the Beast, Holly-
    wood Studios 16, 78
bed & breakfasts 46
Believe, SeaWorld 27, 79
Biergarten Restaurant, Epcot
    12, 98
Big Thunder Mountain Railroad,
    Magic Kingdom 7, 124
Bistro de Paris, Epcot 13, 98
Black Point Wildlife Drive 91
Blue Horizons, SeaWorld 26, 80
Blue Man Group 21
BoardWalk Inn and Villas 38
Bob Carr Performing Arts 29

Boheme, Downtown 28, 109
Bohemian Hotel Celebration 19,
    41
budgeting 56–9
Buena Vista Palace 40, 97

C

Café de France, Winter Park
    30, 111
Camp Minnie Mickey, Animal
    Kingdom 14–5
Canada Pavilion, Epcot 13
Canaveral National Seashore
    33, 90–1
Caribbean Beach Resort 38
Caribe Royale 44
Cat in the Hat, Islands of
    Adventure 23
Celebration 18–9
    accommodations 41–2
    restaurants 103–4
Celebrity Resorts 42
Celt Irish Pub, Downtown 29,
    52, 110
Central Florida Ballet 88
chain hotels 45
Charles Hosmer Morse Museum
    of American Art 30, 85
Chefs de France, Epcot 13, 99
children 60–61
China Pavilion, Epcot 12
Church Street Station 28–9, 52
Cinderella's Castle 7, 98
Cirque Du Soleil 79
Cityartsfactory 28, 82
CityWalk 51
    bars 51
    nightlife 93
    restaurants 105–6
climate 59, 62
Clyde and Seamore Take Pirate
    Island, SeaWorld 27, 80
Cocoa Beach 33, 111, 117
Comic Book Shop, Islands of
    Adventure 22
Contemporary Resort 36
Coral Reef Restaurant, Epcot
    11, 99
Cornell Fine Arts Museum 31,
    85–6
Coronado Springs Resort 40
Courtyard at Lake Lucerne 47
customs regulations 62–4

D

dance 88–9
delis 69

dinner shows 80–81
DinoLand U.S.A., Animal
    Kingdom 15
DINOSAUR 15, 125
disabled travelers 64, 67
Discovery Cove, SeaWorld 26,
    122
Discovery Island, Animal
    Kingdom 14
Disney's Blizzard Beach 122–3
Disney's Typhoon Lagoon 123
DisneyQuest 120
Dolphin Cove, SeaWorld 26
Dolphin Resort 38
Doubletree Resort Orlando 44
Downtown Disney
    accommodations 40–41
    bars 50
    live shows 79
    nightlife 92–3
    restaurants 101–2
    shopping 112–13
    themed attractions 120
Downtown Orlando 28–9
    accommodations 28, 29, 47–8
    bars 29, 47, 52–3
    nightlife 94–5
    restaurants 28, 29, 48, 109–11
Dragon Challenge, Islands of
    Adventure 23, 126
Dream Along with Mickey, Magic
    Kingdom 7, 76
drinking laws 53, 65, 130
driving 130

E

Eatonville 30–1
Echo Lake, Hollywood Studios
    17
Eighth Voyage of Sindbad,
    Islands of Adventure 23, 79
Enclave Suites Hotel & Suites 44
Eô Inn, Lake Eola 29, 47
Epcot 10–13
    accommodations 38–9
    backstage tours 54–5
    live shows 77
    restaurants 11, 12–3, 39,
        98–100, 103
    thrill rides 11, 124–5
Expedition Everest, Animal
    Kingdom 15, 125

F

Fantasmic!, Hollywood Studios
    16, 78
Fantasyland, Magical Kingdom 8

farmers' markets **68–9**
FASTPASS **59, 124–5**
Festival of the Lion King, Animal Kingdom **14, 77**
Festival Bay Mall **24, 114**
festivals **89**
50s Prime Time Cafe, Hollywood Studios **100**
Finding Nemo – the Musical, Animal Kingdom **15, 77**
fireworks **9, 76–7, 78**
Flight of the Hippogriff, Islands of Adventure **23, 127**
Flights of Wonder, Animal Kingdom **15, 78**
Florida Mall **114**
food and drink **68–9**
Fort Wilderness Resort **39**
France Pavilion, Epcot **13**
Frontierland, Magic Kingdom **7**
Fun Spot Action Park **24, 119–20**
Future World, Epcot **10**

G

Garden Grill, Epcot **12**
Gatorland **18, 118**
Gaylord Palms Hotel **45**
Germany Pavilion, Epcot **12**
golf **42, 44, 45, 46, 70–3**
    Disney World courses **70**
    public courses **73**
    resorts **70–73**
Grand Bohemian Hotel **28, 47–8**
Grand Bohemian Gallery, **28, 82**
Grand Cypress Resort **45, 71**
Grand Floridian Resort and Spa **36–7, 96**
Green Meadows Farm **60, 90**

H

Hard Rock Hotel **43**
Harry P. Leu Gardens **29, 91**
Harry Potter and the Forbidden Journey, Islands of Adventure **23**
health and medical care **65**
Hilton **41**
history **74–5**
Holiday Inn Resort Orlando – The Castle **45**
Hollywood Boulevard, Hollywood Studios **16**
Hollywood Rip Ride Rockit, Universal Studios **20, 126**
Hollywood, Universal Studios **21**
Hollywood Studios **16–17**
    live shows **16–17, 78–9**

fireworks **78**
    restaurants **100–101**
    shopping **112**
    thrill rides **16, 125–6**
Holocaust Memorial Resource and Education Center **86**
Holy Land Experience **79, 120–1**

I

IllumiNations, Epcot **77**
Incredible Hulk Coaster, Islands of Adventure **22, 127**
Indiana Jones Stunt Spectacular, Hollywood Studios **17, 78**
Inn at Cocoa Beach **48**
International Drive **24–5**
    accommodations **24, 44–7**
    bars **25, 51–2**
    live shows **25, 81**
    nightlife **94**
    shopping **24, 25, 114–15**
    restaurants **46, 107–9**
    themed attractions **24, 25, 118, 120, 121**
Islands of Adventure **22–3**
    live shows **23, 79**
    restaurants **23, 105**
    shopping **22, 23, 113**
    thrill rides **22, 23, 126–7**
Italy Pavilion, Epcot **13**
it's a small world, M. Kingdom **8**

J

Japan Pavilion, Epcot **13**
Journey into Narnia: Prince Caspian, Hollywood Studios **17**
Journey to Atlantis, SeaWorld **27, 127**
Jungle Cruise, Magic Kingdom **7**
Jurassic Park, Islands of Adventure **22–3**

K

Kennedy Space Center **32–3, 114**
Kilimanjaro Safaris, Animal Kingdom **15**
Kissimmee **18–19**
    accommodations **42–3**
    restaurants **103–4**
Kraken, SeaWorld **27, 127**

L

Lake Buena Vista **24–5**
    accommodations **44–6**
    shopping **114**

themed attractions **122–3**
Lake Buena Vista Factory Stores **114**
Lake Eola Park **29**
Land, The (Epcot) **11**
Le Cellier Steakhouse, Epcot **13, 99**
Liberty Square, Magic Kingdom **8**
live shows **76–81**
Loch Haven Park **28–9**
Loews Portofino Bay Hotel **43**
Loews Royal Pacific Resort **44**
L'Originale Alfredo di Roma Ristorante, Epcot **99**
Lombard's Seafood Grille, Universal Studios **21, 104**
Lost Continent, Islands of Adventure **23**

M

Magic Kingdom **6–9**
    accommodations **36–8**
    backstage tours **54**
    fireworks **9, 76–7**
    live shows **7, 9, 76**
    parades **9, 76**
    restaurants **7, 36–7, 98, 102–3**
    shopping **6, 112**
    thrill rides **8, 9, 124**
Magical Midway **24–5, 120**
Main Street Electrical Parade, Magic Kingdom **9, 76**
Main Street, U.S.A., Magic Kingdom **6**
Maitland **30–1**
    accommodations **48**
    restaurants **111**
Maitland Art Center **31, 86–7**
Maitland Historical Museum and Telephone Museum **31, 87**
Mall at Millenia **114**
Mama Melrose's Ristorante, Hollywood Studios **100**
Manta, SeaWorld **27, 127**
Marvel Super Hero Island, Islands of Adventure **22**
Medieval Times **19, 81**
Mennello Museum of American Art, Loch Haven **29, 83**
Merritt Island National Wildlife Refuge **33, 91**
Mexico Pavilion, Epcot **12**
Mickey Avenue, Hollywood Studios **16–7**
Mickey's Toontown Fair, Magic Kingdom **9**

Millenia Fine Art Gallery **87**
Mission: SPACE **11, 124**
money **66**
Morocco Pavilion, Epcot **13**
museums and galleries **82–7**
music **88**
Mystic Dunes Resort and Golf
    Club **42, 71–2**

N

nature **90–91**
New York, Universal Studios
    20–1
nightlife **92–5**
Norway Pavilion, Epcot **12**

O

Old Key West Resort **38**
Old Town **18–19, 93**
Omni Orlando Resort **42**
Orange County Regional History
    Center **28–9, 83–4**
Orange Lake Resort **72**
Orlando Ballet **88**
Orlando Magic **29**
Orlando Museum of Art **29, 84**
Orlando Philharmonic **88**
Orlando Science Center **29, 84**
Orlando Shakespeare
    Theater **29, 89**

P

Palm Lakefront Hostel **42**
parades **76, 78**
Park Avenue, Winter Park **30**
parks and gardens **90–1**
Park Plaza Hotel **41**
Peabody Orlando **45**
Pirate's Dinner Adventure **25, 81**
Pirates of the Caribbean **7**
Pointe Orlando **25, 114–5**
Polynesian Resort **37**
Pop Century Resort **40**
Port Orleans French Quarter **38**
Port Orleans Riverside **39**
Premium Outlets **25, 115**
Production Central, Universal
    Studios **20**

R

Rainforest Cafe, Animal King-
    dom **14, 100**
Renaissance Orlando at
    SeaWorld **46**
Rep Theater **29, 89**
Restaurant Marrakesh **13, 99**
restaurants **98–111**

Revenge of the Mummy,
    Universal Studios **20, 126**
Richard Petty Driving
    Experience **121**
Ripley's Believe It or Not! **25,
    118–9**
Ritz Carlton Orlando Grande
    Lakes **46, 72, 96**
Rock 'n' Roller Coaster, Holly-
    wood Studios **16, 125**
rodeo, Kissimmee **18, 116–7**
Rollins College **30–31**
Ron Jon Cape Caribe Resort **48**
Ron Jon Surf Shop **24, 115**
Rosen Shingle Creek **46,
    72–3, 97**
Royal Plaza Hotel **41**

S

San Angel Inn Restaurante,
    Epcot **12, 100**
San Francisco, Universal
    Studios **21**
Seafire Inn, SeaWorld **27, 109**
SeaWorld **25, 26–7**
    backstage tours **55**
    live shows **26–7, 79–80**
    restaurants **27, 109**
    thrill rides **27, 127**
Seralago Hotel & Suites **43**
Seuss Landing **23**
Sharks Underwater Grill,
    SeaWorld **27, 109**
Sheraton Safari Hotel **47**
Sheraton Studio City **24, 44–5**
shopping **112–15**
    independent shops **115**
    malls **24–5, 114–15**
Shuttle Launch Experience
    32–3, 127
Sid Cahuenga's One of a Kind,
    Hollywood Studios **16**
Simpsons Ride, Universal
    Studios **21**
Sleuth's Mystery Dinner Show
    25, 81
Space Coast **32–3**
    accommodations **48–9**
    restaurants **111**
    shopping **114, 115**
    themed attractions **119**
    thrill rides **127**
Space Mountain **9, 124**
Spaceship Earth, Epcot **10**
spas and beauty treatments **45,
    46, 47, 96–7**
Splash Mountain **7, 124**

sport **116–17**
Star Tours, Hollywood Studios **17**
Star Wars: Jedi Training Acad-
    emy, Hollywood Studios **17**
Streets of America,
    Hollywood Studios **17**
student travelers **57–8**
Sunset Boulevard,
    Hollywood Studios **16**
supermarkets **69**
Swan Resort **39**

T

Teppan Edo, Epcot **13, 100**
Test Track **11, 125**
theater **89**
theme parks
    age groups **60–61**
    opening hours **58**
    readmission **57**
themed attractions **118–23**
Thornton Park **29**
thrill rides **124–7**
    for younger children **125**
Thurston House B&B **48**
Ticket and Transportation
    Center, Magic Kingdom **6**
tickets **57**
Titanic Dinner Event **25, 81**
Tomorrowland **9**
Tomorrowland Indy Speedway **9**
Tom Sawyer Island **7**
Toon Lagoon, Islands of
    Adventure **22**
tourist information offices **67**
Toy Story Mania!, Hollywood
    Studios **17**
transportation **128–31**
Treasure Tavern **81**
Tutto Italia Ristorante, Epcot **13,
    100**
Twilight Zone Tower of Terror,
    Hollywood Studios **16, 125–6**

U

United Kingdom Pavilion,
    Epcot **13**
U.S. Astronaut Hall of Fame
    33, 119
Universal Express **58**
Universal Studios **20–21**
    accommodations **43–4**
    bars **51**
    restaurants **21, 104–5, 106–7**
    thrill rides **20, 126**
Universe of Energy, Epcot **10–11**
Urban Spa **29, 97**

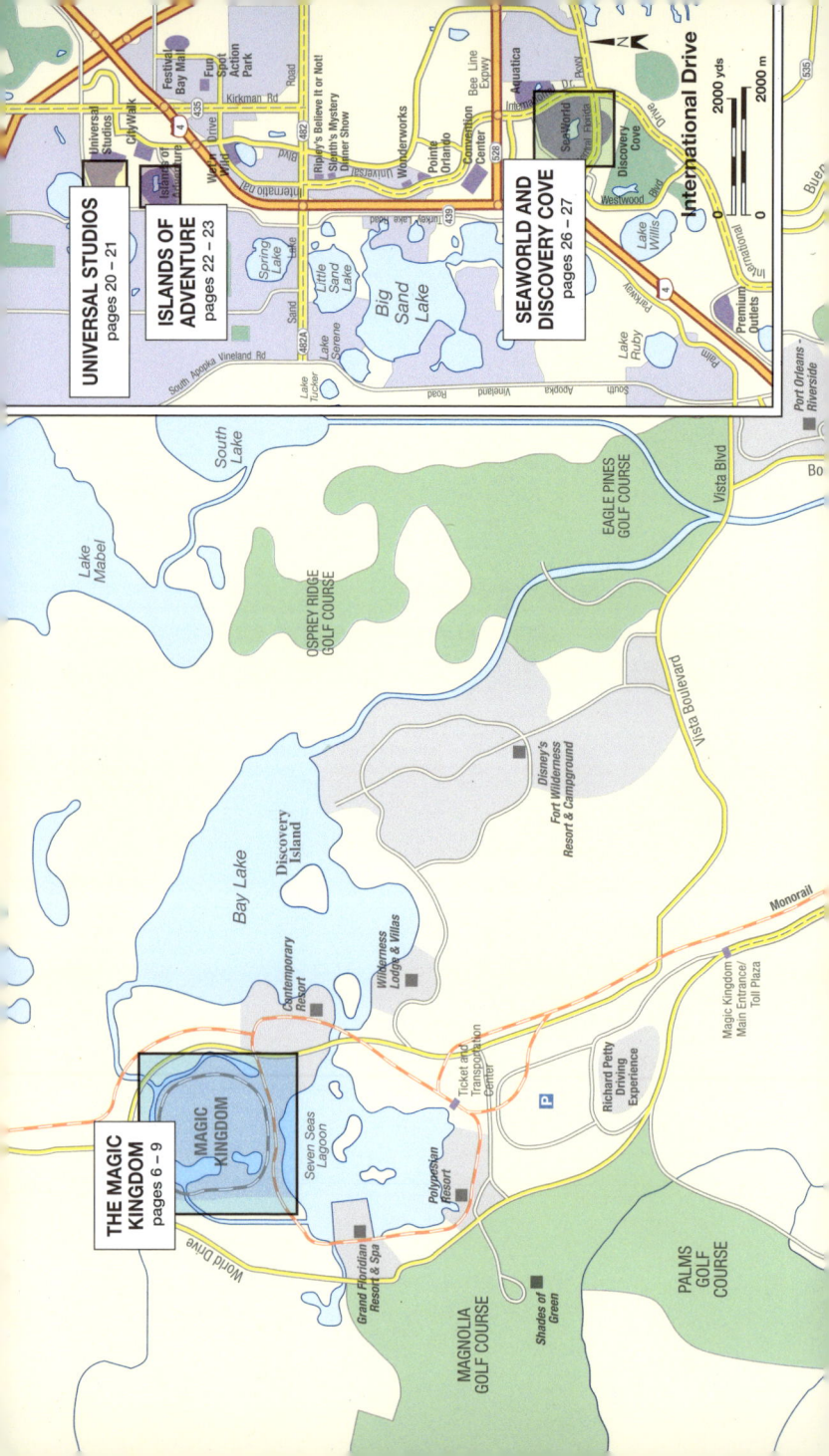

N

2000 yds

2000 m

0

International Drive

UNIVERSAL STUDIOS
pages 20 – 21

ISLANDS OF ADVENTURE
pages 22 – 23

SEAWORLD AND DISCOVERY COVE
pages 26 – 27

Universal Studios

CityWalk

Islands of Adventure

Festival Bay Mall

Fun Spot Action Park

Kirkman Rd

Wet 'n Wild

Ripley's Believe It or Not!

Sleuth's Mystery Dinner Show

Wonderworks

Pointe Orlando

Convention Center

Aquatica

SeaWorld

Discovery Cove

Westwood

Premium Outlets

Port Orleans - Riverside

Buena

Bee Line Expwy

International Drive

Universal Blvd

Turkey Lake Road

Sand Lake Road

Spring Lake

Sand Lake

Little Sand Lake

Big Sand Lake

Lake Serene

Lake Tucker

South Apopka Vineland Rd

Lake Willis

Lake Ruby

South Apopka Vineland Road

Palm Parkway

International Drive South

South Lake

Lake Mabel

EAGLE PINES GOLF COURSE

Vista Blvd

Bo

OSPREY RIDGE GOLF COURSE

Vista Boulevard

Disney's Fort Wilderness Resort & Campground

Bay Lake

Discovery Island

Wilderness Lodge & Villas

Contemporary Resort

Monorail

Magic Kingdom Main Entrance/ Toll Plaza

Ticket and Transportation Center

Richard Petty Driving Experience

THE MAGIC KINGDOM
pages 6 – 9

MAGIC KINGDOM

Seven Seas Lagoon

Polynesian Resort

World Drive

Grand Floridian Resort & Spa

MAGNOLIA GOLF COURSE

Shades of Green

PALMS GOLF COURSE